ELVIS INC.

ELVIS

Inc.

THE FALL AND RISE OF THE PRESLEY EMPIRE

Sean O'Neal

PRIMA PUBLISHING

PRIMA PUBLISHING and colophon are registered trademarks of Prima Communications, Inc.

Project Editor: Stefan Grünwedel

Library of Congress Cataloging-in-Publication Data

O'Neal, Sean
Elvis inc. : the fall and rise of the Presley empire / by Sean O'Neal.
p.   cm.
Includes bibliographical references and index.
ISBN 0-7615-0398-6
1. Presley, Elvis, 1935-1977—Estate.   2. Elvis Presley Enterprises.   3. Presley, Priscilla Beaulieu.   4. Presley, Lisa Marie, 1968- .   I. Title.
ML420.P96054 1996
782.42166'092—dc20   96-1427
                                                                                                                CIP
                                                                                                                MN

96 97 98 99 00 01 AA 10 9 8 7 6 5 4 3 2 1
Printed in the United States of America

HOW TO ORDER:
Single copies may be ordered from Prima Publishing, P.O. Box 1260BK, Rocklin, CA 95677; telephone (916) 632-4400. Quantity discounts are also available. On your letterhead, include information concerning the intended use of the books and the number of books you wish to purchase.

For Tracy, Lauren, Mom, and Dad

CONTENTS

ACKNOWLEDGMENTS

My thanks to Jennifer Basye Sander, Stefan Grünwedel, John Waters, Jeff Campbell, and the Prima Publishing staff. They were a pleasure to work with.

Invaluable research assistance was provided for this book by Mary Ball, Al Gabbelli, Tony Haley, Mary Hilton, Bill O'Neal, Mickey Poppy, Christine Russ, W. C. Shipley, Adeal Simmons, and Dee Webb.

Thanks to Joe Tunzi for assisting with photographs.

Special thanks to Tracy O'Neal for all the hours she spent transcribing, editing, and critiquing the manuscript.

Lastly, thank you to Doris O'Neal who has told me for the last twenty-five years that I should write a book.

INTRODUCTION

On January 4, 1954, a young truck driver from East Tupelo, Mississippi, walked into the studios of the Memphis Recording Service, paid a four-dollar fee, and recorded two songs, "I'll Never Stand in Your Way" and "It Wouldn't Be the Same Without You." Just four days shy of his nineteenth birthday, the unknown singer was hoping to meet and impress Sam Phillips, who had set up the recording service as a sideline in his now legendary Sun Records studios.

It was four dollars well spent. Phillips heard something in the young man's voice he'd been hoping to find for a long time. Here at last was "a white man with the Negro sound and the Negro feel." Phillips signed the unknown singer to a recording contract, and within a few months "That's All Right" had been pressed into vinyl and Elvis Presley was on his way to becoming the most successful recording artist of all time.

Elvis took that four-dollar acetate recording home with him, but no one knew exactly what became of it after that. For all intents and purposes, it simply disappeared. It's been said that Elvis was deeply disappointed by what he heard on that record, so some supposed he'd destroyed it. Many doubted it ever existed at all, believing instead that the story of the "lost songs" was just another bit of Elvis lore invented by the publicity-conscious Colonel Parker. The true fate of the lost songs remained a mystery for nearly forty years.

I saw Elvis perform for the first and last time in June, 1977. I'd always enjoyed his music, but seeing him live in concert only two months before his death intensified my interest. I saved my concert program and ticket stub from that show, and soon, almost without realizing it, I began to build a serious collection of Elvis memorabilia.

Sixteen years later, on August 20, 1993, I received a phone call at work from my wife, Tracy. She called to tell me about an ad she'd seen in the classifieds about the sale of a collection of rare Elvis memorabilia. (She's also a fan, but not nearly as obsessed as I am.) Over the years we've responded to similar advertisements more times than I care to remember. More often than not, the "rare memorabilia" turns out to be nothing more than a couple of back issues of *The National Enquirer* announcing that Elvis has been spotted at a Burger King in Des Moines. Still, I knew that real gems could be found almost anywhere, so we made arrangements to see the collection.

This time, we struck gold.

The collection was an incredible find! It included three autographs, the original script from *G.I. Blues,* and Elvis's first musicians' union card. There were around a hundred unpublished photographs, including snapshots of Elvis at ages twelve and sixteen, photos of Elvis in concert, and candid shots of Elvis at Graceland.

The more I saw, the more excited I became, but it was the last item in the collection that nearly stopped my heart. It was a thin, two-sided disc in a sleeve labeled "Memphis Recording Service—Elvis Presley." I literally held my breath as I gently slid the ten-inch acetate record from its sleeve. Side one read, "I'll Never Stand in Your Way"; side two, "It Wouldn't Be the Same Without You." I now knew what had become of the legendary lost songs—I was holding them in my hand!

I took a moment to catch my breath, talked with Tracy, and then made a deal to buy the entire collection on the spot. We had to put our plans to buy a house on hold for a while, but it was worth it. We now owned one of the most valuable recordings in the world. It was an Elvis collector's dream come true. I couldn't have been more excited if I'd met Santa Claus.

Needless to say, I was anxious to explore the possibility of getting the songs released by a record company. While it's true I wanted to recoup our investment through sales of the songs, as an Elvis fan, I also wanted very much to share my discovery with the rest of the world. Of all things Elvis, nothing could be more exciting than the release of a "new" recording. This was going to generate some real excitement in the Elvis world!

Unfortunately, selling the lost songs wouldn't be as easy as I'd imagined. Soon after I began making inquiries at record companies, I received a letter from an attorney representing the Elvis Presley estate. It was a warning. Since the estate had not granted me permission to sell the recordings, the letter read, I could not legally do so. If I tried to sell the songs without the estate's permission, I would face "legal action."

I couldn't believe what I was reading! How could the Presley estate stop me from selling property to which I had legal title, a recording most people didn't even believe existed? I would later learn that sending letters like the one I'd received is a common practice of the Presley estate—a very effective one. Most people are easily coerced into paying a fee for the estate's blessing in any Elvis-related venture.

I, however, chose to ignore the letter and continued my efforts to sell the lost songs, but my curiosity was aroused. I began to search for more information about the activities of the Presley estate. My inquiries led me into an investigation of a multimillion-dollar industry. Nearly two decades after the death of the man whose life and music made it possible, the Elvis business is doing better than ever. In the course of my investigation, I discovered things that simply amazed me, both about Elvis and about the money machine that still bears his name. (I am currently in negotiations with a major record company for the release of the songs. The sale will be made without the permission of the Elvis estate, and I will keep the actual acetate, which I may sell at some later date.)

I've gathered together in these pages the things I've learned about this remarkable phenomenon. Elvis is a cultural icon today, but he didn't become that way simply because of his talent and good looks. There was money to be made from it, so a company was founded to create this icon, and it has controlled his image and the flood of cash as tightly as is humanly possible, establishing new legal precedents in the process. Elvis is not dead. He lives on—as an image, a face, a symbol. And he will continue to do so as long as that image sells.

1

DEATH OF ELVIS, BIRTH OF AN INDUSTRY

WHEN ELVIS PRESLEY AWOKE on August 15, 1977, it was already late afternoon. There was nothing unusual about finding him in bed at that hour; Elvis customarily stayed up all night and slept through most of the day. After he'd dressed, he went down to breakfast in the dining room of his Memphis home, the twenty-three-room Graceland mansion. Lisa Marie, his then nine-year-old daughter, came in just as he was finishing. She wanted her father to come out and play, but Elvis was reluctant. The prescription sleep medication he'd taken to fall asleep the night before had left him groggy. Lisa Marie persisted, and Elvis finally relented.

There were always people standing outside the gates of the fourteen-acre Graceland estate. Twenty-four hours a day, seven days a week, 365 days a year, at least half a dozen Elvis fans loitered at the fence in hopes of stealing a glimpse of the King of Rock 'n' Roll. The truly knowledgeable fans stood watch in the wee hours, the best time to spot their decidedly nocturnal idol. Imagine the surprise among the small knot of admirers standing at the gates that afternoon when Lisa Marie suddenly whizzed by in a baby-blue golf cart, her father beside her in the passenger seat. The cart was a Christmas present, just one of many expensive gifts Elvis had given her over the years. "Lisa Marie" was painted along the side. The lucky fans who witnessed father and daughter at play that day would be among the last to see Elvis alive.

Elvis spent the rest of the evening relaxing in the mansion. He finished his dinner at around 10:30 P.M., and then left for an appointment with his dentist, Dr. Lester Hoffman. (Elvis had a cavity.) He drove himself, as was his habit, and his live-in girlfriend, Ginger Alden, came along.

Nineteen years Elvis's junior, Ginger was the daughter of U.S. Army Sergeant Walter Alden, the officer who'd inducted Elvis into the army back in 1958. As a teenager, Ginger had made the beauty pageant rounds with some small successes; she'd earned the titles of Miss Traffic Safety and Miss Mid-South. Elvis saw her for the first time on a Memphis television program and had asked his friend, George Klein, to arrange a date. Elvis's enormous celebrity made it impossible for him to meet women in any conventional way. Klein had been a friend since high school—their class president, in fact—and he regularly functioned as a kind of dating service for his world-famous friend.

Elvis had quickly become infatuated with Ginger, who bore a striking resemblance to his former wife, Priscilla. To demonstrate his growing affections, he had bought her several expensive presents, including a $12,000 Lincoln Continental. Ginger claims Elvis proposed marriage on January 26, 1977, and gave her an eleven-carat diamond engagement ring worth $600,000. She says they were to have been married on Christmas Day that same year.

His cavity filled, Elvis returned with Ginger to Graceland some time after midnight. Elvis spent the next few hours working on the songs he would be singing on his upcoming concert tour. Why Elvis continued to put himself through the stresses and strains of touring and performing was a mystery to many. Though his most devoted fans were only too willing to overlook his appearance and the deteriorating quality of his performances, the truth was, Elvis looked bad and felt worse. His weight problems were obvious; the once high-energy, 175-pound rock 'n' roll heartthrob had become an exhausted, puffy, 275-pound caricature who forgot song lyrics and split his pants onstage. But his obesity was only the most visible of a host of health difficulties—some natural, others brought on by twenty years of prescription drug abuse—including hypertension, an enlarged heart, glaucoma, severe constipation, and chronic fluid retention. At forty-two, Elvis was an old man.

He continued to endure the pressures of performing for two reasons. The first was simply that he loved doing it. Elvis had lost interest in making movies years earlier, and making records no longer appealed to him. In the last years of his life, singing was the only thing that gave him genuine pleasure—that and the roaring approval of a concert hall full of fans.

His second reason for touring was a little-known fact that would surprise all but a few: Elvis needed the money. Amazingly, the most successful entertainer in the history of the world was nearing bankruptcy.

At around 4:30 A.M. (it was now August 16), Elvis went to his private indoor racquetball court to play a few games. He was joined by Ginger, his cousin Billy Smith, and Billy's wife, Jo. Elvis had built the court at the height of the racquetball craze, hoping the exercise would help him stay in shape. It hadn't. Elvis had never been very motivated to exercise—since the mid-1960s he'd buttressed his flagging willpower with crash diets and diet pills whenever he'd had to slim down for films or concert tours. As he got older and his health continued to deteriorate, he was increasingly unable to sustain extended periods of strenuous activity. That morning's game was a short one.

Elvis could, however, still sing. He kept two pianos at Grace-land—one of them inside the racquetball building, just outside the court—and he gave a "performance" nearly every day. The songs he sang that morning were all sad ones. He ended with "Blue Eyes Crying in the Rain."

After Elvis finished at the piano, he and Ginger returned to the mansion and retired for the day. At this point in his life, Elvis rarely fell asleep naturally, but even the pills wouldn't help this morning. He always found the period before a concert tour to be particularly stressful. He tossed and turned for what seemed like hours, and then he finally got out of bed and went into the bathroom to read. Elvis suffered from severe constipation and often spent long periods reading on the commode. In fact, his bathroom was furnished almost like an office. That morning he chose *The Scientific Search for the Face of Jesus,* a book about the Shroud of Turin. Ginger recalls telling him not to fall asleep. "I won't," Elvis said, and closed the door behind him.

Ginger says she woke up that afternoon at about two and noticed immediately that she was alone in bed. She saw that the light was on in the bathroom, so she assumed Elvis was still in there, reading, which would not have been unusual. She reached for the phone and called a friend to chat for a few minutes about life with Elvis. She liked calling her friends, she said, from Elvis's bed.

After she hung up, she says she called out to Elvis. When he didn't answer, she got up to investigate. She found him lying face down on the bathroom floor. His skin was blue, his eyes were rolled back in his head, and his tongue, nearly bitten in half, was almost black.

Ginger ran to the telephone and called downstairs for help. Elvis's foreman, Joe Esposito, and his cousin Patsy Presley raced up the stairs to the bedroom. Esposito attempted to perform mouth-to-mouth resuscitation, but Elvis didn't respond.

When the ambulance arrived twenty minutes later, the para-medics of Unit 16 of the Memphis Fire Department thought at first that Elvis was a black man, his skin was so discolored. Charlie Crosby and Ulysses S. Jones Jr. attempted CPR, but it was too late: there were no vital signs, no pulse or blood pressure. Elvis's body was cold to the touch and had begun to stiffen with rigor mortis.

With the arrival of the paramedics, Lisa Marie rushed into her father's bedroom to see what was going on. She was quickly ushered from the room.

The paramedics later reported they knew Elvis was dead when they loaded him into the ambulance, but they continued life-saving procedures anyway. The driver radioed ahead to the emergency room at Baptist Hospital that they were on their way with a forty-year-old white male. No name was mentioned. The fans standing at the gates that day had no idea the vehicle racing down Elvis Presley Boulevard held the body of their idol.

At the hospital, efforts to resuscitate Elvis continued for thirty minutes, but it was hopeless. At 3:30 P.M., Dr. Jerry Francisco, the Shelby County medical examiner, announced to a shocked nation the death Elvis Aaron Presley. The cause of death was said to be "erratic heart beat and cardiac arrhythmia from undetermined causes." Some years later it would be revealed that Elvis, in fact, died of a drug overdose.

The Reverend C. W. Bradley, pastor of the Whitehaven Church of Christ, presided over the funeral, which was held inside Graceland itself. Afterward, Elvis's body was transported to Forest Hill Cemetery in a white hearse followed by sixteen white Cadillacs. Comedian Jackie Kahane spoke the final words at the Graceland service. He said, "Ladies and gentlemen, Elvis has left the building for the last time."

★ ★ ★

During the course of his amazing career, Elvis Presley recorded 114 Top-40 songs, including a dozen number-one hits. He made thirty-three movies, played hundreds of sold-out concerts, and sold 600 million records during his lifetime. His popularity lasted well beyond the glory days of the 1950s, and even today his recordings continue to sell at an astounding rate. Of the 600 million records sold during his lifetime, 150 million were sold during the last eighteen months of his life. As of this writing, that total has surpassed a billion. If they were laid end to end, all the Elvis LPs and CDs sold to date would encircle the earth—*twice*. The biggest selling album of all time is Michael Jackson's *Thriller*, to match Elvis's career total, Mr. Jackson would have to release recordings just as successful every year for three decades.

Then there was the money, a veritable ocean of it, with tributaries that continue flowing to this day. Elvis was the only performer in history to generate revenues of more than a billion dollars; some estimates put his lifetime total (from both music and other promotional sources) at more than *$4 billion*.

His death didn't end the inexorable flood of cash. As a matter of fact, it didn't even slow it down. At the apex of his career, Elvis was earning—after all his taxes and bills were paid—around a million dollars annually. From the date of his death, August 16, 1977, to the end of that same year—a period of less than five months—the Presley estate brought in over twice that amount. Since his death, roughly 500 million more of his recordings have sold, producing additional revenues of around $4 billion.

Yet, when he was alive, only a relative trickle of that vast reservoir of wealth found its way to Elvis himself. When he died, he left behind an estate worth less than $7 million. In comparison, John Lennon, who sold far fewer records than Elvis, performed in relatively few concerts, and appeared in only four movies, left an estate of $200 million. How could the greatest money-making performer who every lived, a man who should have been the richest rock 'n' roller on the planet, leave behind such a paltry estate? Where, in other words, did all that money go?

One commonly accepted explanation is that he simply spent it all—on high living; on a swarm of friends, family, and hangers on; and on extravagant gift giving. (He did, after all, give away Cadillacs to perfect strangers.) Another version paints Elvis as a talented-but-gullible country boy whose innocence was exploited by self-serving relatives, greedy managers, and ruthless record companies.

Both stories are aspects of the truth. Elvis *did* spend money at an unbelievable pace, and he *was* given an awful lot of bad advice. But the complete picture is much more convoluted. In fact, he and his handlers were so profligate it's a wonder there was anything left when the King finally died.

★ ★ ★

The Last Will and Testament of Elvis Presley was read in the Probate Court of Shelby County, Tennessee, on August 24, 1977. The document was thirteen pages long, but its primary message was simple: Lisa Marie would get it all. Since she was only nine years old at the time of her father's death, the will specified that Elvis's assets would be held in trust for her until February 1, 1993—her twenty-fifth birthday. While the trust remained in effect, the income from the estate was to be used to support Lisa Marie, Elvis's father, Vernon Presley, and his grandmother, Minnie Mae Presley.

The will named Vernon executor of what was now Lisa Marie's estate. He'd served as his son's financial manager since 1956; the will effectively allowed him to continue in that position. He was authorized by the will to provide for the health, education, and welfare of any of Elvis's relatives who were, in Vernon's opinion, in need of assistance. This assistance was to end upon Vernon's death.

Several others had also expected to be included in the will. Elvis had had the document rewritten just six months before his death. Perhaps his "fiancée," Ginger Alden, thought he was doing so to include her. If so, she was mistaken. Elvis left nothing to Alden, or to his former wife, Priscilla. Several of Elvis's friends and associates were also certain he would be leaving them something, but they were excluded as well. Charges were made by some of the more bitter losers that the will was a fraud. The judge, however, certified it as authentic.

The probate session lasted only twenty minutes. When it was over, the total value of the estate was still not known. It would take another sixty days to complete a thorough inventory. After leaving the courtroom, Probate Judge Joseph Evans was asked his opinion of the value of the estate. His reply was that it would probably be the largest estate ever filed in the state of Tennessee. Estimates in the media placed the likely value in excess of $150 million. No one had the faintest idea of the real story.

★ ★ ★

While today Lisa Marie remains the sole legally recognized heir to Elvis's estate, what her father's will had actually stated was that his property should be divided equally among all his offspring. As far as he knew, Lisa Marie was his only child, but in that statement he'd provided for the possibility that a half brother or sister might surface. Like most rock stars, Elvis had been involved with a great many lovers over the years. No one was surprised when, in the aftermath of his passing, several came forward with paternity claims.

The majority of the paternity claims that have been issued against the estate of Elvis Presley have been filed after his death, but a few were made during his lifetime. In 1970, Patricia Parker, a waitress from Hollywood, California, filed a lawsuit alleging that Elvis was the father of her son, Jason. Elvis took and passed both a blood test and a lie detector test, and the suit was dismissed.

In 1972, a young man approached Elvis during a concert in Little Rock, Arkansas, and introduced himself as his son. Elvis later found out that the man was actually a woman, and that her real name was Lisa Marie. The young woman's mother had been so obsessed with Elvis, had so desperately wanted to be the mother of his child, she had severely warped her own daughter.

After Elvis died, the number of paternity claims skyrocketed. Many claimants no doubt believed it would be easier with no "father" around to dispute the allegation. Billy Joe Newton claimed to have given birth to three children fathered by Elvis, the first when she was nine years old. She also claimed that she and Elvis were once married, but that Colonel Thomas Parker, Elvis's long-time manager, had insisted on a divorce when he began working with the young singer. Ms. Newton never presented any documentation or other proof of the union; she'd "lost" it, she said.

Lucy DeBarbin's claim turned out to be a profitable one, despite the fact that the truth of it was never established. She claimed to have met Elvis in Monroe, Louisiana, in 1953. Five years later, she said, she gave birth to Elvis's daughter, Desiree Presley. Lucy told the story of her relationship with Elvis in a book, *Are You Lonesome Tonight?*, which she wrote with the help of a former *National Enquirer* reporter. The book sold over two hundred thousand copies and provided Desiree with a considerable "inheritance."

Barbara Lewis claimed that she met Elvis in 1954. They dated for a year, she said, and Barbara gave birth to Elvis's daughter, Deborah Delaine Presley, in June 1955. Years later, while she was in the hospital recovering from gallbladder surgery, Ms. Lewis told Deborah that Elvis was her father. Deborah shopped a manuscript of her life story titled *The Lost Princess,* but she never managed to interest a publisher. She filed an unsuccessful suit against the Presley estate in 1988 for her "fair share."

Barbara Young claimed that she had had an affair with Elvis in 1955, which resulted in the birth of a girl, Deborah Presley, on March 4, 1956. In 1987, Ms. Young filed a $125 million lawsuit against the Presley estate on behalf of her daughter. The court ruled against her.

As of this writing, Lisa Marie is still an only child.

★ ★ ★

When the inventory of the Elvis Presley estate was finally completed, the resulting list was seventy-six pages long. It included two jet airplanes, including the commercial-size *Lisa Marie* and another, nine-passenger aircraft; a checking account with a balance of $1,055,173; the Graceland mansion and grounds, valued at

$500,000; eight cars; seven motorcycles; seven golf carts; two trucks, including a wrecker/tow-truck; a large gun collection; various awards and trophies; thirty-two photo albums containing stills from each of Elvis's movies; insurance policies worth $96,000; jewelry, including a gold cross inlaid with 236 diamonds; a personal wardrobe filling several closets; miscellaneous property valued at $500,000; and promissory notes on money loaned to various individuals totaling $1.3 million dollars, including $270,000 in loans to Dr. Nichopoulos, Elvis's personal physician. Total value: $7 million, a far cry from previous estimates. It wasn't even the largest estate ever filed in Tennessee, as Judge Evans had predicted it would be.

★ ★ ★

Elvis never actually knew how much money he was making. According to a friend, Elvis said he never really wanted to "hoard up a lot of money." He was almost embarrassed at the level of financial success he achieved, and he relied exclusively on his personal manager and his father to handle his financial affairs. As long as there was enough money on hand to buy whatever Elvis wanted, the details of his financial situation were of no concern to him. He instructed his father, Vernon, to make sure there was at least a million dollars in his checking account at all times. This was Elvis's measure of true wealth. He never expressed any concern over the amount of money he had or made as long his checking account was fully stocked.

Both Vernon and Elvis were extremely secretive about financial matters, and they trusted no one outside the family when it came to money. Elvis had made Vernon his business manager in part because he knew that his father would be as tight-lipped about his money as he was himself. Keeping your bank balance a closely guarded secret is something you learn to do out of pride when you have no money. Since Vernon hid his finances from prying eyes when he had none to speak of, he could be counted on to guard the details of Elvis's wealth with the same zealousness.

Unfortunately, Vernon was not as adept at managing money as he was at keeping secrets. He only made one real investment for Elvis, and it lost over a million dollars. After that, he kept his son's money in the bank, mostly in non-interest-bearing checking accounts.

Vernon had much less money to manage than he might have. Elvis kept less than twenty cents out of every dollar he earned during much of his career. The rest went to Colonel Parker, the William Morris Agency, and the Internal Revenue Service.

In 1965, for example, Elvis's income totaled $5,225,000, a staggering sum at the time. That total included $2 million for the three movies he'd starred in that year, $1,525,000 in record and music publishing royalties, and $1,700,000 from movies he'd made in previous years. But after he paid his manager, his agent, and the IRS, Elvis was left with only $1 million. A million a year was hardly the poor house, but it was a far cry from the more than $5 million he'd started with.

That same year, Colonel Parker confirmed to the press that, at a million a year, Elvis was the highest paid entertainer in the world. What the Colonel failed to mention was that he himself was the highest paid manager in the world; his 1965 commission for managing Elvis Presley was $1.3 million—$300,000 more than his client!

Elvis's contract with Parker was the single greatest drain on his income. Amazingly, the agreement gave the Colonel half of Elvis's earnings. Parker's share was truly outlandish. A standard contract between a star of Elvis's magnitude and a personal manager would call for a commission of no more than 10 to 15 percent. Apparently, no one in Elvis's inner circle knew about his deal with the Colonel. Priscilla didn't learned the details of the arrangement until after her former husband's death.

For the most part, Colonel Parker completely misled Elvis financially. However, according to Joseph Hanks, who was Elvis's accountant for the last eight years of his life and later a coexecutor of his estate, Colonel Parker once told him he had advised Elvis to get professional financial advice, to invest his money, and to seek help in finding tax shelters. Elvis's response, Parker said, was that the Colonel should stick to worrying about keeping the money coming in; Elvis and Vernon would take care of how it went out. But several others close to Elvis have stated that Colonel Parker advised his client *against* retaining professional financial advisors.

The William Morris Agency received another 10 percent of Elvis's income, bumping his managerial fees to an unheard-of 60 percent. Elvis's manager and agent received more income from Elvis's work than he did himself. Excessive managerial fees cost Elvis well over $100 million during the course of his lifetime.

In exchange for Colonel Parker's incredible remuneration, Elvis received less than stellar management, most observers agree. Many of the deals Colonel Parker made for Elvis—especially during the 1970s—cost him millions. Particularly damaging was an agreement with his record company, RCA.

Elvis was completely out of touch with what would have been a reasonable royalty rate for an artist of his stature. He often bragged to his friends that he received a nickel for every one of his records sold. In fact, a star like Elvis could have commanded twice that amount from any other record company. Colonel Parker was unwilling, for a variety of reasons, to press RCA for a higher royalty. There seemed to be no one around to tell Elvis that five cents a record wasn't such a good deal, and certainly no one at RCA seems to have made him aware of that fact.

Elvis once said, "I would rather pay my taxes than worry about them." And pay them he did. While Colonel Parker was taking an enormous bite out of Elvis's earnings, the Internal Revenue Service was equally ravenous. Elvis, who was highly unsophisticated about tax matters, was only too willing to feed the government all it could swallow. Most individuals with incomes the size of Elvis's retain expert financial advisors to deal with the IRS and minimize their tax burdens; Elvis's one-and-only tax advisor was his father, Vernon, a man with a seventh-grade education and no accounting experience at all.

Vernon Presley was deeply frightened of the government in general and of the IRS in particular. He lived in fear that his son would lose all his money and return the Presley family to the poverty from which it had risen. He was afraid that if he let an accountant prepare Elvis's tax returns, a mistake would be made or an illegal deduction taken, resulting in huge, crippling tax penalties. To make absolutely certain nothing like that ever happened, Vernon allowed the IRS to calculate Elvis's taxes each year.

Colonel Parker agreed that Elvis should let the IRS calculate his annual tax liability. He furthered the family's general paranoia by telling Elvis he didn't want him to end up like heavy-weight boxing champion Joe Louis, who had been financially ruined in a celebrated encounter with the IRS.

With the foxes guarding the chicken coop, Elvis could rest assured he was paying everything he owed, and then some. Over the years, he would take only a fraction of the deductions to which he was legally entitled, and the government would make certain he paid the maximum tax possible. Elvis was usually in the 75 percent tax bracket.

In a press release, Colonel Parker once stated that Elvis Presley was the highest single taxpayer in the United States. Parker seemed to think paying more income taxes than anyone else was something to brag about. In reality, it was further evidence that Elvis was receiving no professional financial advice. The incompetence with which his tax situation was handled probably cost Elvis around $100 million.

★ ★ ★

Of course, once everyone else was finished, Elvis had no trouble at all spending the rest of the money that came in. In the latter years of his life, he was spending it faster than he earned it. Elvis's genius as a performer was equaled only by his talent for finding ever more expensive toys to buy.

Instead of chartering flights for his concert tours, Elvis purchased his own commercial jet airliner. He paid $1.2 million dollars for a Convair 880, christened it the *Lisa Marie,* and spent another $750,000 customizing it. The jet featured two bathrooms, complete with 24-karat gold sinks, and a bedroom with a queen-size bed. Elvis took friends for rides in the *Lisa Marie* the way most people go for rides in their car. Each time the plane took off, it cost him several thousand dollars.

In 1967, Elvis bought a 163-acre ranch in Mississippi, for which he paid $500,000. This was an outrageous price to pay for land in Mississippi. The asking price had escalated when the owner had found out that Elvis Presley was interested in buying the property. Elvis named the ranch the Circle G, in honor of his mother, Gladys. Once he owned a ranch, he had to furnish and equip it. He spent $150,000 on twelve trailers for the ranch, so that members of his entourage, dubbed by the press as the "Memphis Mafia," would have a place to stay. He spent $100,000 on twenty-five pickup trucks for himself and his friends. He even gave trucks to the three carpenters he'd hired to build a new barn at the ranch. Then he bought horses and horse trailers for everyone.

When the neighbors complained about the noise and construction taking place at the Circle G, Elvis had an eight-foot, solid wood fence erected around the perimeter of the ranch. When the complaints continued, he sent one of the guys around the neighborhood with a checkbook, offering to buy all of the surrounding property.

Eventually, Elvis grew tired of the Circle G and Vernon convinced him that the ranch was a financial drain he could not afford. So he sold it. After Elvis's death, the Circle G's enterprising owner offered tours of the ranch, and for the first time since Elvis had bought it, the ranch turned a profit.

Elvis was also a well-known gun buff. In the latter years of his life, he almost always carried a pistol. He converted an old smokehouse behind Graceland mansion into a firing range, and he and the boys pursued his hobby with vigor. He often had his guns customized with gold inlay. Though he continued to buy guns throughout his life, in one notable month, Elvis purchased $19,000 worth of firearms.

But for cars Elvis had a particular fondness, buying them like candy whenever the spirit moved him. He thought nothing of stopping at a car dealership on a whim and paying cash for a Ferrari. He once spotted a stretch Lincoln Limousine in the movie *Shaft*. When the film was over, he went right out and paid $55,000 for a Lincoln identical to the one he'd seen on the screen. (Even going to the movies was an extravagance: since there was no screening room at Graceland, whenever Elvis wanted to see a film, he just rented an entire movie house for the evening, usually the Memphian Theater.)

During his lifetime, Elvis bought around two thousand cars, most of which he gave away. One Christmas he purchased ten Mercedes as presents. On another occasion, he bought and gave away over $100,000 in Lincolns and Cadillacs in a single day. While on vacation in Denver, Elvis stopped at a car dealership and bought five automobiles at a total cost of $70,000.

On another occasion he bought and gave away fourteen Cadillacs in one day. Visiting the showroom at the time was Mrs. Minnie Person. Mrs. Person had been admiring a Cadillac for some time when a man approached her and introduced himself as Elvis Presley. He asked her if she liked the car, and she replied that, indeed, she did. He then asked if she would like to have the car, and Mrs. Person replied that she certainly would, but there wasn't any way she could afford it. "There is a way you can afford it," Elvis told her, "because I just bought it for you."

Elvis's love of vehicles was not restricted to the four-wheeled variety. One day in the 1960s he bought eleven Harley Davidson motorcycles. He kept one and gave the rest away to his friends, instantly creating the "El's Angels."

Elvis's generosity is the subject of legend. He routinely gave away expensive jewelry and even homes. He gave incredibly costly gifts to family, employees, long-time acquaintances, and complete strangers.

His extravagant gift giving cost Elvis hundreds of thousands—if not millions—of dollars. Spending money on others seemed to bring him more pleasure than spending it on himself, as though the look on a person's face as he or she received a Cadillac or a diamond ring was irresistible.

One of Elvis's favorite gifts to give was jewelry. His personal jeweler, Lowell Hayes, traveled on tour with Elvis, carrying a mobile jewelry store with him. In the last five years of his life, Elvis bought $650,000 worth of jewelry from Hayes, most of which he gave away. One night in the middle of a concert Elvis presented backup singer J.D. Sumner with a $40,000 ring. While appearing in a concert in Asheville, North Carolina, in 1975, Elvis passed out jewelry worth $220,000 to his band and the audience.

Elvis also enjoyed giving gifts to other celebrities whom he admired. He once gave boxer Muhammad Ali a $10,000 robe with Ali's name and "The People's Champion" embroidered on back. Ali wore the robe in a losing effort against Ken Norton and never wore it again.

Occasionally, Elvis's gifts were literally as big as a house. Vernon Presley's home was purchased by Elvis, and he helped Ginger Alden's mother buy her house. Elvis even bought a house for one of his cooks, Mary Jenkins, which she lives in today.

Even in death, Elvis managed to keep on spending. The cost of his funeral, including the cost of his solid copper casket and the hiring of several members of the Memphis police force for crowd control, was $52,000.

★ ★ ★

Elvis also gave prolifically to charities. In almost every instance his giving was done anonymously. Each Christmas, he donated $2,000 each to fifty Memphis-area charities. Some estimates place his total lifetime charitable contributions as high as $20 million. None of these charitable contributions were taken as tax deductions; Elvis believed that using gifts as tax deductions defeated the spirit of giving.

His poverty-stricken childhood made Elvis particularly interested in supporting children's charities. He performed concerts in his birthplace, Tupelo, Mississippi, in 1956 and 1957 to raise funds for the construction of the Elvis Presley Youth Foundation. Thereafter, he donated $100,000 a year for the upkeep of a youth center constructed by the foundation. In 1968, Elvis auctioned his Rolls Royce and donated the $35,000 in proceeds to a charity for retarded children.

In 1973 Elvis gave a concert in Hawaii that became the first worldwide satellite television program. The proceeds from that performance were donated to a cancer research organization. In January 1975, Elvis performed a benefit concert for victims of a tornado in southern Mississippi, and he donated the concert's entire proceeds: $109,000.

He also gave his support to other entertainers in need. When country singer T. G. Sheppard was just starting out, he needed a bus to tour in. Sheppard, a Memphis resident, met Elvis at a roller skating party. Later, Elvis showed up at his house to surprise him with a brand new bus. When Jackie Wilson, one of Elvis's favorite singers, suffered a debilitating stroke in 1975, Elvis sent his wife a check for $30,000 to help make ends meet. He also donated $50,000 to the Motion Picture Relief Fund, an organization that assists needy retired actors. Elvis's contribution was the largest ever made by an individual.

On some occasions, Colonel Parker helped Elvis decide where to make his donations, sometimes with embarrassing results. For example, in late 1963, Parker heard that Franklin Roosevelt's presidential yacht, *The Potomac,* was deteriorating and scheduled for destruction. The Colonel thought it would be a good publicity stunt for Elvis to save the famous boat from destruction. At the Colonel's suggestion, Elvis bought the yacht for $55,000.

The Potomac was in complete disrepair, so the Colonel had it painted so it would look good when it was photographed for the newspaper. What most people didn't realize was that he'd painted only one side.

Colonel Parker then decided the boat should be given to charity to create yet another media event, but giving the boat away wasn't easy. It was in such bad condition the cost of restoring it would exceed its value. Even the March of Dimes, FDR's pet charity, refused to accept the boat.

Finally, actor/entertainer Danny Thomas agreed to accept *The Potomac* on behalf of St. Jude's Children's Hospital in Memphis. At the donation ceremony, while they were both smiling for the cameras, Thomas reportedly whispered to Elvis, "Why did you buy this piece of crap?" Elvis was too embarrassed to admit that Colonel Parker had coerced him into buying the wreck.

★ ★ ★

One could argue that Elvis's largest charitable contribution was to the so-called Memphis Mafia, the group of close friends who seemed to swarm around him wherever he went. They all worked for Elvis in one capacity or another, providing everything from bodyguard services to schlepping water and handing out scarves during his performances. Their salaries were modest, but Elvis also took care of most of their personal expenses, such as housing, food, medical (including a nose job for George Klein), and even dental expenses. He paid a total of $14,000 in dental bills incurred by his friends. (All the money went to a Los Angeles dentist named Max Shapiro, whom Elvis visited on several occasions, sometimes for dental work, other times to get prescription medication. The Memphis Mafia also made extensive use of Dr. Shapiro's services.)

Some of his friends acted as personal bodyguards, sometimes with disastrous—and expensive—results. On one occasion, they severely beat a man who was trying to sneak into Elvis's hotel suite. Elvis was subsequently sued by this individual for $6 million. The case was settled out of court for considerably less. In 1973 Elvis was forced to hire attorneys to defend another lawsuit brought by four men alleging that his bodyguards beat them up at the Las Vegas Hilton. The $4 million lawsuit was eventually dismissed by a Los Angeles court.

Despite the aggravation they sometimes caused him, Elvis continued to treat the Memphis Mafia like family. These men enjoyed a lifestyle as grand as Elvis's own. When he vacationed in Vale, Hawaii, and Palm Springs, he usually paid for his friends and their wives to come along.

Once, during the Christmas holidays, Elvis decided to test the Memphis Mafia to see whether they were taking him for granted. When Christmas day arrived, he handed each one an envelope. Instead of the generous checks they expected, each envelope contained McDonald's gift certificates. Elvis quickly revealed his joke and produced the expected pile of cash. Some years later, one of those gift certificates sold at an auction of Elvis memorabilia for a thousand dollars. Not a bad return on Elvis's one-dollar investment.

In truth, Elvis may have been right to be suspicious. After years on the Elvis dole, his friends seemed to expect the royal treatment, and they weren't above suing him. During his racquetball phase, Elvis had been convinced to lend his name to a chain of racquetball facilities and to supply the initial financing for the construction of the courts. The venture was called Presley Center Courts, and Elvis, his foreman, Joe Esposito, and his personal physician, George Nichopoulos, were partners. Both Esposito and Nichopoulos had a history of counting on Elvis to meet their financial needs. Elvis had supported Esposito for years, and he had already made personal loans to Nichopoulos totaling over $300,000.

When Elvis later decided he couldn't afford to participate in the venture, Esposito and Nichopoulos sued him for damages of $100,000 and enforcement of the agreement. Elvis settled the suit by borrowing $1.3 million from the National Bank of Commerce, putting up Graceland as collateral to fulfill his obligation.

Another $100,000 a year went to pay Elvis's personal singing group, Voice. The group didn't perform or record with Elvis very often as time went on. Group members were simply required to be on call to sing with Elvis in private, at his $200,000 Graceland recording studio, for fun.

Even Elvis's pets seemed to be expensive. When his eighteen-year-old Chow dog, Getlo, developed kidney problems, Elvis spared no expense to save the animal. He flew Getlo to the New England Institute of Comparative Medicine in Boston for treatment. The dog was operated on for a considerable sum but died a few months later.

★ ★ ★

The divorce settlement with Priscilla was yet another drain on Elvis's bank account. Originally, she agreed to a $100,000 lump-sum payment, plus $1,000 a month for herself and $5,000 a month for Lisa Marie. Later, a friend convinced her that she was crazy to have accepted such a ridiculously small settlement from her multi-millionaire ex-husband. Eventually swayed, she hired an attorney and went back to the well for another drink. In the court filing, Priscilla claimed that she had never known the true extent of Elvis's financial holdings.

Elvis made no attempt to argue with Priscilla, but instead pushed for a quick resolution of the issue. He eventually agreed to another lump-sum payment of $2 million, plus $8,000 a month for ten years and child support of $4,000 a month. Priscilla also received the proceeds from the sale of a home in California and a 5 percent interest in two of Elvis's music publishing companies.

Priscilla had always assumed that Elvis was fabulously wealthy. When he died, she was shocked to learn the true extent of his estate. Financial mismanagement and lavish spending had left her daughter with a much smaller inheritance than anyone would have guessed. The future of that inheritance was now in the hands of a man ill-equipped to handle it, a man who hadn't yet realized how close he was to disaster—Elvis's father.

2

VERNON PRESLEY, EXECUTOR

THE MAN LEFT IN CHARGE of what remained of the Elvis estate was born in Fulton, Mississippi, on April 19, 1916. As a boy, Vernon Elvis Presley was close to his mother, Minnie Mae, but his relationship with his father, J. D. Presley, was always distant, at least in part because the boy was "work shy." By the time Vernon was fifteen, J. D. had sent him to live on a relative's farm in the hopes that farm life would instill some kind of work ethic in the boy. Young Vernon used his banishment from the Presley household as an excuse to drop out of the eighth grade.

With little education or ambition, Vernon had trouble finding and sticking to jobs for most of his life. He worked variously as a farmer, truck driver, and painter, but never for very long. In 1933, when he was seventeen, he met Gladys Love Smith at church, who was four years his senior. Two months later they eloped, and two years later, on January 8, 1935, Gladys gave birth to twin boys. The first, Jesse Garon, was stillborn. Jesse was buried in an unmarked grave in the Priceville Cemetery in Tupelo. The second baby, Elvis Aaron, would grow up an only child.

With the Great Depression in full swing, times were hard, particularly in the rural South. In 1938, times got even harder for the Presley family. Vernon was forced to sell a hog to one Orville Bean for four dollars. Partly out of anger at having been forced to part with the animal for so little, and partly out of dire need, Vernon altered the amount on the check from four to forty dollars. He was caught and sentenced to three years in Parchman Prison in Sunflower County, Mississippi. He was released after serving nine months of his sentence.

While Vernon was in jail, Gladys and Elvis made out as best they could. They moved in with Gladys's first cousin, Frank Richards, and Gladys worked as a seamstress so she could stay at home and take care of her three-year-old son. She and Elvis were forced to rely on government surplus commodities for much of their food.

Gladys never seems to have blamed Vernon for her family's hard times. Even when her anger was wholly justified, she excused all of her husband's faults and failings without complaint. Yet Gladys also had a great deal of pride, and she was ashamed of having to accept welfare while Vernon was in prison. Whenever she had to go to the local welfare office, she brought a group of people with her so it wouldn't be obvious who was seeking assistance.

After his release from prison, Vernon took a job with the Works Progress Administration of President Franklin Roosevelt. For a while, he built public toilets in Pascagoula, a small town at the southernmost tip of the state, near Biloxi, but he soon tired of the hard work and the heat, so he quit.

Vernon and his brother, Vester, decided to try their luck in Memphis, a hundred miles northwest of Tupelo. Work was more plentiful in the larger city, and the two brothers quickly found jobs as factory workers. For the next two years, they spent the week in

Memphis and the weekend back home in Tupelo. When World War II ended, the work at the factory slowed and Vernon lost his job.

Back in Tupelo full-time now, Vernon worked first as a laborer at a lumberyard, then he took a job driving a truck for twenty-two dollars a week, a respectable wage at the time. The job made it possible for Vernon to move his small family into a lower-middle-class duplex. For a while, the future began to seem a little brighter for the Presleys. Then Vernon's boss spotted him driving his work truck for personal use, and he fired him.

In 1948 Vernon, Gladys, and Elvis moved to Memphis. The Depression was over, and work was easier to come by, but Vernon was no better at keeping a job. No sooner would he find what seemed to be permanent employment than his "bad back" would act up and he'd quit.

By 1953, Vernon's teenage son was on his way to becoming the real breadwinner of the Presley family. Just out of high school, Elvis was driving a truck for Crown Electric and planning to pursue the trade full-time. He was even wearing his hair in the long pompadour style currently favored by other truckers.

That summer, Elvis visited the Memphis Recording Service to make an acetate demo recording. Elvis had always had a nice singing voice. He sang regularly at the Pentecostal services of the First Assembly of God Church his family attended. In 1945, when he was ten years old, he'd won second prize at the Mississippi-Alabama Fair and Dairy Show for his rendition of Red Foley's "Old Shep." Gladys gave him a guitar for his birthday the following year. His curiosity about what he might sound like on a record was understandable.

(Elvis had actually wanted a rifle on his eleventh birthday, but his mother thought a gun was too dangerous, so he settled for the guitar. He found the one he wanted in a Tupelo hardware store. That store is still standing today, and thousands of visitors come to Tupelo every year to see the display case where the King of Rock 'n' Roll found his first guitar.)

Though Elvis was reportedly very disappointed by what he heard on that first record, he returned on January 4, 1954, and recorded two more songs. This time he met the owner, Sam Phillips, who had established the recording service as a sideline to his Sun Records studios. The Alabama-born Phillips had found some success—and notoriety—as the first white man to record black R&B and blues artists. With the advent of several competing black labels, he'd begun looking for a white artist "with the Negro sound and the Negro feel." Phillips thought he might have found what he was looking for in Elvis. He called him back later that spring to rerecord a song he'd received on demo, but the session didn't go well. Reportedly, Elvis failed miserably.

Phillips then introduced Elvis to guitarist Scotty Moore and bassist Bill Black, who were playing country music at the time with the Starlight Wranglers. The three rehearsed together for a few months, and then, on July 5, they recorded several songs for Phillips, including Arthur "Big Boy" Crudup's "That's All Right," which became a local hit and marked the start of Elvis's career.

When Elvis began to sing professionally, Vernon was opposed to his son's career choice. He told Elvis he had never met a guitar player who was worth a damn. Vernon's support for his son's singing career seems to have begun when the money started rolling in. Even when Elvis was playing small, local clubs and shows he was bringing in more than his father; he often made more money in one night than Vernon made in a week.

Elvis's recording of Junior Parker's "Mystery Train" hit the number-one spot on the country charts in September 1955. That same year, Phillips—to his undying regret—sold Elvis's recording contract to RCA for $35,000—a huge price for the time. Elvis himself received a $5,000 advance, and promptly bought his mother a pink Cadillac. When Elvis became a national star in 1956, Vernon quit his job and, at his son's request, went to work as Elvis's business manager.

Vernon Presley, Executor   2 5

Elvis was apparently unconcerned that his father was unquali-fied for the job and had never managed to work long at anything in his life. Throughout his career, Elvis surrounded himself not with the most qualified professionals but with friends and family, the only people he ever really trusted. Elvis didn't care if Vernon knew about managing or not; his father was simply a man he could trust with his money.

While Gladys always hated the limelight, Vernon enjoyed his son's notoriety. Elvis's fame brought him the respect he had never been able to attain on his own, and he wasn't above flaunting it. In one story, Vernon and Gladys attended their son's 1956 Tupelo per-formance, and as they approached the entrance to the concert venue, they were asked for their tickets. Vernon reportedly pulled out a hundred dollar bill and handed it to the ticket taker and said, "Here are our tickets."

By the time his son died, Vernon seemed to believe that his own vicarious fame would continue unabated. Shortly after the funeral, he signed an agreement with the William Morris Agency, engaging them to deal with anticipated interview requests. His ask-ing price was $25,000 per engagement. There were few takers.

The relationship between Vernon and his son was cordial but not intimate. However, Elvis was very close to his mother. The way in which Vernon responded to her death in 1958 would remain a sore subject between the two men for many years.

When Gladys died, Elvis was devastated. He was serving in the military at the time, and some said her fear about what would hap-pen to her son while he was in the army caused her death. It's much more likely that her death was the result of years of alcohol abuse. Elvis took a few months leave shortly after his induction to be with his ailing mother; she died the day after he arrived at Graceland. Elvis would call his mother's death the great tragedy of his life.

When Elvis's army unit shipped out to Germany, his grieving father went along. Soon after arriving in Bremerhaven, Vernon met

the still-married Davada "Dee" Stanley, and she assuaged his grief
rather quickly. In July 1960, Vernon and Dee were married. Elvis
was opposed to his father's marriage so soon after the death of his
mother, and he did not attend the wedding. When Elvis returned
from the army to discover that Dee had redecorated Graceland
(Gladys had been the original decorator), he made arrangements for
his father and his new wife to live elsewhere. He didn't send them
far, though; Elvis bought them a house down the street with a backyard adjacent to the Graceland property. Vernon was living in that
same house when Elvis died.

★★★

Those around at the time recall that Vernon was shocked and
surprised by his son's death, despite Elvis's obvious poor health. It's
hard to imagine how anyone couldn't have seen it coming. However, Vernon was so disturbed that many feared it would aggravate
his chronic heart trouble and kill him. He was completely distraught
and clearly unprepared to envision life without his son—which is
perhaps understandable since for the past twenty years Elvis had
provided him with work, unimagined wealth, worldwide fame, and
a reason for living.

With Elvis dead and the financial future of the Presley estate
unexpectedly resting entirely on his shoulders, Vernon knew he
needed help. Not surprisingly, he turned to Colonel Parker, the man
he believed was responsible for so much of his son's success.

Vernon had always held Parker in high regard. In an interview
for CBS television, shortly before Elvis's death, Vernon said,
"Colonel Parker's an honest guy. Once you find out you don't have
to worry about a guy being your manager, what he will do for you
[sic]. He handles it, you do the show, and everything works out
wonderfully."

It was actually Parker who first contacted Vernon when he
learned of his client's death. The vultures were circling, the Colonel
warned. People everywhere would be making moves to cash in.

Something had to be done to take control, *now.* A former employee of Parker's recalled his boss's side of that conversation years later: "We must immediately make sure that the outsiders cannot exploit the name of Elvis Presley," the Colonel said. "We can mourn, but a long and inactive period of grief over Elvis will prove disastrous for you, for his daughter, for his estate, and for his legend."

Vernon, nearing collapse over his grief and his fear about the future, eagerly signed an agreement to continue employing Parker at his old commission rate. On August 23, Vernon sent the Colonel the following letter:

Dear Colonel:

I know you have many details to straighten out pertaining to the commitments you had for Elvis. I am deeply grateful that you have offered to carry on in the same old way, assisting me in any way possible with the many problems facing us.

As executor of Elvis's estate, I hereby would appreciate it if you would carry on according to the same terms and conditions as stated in the contractual agreement you had with Elvis dated January 22, 1976, and I hereby authorize you to speak and sign for me in all these matters pertaining to this agreement.

I will rely on your good judgment to keep the image of Elvis alive for his many fans and friends. I will call on you from time to time to help me with many other phases and future problems.

Sincerely and Many Thanks,

Vernon Presley

★★★

When the news of Elvis's death became public, his fans began to converge on Graceland like locusts. The faithful came from all over the world to mourn their idol. Demand for air travel to Memphis was so great airlines added extra flights to their daily schedules. A group of 220 Canadians resorted to chartering their own plane.

The crowds gathering outside of Graceland quickly numbered in the hundreds of thousands. The Memphis heat was unbearable that August, and ambulances regularly whisked away dehydrated mourners. The crowds remained at the mansion until Elvis was buried. In the weeks that followed, approximately five thousand people a day visited his grave.

Along with the crowds of mourners came dozens of enterprising vendors eager to take advantage of the grieving throng. The wake quickly took on the atmosphere of a carnival. The day after Elvis died, there were "Elvis Presley Memorial" T-shirts for sale at ten dollars each. One ingenious entrepreneur purchased all of the copies of the *Memphis Commercial Appeal* announcing Elvis's death from the machines near Graceland and then resold the fifteen-cent newspapers for five dollars apiece. For those fans on a more limited budget, ten-cent postcards of Graceland could be had for only $1.50. Elvis bumper stickers that cost around fifty cents the day before were now available for two dollars. And, of course, food vendors lined Elvis Presley Boulevard, selling soda and ice cream at greatly inflated prices.

But someone had begun exploiting Elvis's death even before he'd been declared clinically dead at the hospital. Reporters and photographers from the *National Enquirer* were on the scene at Graceland only minutes after the ambulance left with the moribund Elvis. The tabloid could only have been tipped off by someone inside the mansion.

No one knows for certain—except the guilty party—who leaked the news to the press that morning, but Ginger Alden was certainly in the best position of anyone at Graceland to have made a call to the *Enquirer*. According to a longtime friend of Elvis, the call she made that afternoon came *after* she'd discovered Elvis's body on the bathroom floor, and it wasn't to a friend, but to her mother. Over the next few minutes, the friend says, Ginger and her mother worked out a plan to sell the exclusive story of Elvis's death to the tabloid for $100,000. Ginger telephoned a contact at the *Enquirer* and made the deal. *Then* she called for help. Additionally, Joe Esposito and the others who raced to Elvis's room in response to Ginger's call later reported that she didn't look as though she had just gotten out of bed. Ginger, they said, was completely dressed and wearing makeup.

If the unidentified *National Enquirer* informant was the first person to cash in on Elvis's death, he or she was soon followed by many others. The distinction for tackiest exploitation should probably go Elvis's cousin Bobby Mann. He took a picture of Elvis lying in his casket and sold it for $78,000 to the *National Enquirer,* which splashed it across the tabloid's cover.

Exploiting Elvis's death was not by any means exclusive to his friends and relatives, either. Former American Bandstand host and well-known music business figure Dick Clark was the first to complete a movie based on Elvis's life. He produced the film without the participation or permission of the Presley estate, though Priscilla was hired for $50,000 to review the script for accuracy. When *Elvis* was televised on February 11, 1979, it was the highest-rated program in its time slot by a wide margin. (Kurt Russell portrayed Elvis in the film.)

But not every attempt to cash in on the Elvis name was successful. A Memphis man thought he could make a few bucks off of Elvis's old ranch, the Circle G. His plan was to subdivide the property into one-inch-square plots and sell them for five dollars each. If the plan worked, he stood to make several million dollars. However, he found few buyers interested in a handful of dirt. To help pay the mortgage, he was forced to also offer seven-inch strips of the wooden fence surrounding the ranch. Elvis's cousin Billy Smith signed certificates of authenticity to accompany each piece of the fence.

But Colonel Parker became the main player in the Elvis exploitation game—in fact, he very quickly controlled the entire board and revised the rules for his own benefit. For instance, one year after Elvis died, in September 1978, Parker organized a week-long Elvis convention at the Las Vegas Hilton. He called the convention "Always Elvis." It included a few attractions, such as continuous

Elvis movies and music, but the only truly noteworthy event was the appearance of Vernon, Priscilla, and Lisa Marie together in public for the first time since Elvis's death. They unveiled a life-sized bronze statue of Elvis outside the Hilton showroom. But what most fans got for their fifteen dollar entrance fee was the opportunity to buy more Elvis products from vendors, who had each paid $2,500 to secure a booth. In the end, after the Presley estate received fifty percent of the proceeds, everyone but Parker came away empty. Word quickly circulated that "Always Elvis" was a rip-off, and only a few hundred fans attended the convention. Many vendors didn't even make enough to cover their booth fee.

This was just how the Colonel liked to arrange his schemes, so he made money both ways, whether anyone else did or not. Almost immediately after Elvis's death, Colonel Parker turned his attention to gaining complete control of the burgeoning world of Elvis merchandise. Parker wanted an exclusive licenser, a company that would manage and protect the merchandising of the name and likeness of Elvis Presley and all associated products (except records—the Colonel had already sold the rights to Elvis's music to RCA). To do this, Parker turned to Harry Geissler.

Geissler owned Factors Etc. Inc., a merchandising company known for its handling of such big-name clients as *Star Wars, Rocky, Grease,* and Farrah Fawcett Majors. Geissler, a third-grade dropout, was a steelworker before he went into in the merchandising business. He had built Factors into the country's largest mass merchandiser.

Before achieving its first big success with the once-ubiquitous Farrah Fawcett swimsuit poster, Geissler's company was probably best known for its legal difficulties. Factors paid $100,000 to settle highly publicized charges that it was selling unauthorized merchandise. But Factors also had a reputation for aggressively pursing violators of its own exclusive licensing agreements. Bootleg products had plagued the Elvis market for years, and the Colonel was eager to let Factors foot the bill for chasing down the new crop of *post mortem* opportunists.

Also, Factors was a multimillion-dollar operation that was capable of handling the licensing of a star the magnitude of Elvis Presley. Yet the company wasn't so large that the Presley estate wouldn't be an important account.

Colonel Parker flew to New York to finalize negotiations with Harry Geissler, and they quickly came to an agreement. In return for a 15 percent royalty on all sales and a guaranteed minimum payment of $150,000 a year, Factors was granted the exclusive right to exploit the name, likeness, characterization, symbols, designs, and visual representations of Elvis Presley on merchandise throughout the world. The contract was for eighteen months, with four one-year renewal options.

The merchandising agreement with Factors was unusually complex. Rather than contracting directly with the Elvis Presley estate, Parker set up the arrangement between Factors and another company, Boxcar Enterprises. Parker had formed Boxcar in 1974 to license and merchandise Elvis Presley products. At the time, it was a relatively small gear in the Elvis money machine. Typically, rock star merchandise is only in demand when the fan base for the artist is teenagers. (You don't see many Frank Sinatra T-shirts.) But once Elvis died, a license to merchandise suddenly became an extremely lucrative property.

The ownership distribution of Boxcar was also puzzling. The Colonel owned 40 percent, with 15 percent each going to Elvis, the Colonel's long-time assistant Tom Diskin, RCA's George Parkhill, and Hill and Range Music Company's Freddy Bienstock. It's not clear why payments for Elvis Presley merchandising should have gone to Diskin, Parkhill, and Bienstock. When Bienstock's shares in Boxcar were later bought back by the company, Colonel Parker owned 56 percent and Elvis and Tom Diskin each owned 22 percent.

It is quite possible that Colonel Parker formed Boxcar with Elvis's death in mind. Even in 1974, it was obvious that his client was having serious health problems. Most of Elvis's inner circle believed he could go at any time. When Elvis was gone, there would be no more concert income and no more new records—but there might be a heck of a souvenir business.

Factors's agreement with Boxcar called for another seemingly arbitrary distribution: 25 percent of all royalties were to be paid to Parker, 25 percent to the Presley estate (of which the Colonel also collected half), and 50 percent to Boxcar. At the end of this convoluted road, Parker ended up with 53 percent of all royalties on Elvis merchandising. Only 36 cents out of every dollar went to the Presley estate. Adding insult to injury, the ever-present William Morris Agency collected a commission on the deal for "introducing" Harry Geissler to Colonel Parker.

Vernon's decision to agree to this contract was a costly one. With Elvis dead, merchandising was the estate's only major potential income source. Vernon gave away most of it to Colonel Parker.

★★★

Harry Geissler often referred to himself as the "King of the Merchandisers," and he loved the idea of representing the "King of Rock 'n' Roll." Once the deal was set, Factors made a truly royal effort to get Elvis products onto the market in a hurry. Within six weeks of Elvis's death, Factors had assembled a merchandising effort reminiscent of Colonel Parker's 1956 Elvis Presley Enterprises campaign, which generated millions. (Elvis replaced Davy Crockett as the biggest selling character merchandise of the 1950s.) The company embarked on a nationwide tour to exhibit its line of Elvis Presley products. His intention, he said, was to move the Elvis market away from what was largely a collection of junk.

While Geissler promised that his company would only approve the manufacture of tasteful items, in practice, Factors licensed practically anything, as long as the money was right. Items produced by permission from Factors included dollar bills bearing Elvis's picture, gold-plated belt buckles, Christmas tree ornaments, T-shirts, posters, watches, bubble gum cards, and a multitude of other items.

On January 8, 1978, on what would have been Elvis's forty-third birthday, fans by the tens of thousands converged upon Memphis. The Memphis fairground was turned into a giant flea market of Elvis merchandise. Factors was ready for the fans, but the pirates were still testing the company's vaunted reputation for nailing bootleggers. Geissler estimates that in the first two years after Elvis's death his company filed five hundred lawsuits to stop the sale of unlicensed products.

Unlicensed merchandise was even being sold in the strip mall across the street from Graceland. It was a great location; fans making the pilgrimage to Memphis frequented these stores, naturally assuming they were sanctioned by the Presley estate. T-shirts, posters, ash trays, fuzzy dice, lady's underwear, vials of "Elvis sweat"—all were selling well without a license from Factors. The company had been ignoring this small violation (Factors had its hands full already), but when other merchants in the mall who sold only licensed items threatened to stop selling Elvis products, the company took action. Factors sent a letter to the store owners stating, "We are informed that you are presently selling unauthorized Elvis Presley T-shirts, belt buckles, candles, and other merchandise. This letter shall constitute a formal and final demand that you, your agents, employees, and representatives immediately cease and desist." The store owners were given fourteen days to comply with the order or lawsuits would be filed seeking an injunction to shut them down, as well as payment of monetary damages.

Harry Geissler always did his best to portray Factors, Colonel Parker, and Vernon Presley as one big happy family. Factors's efforts on behalf of the Presley estate were presented as entirely benevolent. "We are aggressive in protecting the rights of the Presley organization," Geissler told the *Memphis Commercial Appeal*. "The pirates are literally stealing money from Elvis's family, and remember, it is a family affair from the grandmother all of the way down to little Lisa Marie." In private, Geissler was much more candid about his feelings: "I don't even like Elvis's music, but I always was a fan of Colonel Parker's."

Colonel Parker and Harry Geissler, seeking to justify themselves, at times seemed to be in competition for the tackiest public remark about Elvis. Probably Parker's best was when he said, "We are keeping up the good spirits, we are keeping Elvis alive. I talked to him this morning, and he told me to carry on." Geissler's was less poetic, but just as tasteless: "We are the only protection against people dancing on Elvis's grave."

★★★

With the Colonel in his usual position of running the business of Elvis Presley (while taking as much money for himself as possible), Vernon Presley could turn his attention to the more mundane tasks of wrapping up his late son's estate. But of all the things Vernon expected to deal with in his new role as the estate's executor, grave robbing was probably not one of them. Yet among the thousands of tourists coming to Forrest Hill Cemetery to view Elvis's final resting place, three had something a little more ghoulish in mind than paying their final respects.

On the night of August 29, 1977, Memphis police officers patrolling the cemetery in a squad car spotted three men approaching Elvis's tomb in a suspicious manner. One of the officers called to the men, and they bolted for their car. A lengthy chase ensued, which ended in the arrests of Ronnie Lee Adkins, Raymond Green, and Bruce Nelson on suspicion of attempting to steal Elvis's body and hold it for ransom.

When the police caught the men—all from Memphis, all in their early twenties—they found no digging tools in the car, only a tool kit consisting of a crow bar, bolt cutters, a wrench, and a screwdriver. (It's not clear how they planned to remove and load Elvis's eight-hundred-pound casket into the back of their Chrysler using that particular combination of tools.) It was assumed the digging tools had been thrown out the car window during the chase. Without the tools, the police had no evidence and the men were released.

Later, one of them revealed that the three had planned to steal the body and hold it for a $3 million ransom. Their attorney stated categorically that there was never any real intention to steal the body. The whole affair, the attorney said, was a hoax designed to create a story that one of the men could sell to the *National Enquirer.*

Whether or not the attempted theft of Elvis's body was genuine or not, it disturbed Vernon greatly. In addition, families of others interred at Forest Hill were complaining that they were being inconvenienced by the thousands coming to visit Elvis's grave. Vernon decided to petition the City of Memphis for permission to move the graves of his late son and his wife to Graceland. Permission was granted by the city, and a date of October 2 was secretly set for the move.

At 7:00 P.M. on October 2, two white hearses carrying the remains of Elvis and Gladys Presley drove through the gates of Graceland. The hearses were escorted by eight Memphis police officers, as well as five Shelby County deputies. Amazingly, secrecy was maintained, and only a handful of fans were present at the gates to witness the evening procession.

By 8:30 P.M., both Elvis and Gladys were reinterred behind the pool, in the Meditation Garden. Vernon wanted to make certain that no future attempts would be made to steal his son's body. Elvis's eight-hundred-pound copper casket was encased in a three-thousand-pound vault, with a two-thousand-pound granite slab covering it. An eight-hundred-pound bronze plaque was placed on top of the casket. As a final measure of security, Vernon had the graves guarded twenty-four hours a day and monitored by closed-circuit television.

Immediately after the news of the reburial became public, Vernon was bombarded with requests to open the grave site to the public. He was agreeable, but he wanted to wait until the graves were cosmetically perfect. However, demand was so great that

Vernon feared he was risking endless break-ins if he didn't open the grave site sooner. On November 27, 1977, the grave sites were opened to public viewing. The first day saw eight thousand visitors.

Vernon's brother, Vester, had been the gate guard at Graceland for twenty years. For all those years, his job had been to deny access to the grounds. After Elvis's body was moved to Graceland, he found himself suddenly opening the gates and inviting the world to come in.

As what would have been Elvis's forty-third birthday approached, fans began visiting Elvis's grave in astounding numbers. Between mid-December 1977 and mid-January 1978, around a hundred thousand people made their way through the gates of Graceland. The throngs lining up to view Elvis's grave caused both traffic and litter problems. The trash problem was so bad that the City of Memphis added a full-time employee to supervise cleanup around the neighborhood. The garbage thrown on the ground each day on Elvis Presley Boulevard was equal to the amount of refuse generated by a hundred households in a week. At 3:00 A.M. each day, a street sweeper was dispatched to Graceland to clean the final remnants from that day's visitors.

Meanwhile, Forrest Hill Cemetery, suddenly needing to dispose of Elvis's original tomb, sold the stone crypt to a group of Memphis businessmen. Their plan was to cut the stone into forty-four thousand two-inch-by-one-inch pieces and offer them for sale at eighty dollars each. Sold piecemeal, Elvis's crypt would bring in over $3 million. So what if the idea was in bad taste, the businessmen felt. As one said, "Elvis was the epitome of bad taste. The people who worship him reflect the same bad taste. The typical fan is a woman in her mid-thirties to forties with plastic hair, too much makeup, gaudy clothes, and a gaudy personality; a forty-hour-a-week guy who punches a clock, with a secondary education or less; people from the same social, political, and economic class he was, the lowest."

But Elvis fans surprised the cynical businessmen by refusing to buy the hacked-up tomb, and very few pieces of the crypt were ever sold. Many fans thought of Elvis as a member of their family, and the prospect of owning a hunk of his grave was just too ghoulish.

★★★

With Elvis's body resting securely at Graceland, Vernon turned his attention to the estate's finances. And the first thing he addressed was the payroll. For over two decades, Elvis had surrounded himself with friends and family assigned to a variety of largely invented jobs. Elvis's friends were supported by him and shared in his extravagant lifestyle, ensuring that they would always be available when he wanted them. When Elvis died, many of his "employees" assumed they would continue to work for Vernon as they had for his son. They were mistaken.

Vernon had long resented the Memphis Mafia and others Elvis had put on the payroll. He believed they were nothing but a waste of money—"their" money, the Presley's money. Vernon could be seen wincing whenever Elvis went on another buying spree. Vernon never forgot what it was like to be poor, and he lived in constant fear his profligate son would spend the Presley family back into poverty. He and Elvis argued heatedly about money on more than one occasion.

Vernon voiced no objection, however, when he himself was the beneficiary of Elvis's generosity. When Vernon and Dee split up on May 5, 1977, it was Elvis who paid the divorce settlement. Elvis was only too happy to see her go—he'd never liked the woman, whom his father had married too soon after his mother's death, he felt—but he was *not* happy to shell out $250,000. Fifteen years later Dee Stanley would write an article for the *National Enquirer* entitled "Elvis and His Mother Were Lovers."

Now Elvis was dead and Vernon was the boss. Almost immediately, the Memphis Mafia found itself unhoused and unemployed. Two members of the Mafia thought the layoffs did not apply to them. Joe Esposito, Elvis's foreman, publicly stated that he would be staying on to help Vernon manage what was left of the Elvis business. Charlie Hodge, whose main job had been to hand Elvis his water and scarves on stage, was sure that Vernon would continue to allow him to live at Graceland. Both of them were summarily relieved of their duties; poor Charlie Hodge was kicked out of Graceland after living there for seventeen years.

Vernon's axe was not exclusively applied to hangers-on inside the mansion. Gary Pepper, who had multiple sclerosis and lived in a wheelchair, had worked for Elvis for several years. Elvis first spotted Pepper at the gates of Graceland, in his wheelchair, hoping to catch a glimpse his hero. Elvis sent word to the front gate to bring Pepper up to the mansion. Pepper told Elvis he had started one of the first Elvis fan clubs, and Elvis created a job for him opening his fan mail. Two months after Elvis's death, Vernon fired Pepper, stopping his $400 monthly payments.

Vernon's downsizing radically altered the lives of many people. Overnight, friends who had been living like millionaires suddenly found themselves with no incomes at all. Many lacked, in today's terminology, readily transferable job skills (handing out scarves and opening mail doesn't lead to much else).

A select few members of Elvis's entourage found gainful employment after they left Graceland. Red West went on to costar in the television series *Baa Baa Black Sheep*. Jerry Schilling became the manager of the Beach Boys. But the only thing most of the Memphis Mafia had to sustain themselves with were memories— and luckily, people were willing to pay big money for them.

The remembrances of Graceland insiders soon became closely guarded treasures, gems to be sold one carat at a time to the highest bidder. When George Klein was giving a lecture about Elvis at Memphis State University, he noticed members of the audience taking notes and he became very upset. He demanded that all note taking cease immediately. Klein wasn't about to give away information that movie producers and book publishers would pay money for.

While George Klein still has not gotten around to writing his book, several Presley insiders have. These included Elvis's uncle and former Graceland gate guard, Vester Presley; Ed Parker, Elvis's bodyguard and karate instructor; Marty Lacker, another Memphis Mafia member; Elvis's stepmother, Dee Stanley, and her sons; even Elvis's nurse at Baptist Hospital, Marian Cocke. Within two years of his death, more than twenty books about Elvis had been published, as well as several television specials and movies; all were produced from the recollections of Elvis's friends and relatives.

After being fired by Vernon Presley, Charlie Hodge designated Dick Grob, the former head of security of Graceland, as his manager. Hodge sold his technical advice to Dick Clark for the production of his made-for-television movie about Elvis. Charlie then hit the concert stage, singing with, and presumably handing water and scarves to, an Elvis impersonator. He also regularly appeared at Elvis conventions and started his own Elvis newsletter.

J. D. Sumner, a member of Elvis's backup singing group the Stamps Quartet, made extra money by renting a limousine Elvis had given him for a thousand dollars a weekend. He also continued to perform in concerts billed as "Elvis Tributes."

Even Elvis's discoverer, Sam Phillips, got into the act by changing the call signs of his radio station to WLVS and instituting an all-Elvis format. Sam had missed out when he had sold Elvis's contract to RCA. He was not about to miss his last chance to capitalize on his Elvis connection.

Shortly after Elvis's death, Ginger Alden recorded the song "I'd Rather Have a Memory Than a Dream." She then hit the tabloid circuit. She later moved to New York to pursue a modeling and acting career. She signed with the Ford Modeling Agency, which helped her land work in both magazine advertisements and television commercials. Ginger was proud that she could get modeling jobs from clients who knew nothing about her Elvis connection.

She was not, however, as successful with her acting career. She enrolled in acting classes in Lee Strasberg's famous Actors' Studio, but her one starring role was in a movie called *The Living Legend*. The film was loosely based on Elvis's life. She later revealed that Elvis had come to her in a dream and told her to accept the role.

Until recently, Ginger held the distinction of being practically the only person who was ever close to Elvis and who hadn't written a book, but her story is scheduled to hit the bookstores on the twentieth anniversary of Elvis's death.

In February 1978, Ginger Alden's mother made a final attempt to squeeze some money out of Elvis's estate. She sued for $39,587, which she claimed Elvis had promised her to pay off her home mortgage. Her case was quickly dismissed.

About the same time, Priscilla made a similar claim, though she didn't take it to court. She told Vernon that Elvis had promised to give her father the money to buy a liquor store, but Vernon refused to give it to her.

In January 1978, Vernon secured his own financial future. A Memphis court ruled that he should continue to receive $1,400 a week from the Presley estate. This was his salary when Elvis was alive. He was also granted a sum of $28,000 for his services as executor. At the time, Vernon commented that his salary might look big but not much was left after he finished paying taxes.

★★★

In the months immediately following the funeral, money continued to roll in to the Elvis estate. Indeed, the influx of cash was phenomenal. From August until the end of 1977, the estate earned $2.1 million. At that pace, the estate would bring in $8 million in the first year, easily eclipsing Elvis's peak earnings of a million a year.

The single biggest revenue producer during this period was a television special that aired on October 3, 1977. Filmed in June of that year, *Elvis in Concert* captured Elvis performing in Omaha, Nebraska, and Rapid City, South Dakota, on what would be his final concert tour. The King was grossly overweight and had diffi-culty remembering the words to his songs. His memory was not well served by CBS's airing of this program, but it earned the estate $750,000. Today, the decidedly more image-conscious estate refuses to allow this program to be aired or sold.

The cash continued to flow at a respectable pace over the next year and a half. To an outsider, the Presley estate appeared to be enormously rich. Within two years, however, it was clear that the estate's financial condition was worsening. The public's interest in Elvis had begun to wane. Sales of Elvis merchandise were slowing. Record sales were still high, but the estate was committed to a con-tract with RCA that paid little in the way of royalties.

And there were expenses. Lots of them. The cost of maintaining Graceland alone was $500,000 a year. Much of that money was spent on security. Vernon continued to employ guards to patrol the grounds of Graceland, since break-ins had always been a constant concern and crowds continued to gather at the front gate. And every now and then, a fan would jump the fence. (When Elvis was alive, a then-unknown Bruce Springsteen climbed the wall and made it to the front door before he was apprehended by a security guard.)

Then in February 1978, the National Bank of Commerce sued the estate for payment of three loans totaling $1.4 million. To make matters worse, the IRS increased its valuation of the estate from $5 million to $22.5 million and assessed new inheritance taxes valued in the millions.

The cash on hand to meet the estate's obligations was about a million dollars. In a desperate attempt to raise money, Vernon began selling Elvis's most valuable assets. He started by disposing of his only personal asset: his house. He sold his home for $85,000 and moved into an apartment at Graceland. Next, he sold Elvis's Tri-Star jet, *The Hound Dog II,* to *Hustler* magazine publisher Larry Flynt for $1.1 million. In May, he sold the *Lisa Marie* for $3 million to the First Church of God in Benton, Illinois. The original asking price had been $2.5 million, but Colonel Parker had come up with the idea of charging an extra $500,000 to allow the purchaser to use Elvis's name in conjunction with the plane.

The First Church of God's pastor, the Reverend Lloyd Tomer, bought the *Lisa Marie* with the idea of flying it around the country and charging admission for tours. Reverend Tomer hoped to raise a million dollars to pay off the debt owed on his newly built sanctuary. Unfortunately, the reverend overestimated the public's interest, charging a very unpopular $300 admission fee. An oil company that was originally planning to joint venture the operation with the church pulled out of the deal when it became apparent that few people were willing to pay the exorbitant fee.

Reverend Tomer grew desperate to find a way to make the *Lisa Marie* pay off. He flew the plane to Memphis to coincide with an appearance by the Reverend Billy Graham. The admission price by this time had dropped to five dollars. Still, very few people came to tour the plane. Eventually, Reverend Tomer was forced to default on the loan his church had taken out to purchase the *Lisa Marie*, and the plane was repossessed by the bank.

Vernon continued selling off parts of the estate in what became a virtual Elvis garage sale. It seemed that only Graceland itself was not for sale. For the present, Vernon viewed the mansion as untouchable, but he desperately needed to find a way to pay the expenses of maintaining it.

About this time, the city of Memphis came forward with an idea that just might solve Vernon's financial difficulties. Shortly after Elvis's death, the city had begun to plan an Elvis memorial, but there was considerable disagreement among local officials about what form the memorial should take. The first idea was to erect a statue. That idea soon gave way to the vision of an Elvis Presley museum. The museum idea prevailed because of its obvious profit potential.

In the spring of 1978, the City of Memphis took their museum idea to Vernon. But city officials found Vernon very demanding. He insisted that any such museum be located on property the Presley estate owned across the street from Graceland. He also wanted a portion of the profits from the museum to go to the Presley estate.

Though negotiations had been secret, the *Memphis Commercial Appeal* broke the story of the proposed museum in June, revealing the city's plan to split museum admission fees equally with the Presley estate until the building was paid for. After the costs were recovered, the story disclosed, the city would receive 25 percent and the estate would receive 75 percent. It was also reported that the Schlitz Brewing Company had agreed to donate $25,000 toward the construction of the museum.

In August, Vernon confidently announced that an agreement with the city to build the museum was near completion. He confirmed that the museum would be located across the street from Graceland, on property owned by the Presley estate. Vernon went on to say that the museum would be completed within a year.

Once the announcement was made, however, critics of the plan jumped in. Several citizen's groups were upset that taxpayers would be funding the construction of the museum at a cost of a million dollars. If the Presley estate was going to share in the profits, why wasn't it sharing any of the expenses?

In response to these complaints, the city established a trust fund at the National Bank of Commerce to receive donations for construction of the museum. Only $10,000 came in.

The City of Memphis then decided that an outright purchase of Graceland might be more attractive to the taxpayers. This strategy would also eliminate the continuing involvement of the Presley estate, and the project would return a profit for the city alone. In the city's plan, Graceland would be untouched and the museum itself would be constructed nearby.

But to gain and keep public support for their project, city officials would have to demonstrate that Graceland could be operated at a profit. The State of Tennessee agreed to assist the city in evaluating the possible purchase of Graceland. A consulting firm was engaged to study the economic feasibility of operating the home as a tourist attraction. The consultants' report was to include everything from how memorabilia would be displayed to how many visitors could be expected and what admissions fees would be charged.

Of course, no one had yet run the idea by Vernon. To their surprise, when the city approached him with the idea of purchasing Graceland, they were rebuffed. City officials persisted in their efforts to acquire Graceland and were eventually quoted an asking price of $3 million, which they turned down. Interest in Elvis, city officials believed, would fade in time, and they'd never make their money back.

★★★

The stresses of Vernon's new responsibilities took an immediate toll on his health. He'd been plagued by heart problems for years; his first heart attack had occurred in 1975. In February 1979, after complaining of an irregular heart beat, Vernon received a pacemaker. After that, his health declined steadily. As the pressures of the ailing estate grew, his heart condition worsened. The failure of the museum negotiations was a kind of final blow.

On June 26, 1979, at 9:20 A.M., Vernon's heart stopped. Priscilla, Lisa Marie, Colonel Parker, and Joe Esposito all attended the funeral, as did Vernon's ex-wife, Dee Stanley, and Elvis's ex-girlfriend, Linda Thompson. The occasion of Vernon's funeral would be the last time all of Elvis's inner circle would be together. Vernon was buried beside Elvis and Gladys in the Meditation Garden at Graceland. As the casket was being lowered into the ground, the sound of Elvis singing a spiritual was played over a loudspeaker.

Vernon's death left Lisa Marie and Grandma Presley as the sole beneficiaries of Elvis's estate. The rights of Elvis's other relatives had ended when Vernon died. Of course, Vernon had already cut almost everybody off. The one exception was Elvis's aunt, Delta Mae Biggs.

Ms. Biggs continued to live at Graceland from the time of Elvis's death until her own death some fifteen years later.

Vernon's personal assets were both few and of little value. The only thing of substance he had ever personally owned was the house Elvis had bought for him, and this had already been disposed of. He left his remaining few assets to his nurse and girlfriend, Sandy Miller.

Elvis's will had allowed Vernon to choose his own successor, and everyone was anxious to hear whom he'd left in charge. He surprised everyone by choosing three coexecutors for the declining estate: Joseph Hanks, Elvis's and Vernon's accountant, the National Bank of Commerce, and Priscilla Presley.

At the time of Vernon Presley's death, the financial condition of the estate was truly bleak. It would be up to Priscilla to save her daughter's inheritance. She had said for years that she should have managed Elvis's money. Now she was going to get her chance.

But first, there was the Colonel.

The true master of exploitation was waiting in the wings. He had been preparing for Elvis's death for some time. You might even say he had prepared for that moment since they first met in 1955.

3

THE COLONEL V.
THE GUARDIAN

ON THE AFTERNOON Elvis Presley died, Colonel Tom Parker was in a meeting with his staff in his suite at the Sheraton Hotel in Portland, Maine. Elvis was scheduled to appear for two nights at Portland's Cumberland Civic Center, the first stop of his latest concert tour. The Colonel had begun booking his client in smaller cities like Portland in an effort to hide his increasingly shocking appearance from the media.

A phone call interrupted the meeting; it was Joe Esposito. "Elvis is dead," he told Parker. The Colonel paused for a few moments, those present at that meeting recall, then spoke into the phone. "Nothing has changed," he said, "this doesn't change a thing." After Esposito hung up, Parker placed a call to RCA Records to confirm that the company would still be paying all of the expenses he had incurred in Portland. RCA assured the Colonel that the record company would take care of everything. His expenses covered, Parker left the hotel for the airport. He had unexpected business in Memphis.

Colonel Parker didn't dress the part of a mourner at Elvis's funeral; then 68 years old, the 250-plus pound Parker showed up in a Hawaiian shirt and a baseball cap—he almost always wore some kind of hat to cover his bald spot. He declined an invitation to serve as a pallbearer, and he didn't speak or play any role in the memorial ceremony. In fact, as the final words were being spoken at Elvis's grave, the bulky, beflowered Colonel could be seen sitting on a police motorcycle off in the distance.

Parker had come with a contract in his hand, ready for Vernon's signature. That piece of paper would keep him on as manager, despite his client's death. "His death doesn't change anything," the Colonel was heard to say to Vernon. "If you show signs of weakness at this moment, everything will fall apart." There was never really any doubt the contract would be signed. Vernon had always been something of a pushover as far as the Colonel was concerned. An associate of Parker's from the 1950s recalls Parker commenting that all he ever had to do with Vernon was mention money.

Parker would now manage Elvis Presley's memory. During the days following the death of Elvis, the Colonel was often quoted as saying, "I owned 50 percent of Elvis when he was alive, and I own 50 percent of him now that he's dead."

★ ★ ★

In 1979, after Vernon's death, the principals of the Presley estate were back in Probate Court for the appointment of the new executors and approval of various administrative items. Vernon's chosen successors—Joseph Hanks, the National Bank of Commerce, and Priscilla Presley—received quick approval from Probate Judge Joseph Evans. However, one administrative item caught the judge's eye. The new coexecutors intended to extend Colonel Parker's management contract. The estate needed Judge Evans's permission to continue with the agreement, but his approval was considered a mere formality. No one expected the judge to offer any objections.

The coexecutors wanted to continue the estate's relationship with Colonel Parker because they believed he was the one man who could make the most of whatever opportunities existed to capitalize on the public's continuing but unpredictable fascination with Elvis Presley. Also, they expected that Parker would present Elvis in the same "high-quality manner" he had throughout Elvis's career. On June 29, 1979, they had sent him the following letter:

Dear Colonel:

As the persons named under the will of Vernon Presley to be the successor, coexecutors and cotrustees of the estate of Elvis Presley we would like to extend to you our appreciation for the work you have done for the estate and to let you know that we do want things to continue as they have and as set forth in the letter of August 23, 1977, from Vernon Presley as the then executor of the estate to you.

A copy of that letter is attached hereto as an exhibit and the terms thereof are incorporated herein.

Sincerely,

Joseph A. Hanks, Priscilla B. Presley, the National Bank of Commerce

When Judge Evans learned the details of the estate's agreement with Colonel Parker, he was flabbergasted. What surprised and concerned him most was that the contract gave Parker 50 percent of the estate's income. The judge was amazed that anyone would pay such a huge commission for the management of a living entertainer, let alone a dead one. He began to wonder if Lisa Marie's estate was really in the hands of people who were looking out for her best interests. To everyone's surprise, Judge Evans withheld his approval of the contract. He first wanted a full investigation of Parker's financial dealings, and to conduct it, he appointed a Memphis attorney; the attorney would be Lisa Marie's financial guardian until the matter was settled.

For the first time since they'd met nearly twenty-five years ago, someone was stepping between Elvis and the Colonel.

★ ★ ★

Since 1955, the Colonel's grip on Elvis had continued nearly unchallenged. Back then, Elvis was a hot new country singer on the rise, but hardly a star. His first manager, a Memphis disc jockey named Bob Neal, had asked Parker to help him make some tour arrangements for his young client. Parker was then managing some notable country singers himself, including Gene Austin, Eddy Arnold, and Hank Snow.

In Elvis, Parker knew he'd found something special, and he seems to have had no compunction about going after the young singer. The persuasive Parker convinced Elvis that he could make him a star. But Elvis was still a minor, so it was the boy's parents Parker had to convince to sign a management contract. Vernon was quickly won over, but Gladys took an instant disliking to Parker. For reasons of her own, she didn't trust him. In fact, she vehemently opposed her son having any type of relationship with "that man."

Then, as now, the Colonel was not easily dissuaded. When he learned that Gladys was a tremendous fan of Hank Snow—a major country star of the 1940s and early 1950s, and one of Parker's current clients—he asked him to visit her and plead Parker's case. In his autobiography, Snow wrote that he was under the impression at the time that he himself would receive 50 percent of Elvis's contract if he convinced Gladys to sign.

Snow's intervention did the trick, and Gladys signed. Colonel Parker was now Elvis's "sole and exclusive advisor, personal representative, and manager in any and all fields of public and private entertainment," and he would be for the rest Elvis's life. Snow, by the way, never got a penny.

Only once during their twenty-three-year relationship did Elvis actually try to fire Parker, though friends say he talked about it often enough. During the 1960s, Parker nearly destroyed Elvis by obligating him to star in a series of "B" movies, in which he sang ever more ridiculous songs. Elvis hated making those films, and for a while, they hurt his career. In 1968, a highly rated television special,

Elvis, along with a series of record-breaking Las Vegas concerts, revived his career, but by the mid-1970s, things were beginning to slow down again, and Elvis blamed the Colonel.

However, in one incident, according to members of the Memphis Mafia who were traveling with Elvis at the time, he actually asked for Parker's resignation. Elvis was never known to fire anybody himself, preferring to leave that bit of dirty work to others, typically his father. Even then, it took a fit of anger to move him to actually give the order.

Ironically, the start of the incident had nothing to do with Parker: the Las Vegas Hilton hotel where Elvis was performing fired one of its employees whom Elvis particularly liked. During his performance the next night, Elvis delivered a rambling tirade against the owner of the hotel, Baron Hilton. Colonel Parker stood backstage listening, at first stunned and then angry—Parker and Hilton were friends, and they had worked out a lucrative deal together. When Elvis left the stage, he and Parker argued hotly. The argument ended when Elvis threatened to fire Parker and stormed off to his suite. He immediately called Vernon and demanded that he fire the Colonel. Vernon protested, but Elvis was adamant.

When Vernon arrived at Parker's suite, he couldn't look him in the eye and he mumbled, but he came right to the point: the Colonel was fired. Parker was unruffled. He would dissolve the contract and leave without making a fuss, but first Elvis would have to come up with a little cash—$2 million, in unpaid expenses. He presented Vernon with an itemized bill, most of which was a blatant fabrication. Without questioning Parker's claim or even bothering to review the statement, Vernon backed down.

He went back to his son and convinced him that it would be a disastrous and costly mistake to fire Parker, and Elvis reluctantly agreed to make up with him. Why Elvis didn't realize that he could have gotten any number of people to put up the $2 million to buy his contract from Colonel Parker is anyone's guess.

According to a close associate, Elvis respected Colonel Parker for his ability to manipulate those with whom he negotiated. However, personally, Elvis felt very uncomfortable around the Colonel. Another friend says he never once saw Elvis and Parker together for a social occasion in the twenty-one years he knew them. Elvis kept his business and private lives separate. When he and the Colonel met, it was always to conduct business. After the Baron Hilton incident, their relationship became even more distant.

The truth was, despite the braggadocio, Elvis had been intimidated by the Colonel since they first met. There's no better illustration of the power Colonel Parker exercised over Elvis than his commission structure. For the first eleven years of their relationship, Parker collected a whopping 25 percent on all of Elvis's gross earnings. Though a percentage that size was not unheard of, it was twice the industry standard of the time. In 1967, the Colonel decided it wasn't enough.

One former Elvis associate recalls the incident that triggered Parker's demand for more money. It occurred when Elvis was in Hollywood in the midst of filming *Clambake,* his twenty-fifth movie. According to the associate, Elvis stumbled to the bathroom in the middle of the night and slipped and hit his head on the sink. He suffered a concussion, and the filming schedule was delayed until he recovered.

Parker attributed the fall directly to pills (perhaps rightly so), and he told Elvis he was going to have him constantly watched from now on to make sure such accidents didn't happen again. In return for the extra work, Parker demanded 50 percent of his earnings. If Elvis refused, Parker said, he would resign and Elvis's career would be ruined. Elvis grudgingly agreed to the increase, as the Colonel knew he would, and a letter outlining it was signed on January 2, 1967.

Ironically, in the movie *Fun in Acapulco,* Elvis plays a singer who objects when a manager who wants to represent him asks for half of his earnings. Elvis's character says, "That is pretty much for a commission." Additionally, Colonel Parker acted as technical advisor on most of Elvis's movies, though he was required to do little more than deliver his client. Once all the commissions and side fees were collected, Parker made more from an Elvis movie than Elvis did.

It's not clear why Parker didn't also demand that Elvis stop his self-destructive behavior. Rather than trying to convince his client to get help, the Colonel seems to have used Elvis's drug abuse problem to feather his own nest.

When the State of Tennessee began looking into charges against Dr. George Nichopoulos in 1979 for overprescribing medication to Elvis and others, Colonel Parker denied any long-standing awareness of the problem when he was interviewed by investigators. During that interview, Parker said Elvis had visited him at his Palm Springs home. Elvis appeared ill, the Colonel said, and he had asked if Elvis needed a break. Elvis apparently responded by saying that he was taking drugs, which were making him look sick. The Colonel offered to help, but Elvis refused and told him to mind his own business. Parker claimed that this was the first he knew of Elvis's drug problem.

Yet Elvis's drug-related fall, the one that led Parker to demand a higher commission, happened years earlier. Several people close to Elvis and Parker have confirmed that Parker knew Elvis had a drug problem several years before this supposed encounter. And no one remembers ever hearing Colonel Parker advise Elvis to stop using prescription medication.

The 50 percent commission stayed in place for the rest of Elvis's life. This was the arrangement Vernon Presley had practically begged the Colonel to accept after Elvis died; it's the same deal Vernon's successors were so anxious to renew. It's a testament to the force of Parker's personality that all these people were profoundly grateful when he deigned to accept half the estate's income.

★ ★ ★

The man Judge Evans chose to investigate Parker's relationship with the Presley estate was Blanchard Tual, a Memphis attorney; he would be Lisa Marie's financial guardian *ad litem* (for the time being), or until the issues with Parker were resolved. Later, the judge extended Tual's financial guardianship to Lisa Marie's eighteenth birthday.

Blanchard Tual was one of the few entertainment attorneys practicing in Memphis at the time, and Judge Evans probably chose him for the job because he was the most prominent of those few. Nonetheless, it was a fortuitous choice for the Presley estate; Mr. Tual took his assignment very seriously.

One of Tual's first tasks, in November 1980, was to oversee the filming of *This Is Elvis,* a movie being produced by Warner Brothers. Colonel Parker had sold Warner the rights for $750,000. Tual was on the set to assure himself that the movie was in the best interest of Lisa Marie. After reading the script and observing the production in progress, Tual was convinced the film was in good taste, would serve Lisa Marie's interest, and would make a substantial profit for the estate. Colonel Parker seemed to be off to a good start with Tual. Their honeymoon would be short-lived.

The first step in Tual's investigation was a crash course in the background of Colonel Parker. He interviewed the Presley estate's attorneys, Priscilla Presley, the Colonel, various music publishing attorneys, entertainment attorneys, and several RCA executives.

Tual had barely had time to assemble a thumbnail sketch when Judge Evans increased his responsibilities. On December 10, 1980, the judge authorized Tual to secure any and all tax information from August 16, 1977 to the present concerning Colonel Tom Parker and Boxcar Enterprises, the company Parker had formed in 1974 to manage Elvis-related merchandising. Parker agreed to turn over his and Boxcar's tax returns for 1977-79 under the condition that their contents would be kept confidential. Tual agreed to these terms to avoid a lengthy court battle.

The details of Elvis Presley's dealings with Colonel Parker had always been closely guarded secrets. In fact, before Judge Evans came into the picture, the exact terms of their business relationship were virtually unknown to anyone but Elvis, Vernon, and the Colonel. Tual's investigation would reveal for the first time the specifics of Colonel Parker's dealings with Elvis. The public had yet to discover just how self-serving the flamboyant, charismatic manager had been.

One of Tual's first conclusions was that Parker's 50 percent commission was indefensible. He called the Colonel's continuing claim on Elvis's posthumous earnings "excessive, imprudent, unfair to the estate, and beyond all reasonable bounds of industry standards." He also discovered that the contract raising Colonel Parker's share to 50 percent, dated January 2, 1967, contained no consideration for the increase; therefore, the agreement could be voided for lack of consideration.

In his report to Judge Evans, Tual explained how he believed Colonel Parker had gained such an unprecedented percentage of Elvis's earnings. "Elvis was naive, shy, and unassertive," Tual wrote. "Parker was aggressive, shrewd, and tough. His personality dominated Elvis, his father, and all others in Elvis's entourage."

The deeper Tual dug, the more skeletons he unearthed. In Tual's opinion, Colonel Parker handled the latter part of Elvis's career in an utterly self-serving manner. As evidence, he submitted a report on various side deals Parker had made over the years with people he was supposed to be negotiating with on Elvis's behalf. He cited several clear cases of conflicts of interest.

Parker had what almost amounted to an obsession with receiving extras for himself out of the deals he made for Elvis. Most of Parker's side deals and extras involved considerable amounts of money, but at times the Colonel would ask for worthless tokens just to demonstrate that he was in charge. According to a former Paramount Pictures executive, on one occasion Parker demanded that he be given the ashtray on the conference table before he would sign a contract with the movie studio. (Even an interview with the Colonel had a price tag. His fee was $25,000 for a short interview; $100,000 for a long one. Of course, there were very few takers.)

Colonel Parker's negotiations with the International Hotel in Las Vegas exemplified this pattern of collecting tribute in exchange for a chance to work with Elvis. In 1969, Parker negotiated a five-year contract with the hotel that provided his client with a salary of $100,000 to $130,000 per week. The Colonel often boasted about this deal, and he continued to brag despite the fact that that price was soon surpassed by acts of far less commercial value with far fewer operating expenses; Elvis had to pay a dozen musicians, a backup band, and a chorus, as well as spending hundreds of thousands on his costumes.

What should be understood here is that Las Vegas shows are typically money losers, designed to attract gamblers to the casinos. But with the Colonel's deal, the International was taking in twice what it was paying Elvis from ticket and drink sales alone. During Elvis's first four-week engagement, the hotel's gross receipts totaled $1.5 million. Elvis received $450,000. The net profit to the International for Elvis's four weeks of performances was $1 million, not to mention their increased gambling business.

Alex Shoofey was the manager of the International Hotel during the time Elvis appeared there. He says the contract Colonel Parker agreed to on behalf of Elvis was the best deal ever made by a casino in Las Vegas. Elvis Presley was the greatest attraction in the history of a town known for its stellar attractions. He was the International Hotel's only showroom act ever to show a profit.

What induced Colonel Parker to give the International such a good deal? One likely explanation is Parker's fondness for gambling. Parker became notorious as one of the most reckless gamblers in the history of the International. According to a former manager, "The Colonel was one of the best customers we had. He was good for a million dollars a year." The International provided Parker with a line of credit to support his habit and, in recognition of his economical delivery of Elvis, generous repayment terms for his casino debt. Parker may even have had some of his gambling debts completely forgiven.

In addition to the line of credit, Parker received special favors from the hotel. His freebies included a year-round suite of offices and hotel rooms, food and beverages for his home in Palm Springs, California, and free transportation to and from Las Vegas anytime he wanted it. The International also engaged Parker as a consultant. On April 20, 1972, Baron Hilton, who owned the International as well as the Hilton hotels that bear his name, wrote the Colonel a letter confirming the payment of $50,000 per year over a three-year period for "talent and publicity consulting services." On March 8, 1976, Hilton sent Parker a check for $25,000.

In Blanchard Tual's opinion, these side deals were made in exchange for the Colonel's delivering Elvis to the International at a cut rate. In his report, Tual stated that he believed Colonel Parker's gambling habit created a direct conflict of interest: "The impropriety of a manager losing such sums in the same hotel in which he has to negotiate on behalf of his client goes without saying."

Colonel Parker accepted still more favors from the William Morris Agency. In 1956, the agency was headed by Parker's close friend Abe Lastfogel, whom the Colonel nicknamed "The Admiral." As Elvis's agent, William Morris was entitled to 10 percent of his earnings. However, there is considerable doubt whether Elvis ever signed a contract with the agency; Parker probably made a handshake deal with Lastfogel on Elvis's behalf.

William Morris had very few responsibilities in its representation of Elvis. The agency occasionally provided advice to Colonel Parker concerning the structure of movie and concert deals, and it probably introduced him to a few important people in show business. But Parker always made the vast majority of decisions about Elvis's career on his own.

The person who seemed to have benefited most from Elvis's contract with William Morris was Colonel Parker. The agency gave the Colonel a rent-free office, purchased a home he wanted in Palm Springs, which it then rented it to him under very favorable terms, and it even provided employees of the agency, who worked for Parker at no charge. In theory, these new hires were being "trained" by the Colonel; in reality, they learned almost nothing, except how to prepare Parker's lunch.

Blanchard Tual's most disturbing revelation came after he turned his attention to Colonel Parker's dealings with RCA Records. It was widely assumed that Elvis had left behind an estate worth much more than it actually was. After all, the royalties from his records alone must have been pumping mountains of money into the estate. After his death, his records were selling faster than ever.

In fact, the estate's royalty income was far less than most people knew—thanks to the mysterious machinations of Colonel Parker. On March 1, 1973, Parker completed negotiations for a new seven-year record deal between RCA and Elvis. The contract called for a royalty of ten cents on singles, fifty cents on albums, and one dollar on double albums. The album royalty constituted only a five percent increase from Elvis's original 1955 contract—even though record prices had doubled since then. Other recording artists of the day were receiving $1.10 per album. The contract also called for a flat royalty rate, which meant that as record prices rose, Elvis's percentage would actually decrease.

In his report, Tual pointed out that under this agreement Elvis's royalty rate was only half that of artists like the Rolling Stones, Elton John, and the Beatles. A star of Elvis's magnitude should have commanded a royalty several percentage points higher. At the very least, the deal should have included a royalty rate that increased as sales for a particular album reached certain thresholds.

Stranger still, Parker had actually negotiated six separate agreements with RCA, all dated March 1, 1973. Four of those agreements called for RCA to make questionable payments to Parker. Those four agreements are summarized as follows (the "All Star Shows" referred to below was owned by Colonel Parker):

AGREEMENT 1: dated March 1, 1973, between RCA, All Star Shows, and Elvis Presley. Whereby as an inducement to Elvis to sign the seven-year exclusive recording agreement, RCA agreed to pay Elvis and All Star Shows the sum of $100,000 upon the expiration of the seven-year agreement. The payment to All Star Shows was in connection with Colonel Parker's merchandising that exploited RCA's interest in Mr. Presley and the records of Mr. Presley. The agreement was signed by Elvis and Colonel Parker.

AGREEMENT 2: A seven-year agreement dated March 1, 1973, between RCA, RCA Record Tours, and All Star Shows. All Star Shows agreed to furnish the services of Colonel Parker to assist RCA Records in planning, promotion, and merchandising in connection with the 1972 tour agreement concerning Elvis Presley. RCA agreed to pay All Star Shows a total of $675,000, payable $75,000 the first year and $100,000 per year for the remaining six years. In addition, RCA Record Tours also agreed to pay All Star Shows a total of $675,000, payable $75,000 the first year and $100,000 for the remaining six years. In sum, a total of $1,350,000 would be paid by RCA to Colonel Parker. In addition, RCA agreed to pay All Star Shows 10 percent of RCA Record Tours net profits. Elvis did not receive any moneys pursuant to that agreement.

AGREEMENT 3: A five-year agreement dated March 1, 1973, among RCA, All Star Shows, and Colonel Parker. All Star Shows was bound for the services of Colonel Parker for five years to consult with RCA Records and assist RCA Records in the exploitation of Elvis's merchandising rights. RCA agreed to pay All Star Shows $10,000 per year for a total of $50,000 over the five-year period. Elvis did not receive any moneys pursuant to this agreement.

AGREEMENT 4: A seven-year agreement dated March 1, 1973, between All Star Shows and RCA Record Tours. All Star Shows was bound to furnish the services of Colonel Parker to assist RCA Records in planning, promotion, and merchandising in connection with the operation of the tour agreement. RCA agreed to pay All Star Shows a total of $350,000, payable $50,000 per year over a seven-year period.

Why was the royalty rate for the new seven-year recording agreement so far below industry standards for an artist of Elvis's stature? Tual believed that Colonel Parker had looked out for his own interest when he negotiated the deal. In Tual's opinion, the over $2 million payment made directly to the Colonel in those additional four agreements induced him to agree to a relatively low royalty rate in Elvis's new contract.

The side deals between RCA and Colonel Parker did not end there, but continued after Elvis's death. As a result of new deals Parker made with RCA after Elvis died, the Colonel received at least $950,000 from September 15, 1977, to February 15, 1980, including $675,000 for services related to promotion, merchandising concepts, and packaging suggestions on RCA Record Tours; $165,000 in "consulting fees"; $175,000 for "extra services in preparing product promotion cost merchandising"; and $50,000 more for promotion, merchandising concepts, and packaging suggestions.

It should be noted that none of the later, 1977 agreements with RCA were approved or acknowledged by Vernon Presley, who was executor of the estate at the time, or by anyone connected with the estate. Consequently, it must be assumed that Vernon was unaware of them.

The final agreement signed by Colonel Parker on that fateful March day in 1973 may have been the single most financially damaging contract in the history of the music industry. It called for Elvis to sell the rights to all the songs he recorded before that date—seven hundred of them—to RCA for approximately $5.4 million dollars. It was a substantial amount of money, and Elvis was glad to get it at the time, but it was insignificant compared with the amount Elvis would have received over the years had he kept ownership of his songs. And remember, the Colonel got half and the IRS got half of Elvis's share. When all was said and done, only $1.35 million remained from the original payment—and most of that went to Priscilla to fulfill the terms of their divorce settlement. Elvis sold the rights to the greatest master catalog in music history and was left with virtually nothing to show for it. Thereafter, his estate received no royalties at all for any songs Elvis had recorded prior to March 1973.

The deal was a very unusual one; record companies rarely buy an artist's master catalog. Elvis is the only artist from whom RCA ever made such a purchase. But most puzzling of all was why Parker had allowed the sale to take place. It was this deal that Blanchard Tual believed to be the most serious transgression committed by the Colonel.

"The critical point in the RCA/Elvis Presley relationship was March 1, 1973," he wrote in his report, "with an agreement negotiated by Colonel Parker on behalf of Elvis for RCA to purchase Elvis's royalty rights for $5.4 million. The selling price was a fraction of their worth. The agreement was unethical, fraudulently obtained and against all industry standards. The tax implications alone should have prohibited such an agreement or at least prohibited it without further investigation."

As should have been obvious to anyone, then or now, this was an abominable transaction, especially considering the status of Elvis's career at the time. In 1973, Elvis was reaching another career peak. The *Aloha from Hawaii* NBC television special had aired on January 14. At a cost of $2.5 million, it was the most expensive entertainment special ever produced, but it was seen around the world by over a billion people. RCA later released a two-record album of the *Aloha from Hawaii* concert, which sold over 2 million copies. That year, Elvis was only thirty-seven years old, riding high, with no reason whatever to consider selling off an almost certain lifetime annuity.

On the other hand, Colonel Parker might have found a buyout very appealing. In 1973, Parker was sixty-three years old, overweight, and recovering from a heart attack. As a result of the agreements with RCA, he received $2.5 million. He was guaranteed to receive another $3,700,000 over the next seven years, in addition to 10 percent of the net profits from RCA Record Tours. The guaranteed payments to Colonel Parker provided a great deal of income to a man approaching the twilight years of his life.

Also, by 1972 Elvis's health had begun to fail, perhaps motivating the Colonel's actions. According to Tual, "It is not a coincidence that most of the side agreements that Colonel Parker made with RCA and the International Hotel were entered into after 1972. Colonel Parker had to be aware of Elvis's mental and physical deterioration."

In April 1977, only months before Elvis died, rumors circulated that Colonel Parker was putting Elvis's management contract up for sale. Parker denied the rumors then and continues to deny them today. Yet, a contract sale would have made sense, given what he must have thought about Elvis's future as a performer. He'd cashed out with the RCA royalty sale; selling Elvis's management contract would have provided Parker with a final, gigantic score.

At the time, Colonel Parker justified the RCA deals by saying, "The old records don't sell no more." Later, Parker would say the sale had been Elvis's and Vernon's idea. In his version of the events, RCA approached Elvis with a $3 million offer for his royalty rights. Elvis and Vernon were excited about the possibility of a quick infusion of cash. Colonel Parker thought it was a terrible idea and recommended against it, and in the end it was Elvis's decision to sell the songs. Colonel Parker simply carried out his instructions. It's hard to imagine Parker ever just following instructions, unless he would have benefited as a result. He was, however, successful in convincing RCA to pay almost double their original $3 million offer.

The RCA executive who signed the buyout agreement, Mel Ilberman, confirmed that $3 million was RCA's initial offer to purchase Elvis's masters. However, on other occasions, the same individual has stated that it was Colonel Parker who initiated the buyout, and others told Blanchard Tual that it was all the Colonel's idea. However, whoever initiated the buyout, the beneficiaries are clear.

The travesty of the RCA royalty sale was magnified when Elvis's death drastically increased the demand for his records. The backlog of Presley records in the RCA warehouses was eliminated almost overnight. RCA's first posthumous release, *Elvis in Concert,* sold more than a million copies in the first few days of its release. Orders for Elvis records came in to the RCA pressing plant with such velocity the computer system overloaded and shut down. Demand was so great RCA resorted to contracting with outside record-pressing plants. In England, an RCA record-pressing plant was reopened to help meet the demand for Presley products. This tremendous surge in demand for Presley albums affected the entire record industry. New releases by other artists were delayed because so much of the record industry's production capacity was being devoted to pressing millions of Elvis's albums.

How much did the Presley estate lose because of the royalty sale? In the four months following Elvis's death, RCA sold 200 million of his records. In January 1978, RCA reported record-setting profits for the first quarter due to what it termed the "extraordinary posthumous demand" for Elvis records. Approximately 500 million Elvis records have been sold since his death. At a conservative average retail price of $8 per unit, the total revenue from them must be around $4 billion. The Presley estate would have received 8 percent, or $320 million in royalties.

In Tual's opinion, "Colonel Parker's side deals with the International Hotel and RCA which Elvis did not approve, or acknowledge, were instances of paying Colonel Parker, not for services rendered to Elvis, but for services rendered to RCA and to the International. This is a clear, textbook conflict of interest, which no reputable manager should have even considered. RCA must also share the responsibility and blame along with Colonel Parker for the 1973 agreement. The executives who worked with Colonel Parker were not naive. They realized that the key to Elvis was Colonel Parker and that control of Elvis meant millions of dollars for RCA."

★ ★ ★

During his investigation, Tual also became interested in the activities of Boxcar Enterprises. It was through Boxcar that the Colonel had made the merchandising deal with Factors Etc. after Elvis's death.

What Tual found was that not only did Parker own a controlling interest in Boxcar but he also received the lion's share of the company's salary disbursements. From 1974 to 1979, Boxcar salaries were incredibly lopsided, and they grew more so with each passing year:

    1974: Elvis $2,750, Parker $27,650

    1975: Elvis $6,000, Parker $24,000

    1976: Elvis $10,500, Parker $136,000

    1977: N/A

    1978: Elvis Presley estate $161,000, Parker $351,000

    1979: Elvis Presley estate $273,000, Parker $468,000

Tual wondered why Elvis received such a small share of Boxcar, since he was the star and the one being merchandised. A likely explanation was that Elvis was ignorant of the inner workings of the company. When Tual questioned Parker about Elvis's access to information about Boxcar, the Colonel told him that Elvis did attend some Boxcar meetings. Yet, Elvis's signature is not found on any Boxcar documents. Chances are, he was again letting other people "take care of business."

Colonel Parker also used Boxcar to make some interesting arrangements with RCA. The record company partnered with Boxcar in 1974 for the sale of an album entitled *Having Fun on Stage with Elvis*. The album was sold under the Boxcar label, and RCA agreed to distribute the record worldwide and pay Parker an advance of $100,000 against a domestic royalty of one dollar and a foreign royalty of seventy-five cents. While 50 percent of the royalty went to Elvis, there was no contractual obligation for Boxcar to pay Elvis any part of the $100,000 advance. It is assumed that Elvis received none of it. If RCA had paid Elvis directly for this project, his royalty rate per album would have doubled. Thus, RCA helped Boxcar and Colonel Parker gain yet another financial edge over Elvis.

Tual also questioned Parker about the Factors deal. He wondered whether Parker had sought competing offers from other merchandisers. Parker's response was that he did negotiate with several other mass merchandisers. Factors was chosen because the company offered a minimum guaranteed payment of $150,000, Parker said.

But Tual also questioned the integrity of the Factors operation. As evidence of what he felt were questionable business practices, he identified several lawsuits that Factors had been involved in. In 1976, Factors president Harry Geissler paid $100,000 in fines for infringement of the Muppets design, the Peanuts characters, and the characters of Starsky and Hutch. In April 1981, Factors pleaded guilty in federal court in Wilmington, Delaware, on three counts of mail fraud and was fined $100,000. Included in the mail fraud charge was a charge of devising a scheme to defraud three of Factors's licensors of approximately $75,000 in royalties by entering false information into Factors's computerized sales journal.

"Therefore," Tual concluded, "the probability exists that Factors may have defrauded Boxcar and the estate. Sources of income such as foreign merchandising may have been withheld and may show up in an audit which should be conducted immediately."

Acting on the information that Tual presented, the court banned Factors from any further merchandising of Elvis Presley.

★ ★ ★

The luster of Colonel Parker's reputation was badly tarnished by the revelations of Blanchard Tual. One of the Colonel's favorite sayings was, "When I met Elvis Presley he had a million dollars worth of talent; now he has a million dollars." Many would soon agree that he should have added, "And for every million he gets, I get two!"

But while Parker's integrity was open to widespread criticism, few doubted his managerial wizardry. Even today, the public commonly agrees that Colonel Parker was a shrewd and resourceful manager who was greatly responsible for Elvis's phenomenal success. He may have been looking out for himself, but he was still a sharp operator making hot deals.

There is no question that Colonel Parker made some great deals for Elvis in the early years of their relationship. In 1956 he negotiated a record contract that paid Elvis forty-five cents for every album he sold—an exceptional royalty, considering that albums retailed for $3.98 at the time. Under Parker's direction, Elvis became the highest-paid actor in Hollywood. The Colonel's bravado came shining through when he negotiated Elvis's contract for his first movie, *Love Me Tender*. When he demanded a $100,000 for his client, the producer responded that Jack Lemmon didn't even make that kind of money. The Colonel's response was that maybe Lemmon should consider getting a new manager.

However, unnoticed by the public, Parker's effectiveness as Elvis's manager clearly diminished over the years. He made a slew of bad management decisions that hurt Elvis both financially and personally. In Tual's opinion, as time progressed, Parker simply became more interested in making money for himself than for Elvis.

Tual found one of the most glaring examples of this ineptitude in Parker's RCA deal: amazingly, in addition to everything else, it contained no audit clause. In fact, there's a blank space on the page where the audit clause is usually inserted, indicating that it may have been purposefully removed. Auditing a record company's royalty calculation is a normal part of the artist's end of the music business. Most artists are advised to audit their record companies whenever they've had high record sales. Tual believed that if an audit were ever conducted for the period of March 1, 1973, to January 31, 1978, the recovery in unpaid royalties would be substantial.

Furthermore, it seems the accounting provision of Elvis's recording contract has always been ignored by Colonel Parker, up to this day. Since 1973, RCA has regularly mailed accounting statements to Parker, but he has never objected to even one accounting, nor has he ever requested an audit. In fact, Parker always discouraged anyone from questioning the record company's books. At one point after Elvis's death, the coexecutors discussed auditing RCA and Colonel Parker advised strongly against it.

Auditing RCA would simply have been good business practice, which was incumbent upon Parker as Elvis's manager. Objecting to at least a few record company accounting statements is a matter of course to protect the artist and keep the option of an audit open. It's a well-known, industry-wide practice.

"Colonel Parker's practice," Tual wrote in his report, "of not objecting to accounting and not auditing, in light of the agreements and side agreements to Colonel Parker, bolster the argument that Colonel Parker was, in effect, bought off by RCA, either expressly or tacitly, and that for the payments he received, he kept Elvis under control."

Tual also questioned Colonel Parker's decision to turn down several lucrative foreign tour offers. Elvis was even more popular outside the country than he was at home. His following around the world was truly remarkable. When the *Aloha from Hawaii* television special was broadcast in Japan, it attracted 98 percent of the Japanese viewing audience. Yet, unbelievably, Elvis never toured outside the United States. In fact, he was the only American star with an international reputation who never performed beyond United States borders. Elvis himself had always been eager to make such tours, and he constantly discussed the prospect, not only with his entourage, but in press conferences as far back as the 1950s. There were many times when he could have used the money such a tour would have brought him.

Colonel Parker received some incredible offers from foreign promoters. He seems never to have told Elvis about the multimillion-dollar offer for a tour of Japan, or the one-million-dollar offer for a one-night performance in London. He gave a variety of reasons for restricting his client to U.S. appearances. There were always logistical problems, technical problems, security problems, and even tax problems.

Tual didn't learn why Parker refused to let Elvis tour overseas until after his investigation was over. The reason was Parker's most closely guarded secret, beyond any of his financial dealings, and he only revealed it after the Presley estate was suing him and his back was to the wall. For now, though, it seemed like just another mysterious case of managerial incompetence, one that was increasingly easy to imagine.

In his investigations, Tual discovered little things, too, that defied logic, but which made the case for Parker's incompetence stronger. For example, for some reason that has never been established, Parker failed to register his client with BMI (Broadcast Music Inc.) so that he could receive his share of writer's royalties for the songs in which he held a one-half interest. It is unclear how the Colonel could have made such an obvious mistake, especially since he would have shared in any royalties that Elvis received.

Colonel Parker's questionable business decisions also denied Elvis several important honors. Chief among those was a chance to perform for the president of the United States. Most entertainers would rank an invitation to perform at the White House as one of the greatest honors they might receive. But in 1975, when Elvis was invited to sing for President Richard Nixon, Parker declined the invitation because the White House refused to pay a $25,000 fee for the performance. Of course, the president doesn't pay for a performance at the White House, and everybody knew that. The Colonel's

response to criticism at the time was simply that Elvis never performed for free.

★ ★ ★

On July 31, 1981, Blanchard Tual filed a report of his completed investigation with Judge Joseph Evans. In the report, Tual
charged that Colonel Parker cost Elvis "millions of dollars because
of his lack of business savvy." It is unclear whether Parker's managerial omissions were the result of native incompetence or simple
neglect as he turned his talents to maximizing his own income. Tual
also criticized Vernon Presley and his successor executors for not
obtaining opinions from experts before signing agreements with
Colonel Parker.

Tual summarized his investigation into Colonel Parker's management of Elvis with a laundry list of serious allegations: "The
guardian submits that Colonel Parker knowingly violated the
artist/manager trust in 1973 and continued to abuse it until after
Elvis's death. There is evidence that both Colonel Parker and RCA
are guilty of collusion, conspiracy, fraud, misrepresentation, bad faith
and over reaching. The agreements may have been valid on their
face but they are unethical, fraudulently obtained, and against all
industry standards. These actions against the most popular American
folk hero of the century are outrageous and call for a full accounting for whoever is responsible."

In his conclusion, Tual wrote, "Lisa Marie Presley is only twelve
years old and has her whole life before her. She is entitled to the
benefits of her father's talents and should not be deprived of them
due to the self-dealing of her father's manager and record company."

The guardian *ad litem* went on to recommend that:

- The court deny the coexecutors petition to approve the
  compensation paid to Colonel Parker.
- The court direct the coexecutors not to enter into any
  future agreements with Colonel Parker.

- The court direct the coexecutors and the estate's attorneys to file a complaint against Colonel Parker seeking to void Colonel Parker's contracts with Elvis Presley and with the estate on the following grounds: a.) breach of contract; b.) breach of fiduciary duties; c.) negligence for failure to object to RCA's accounting; and d.) collusion and conspiracy with RCA Records to defraud Elvis Presley of royalties pursuant to the 1973 buyout.

- The court direct the coexecutors to cease paying any commissions to Colonel Parker.

- The court direct that any income that in the past may have gone through Colonel Parker or the estate be paid directly to the estate.

- The court direct the coexecutors to file a complaint against RCA in the proper court seeking to void the 1973 master buyout agreement alleging collusion and conspiracy with Colonel Parker in an effort to defraud Elvis of his royalties from such masters.

- The court direct the coexecutors and the estate's attorneys to continue its audit against RCA, and that if RCA raises any defenses of the estate's right to audit back to 1973, then the estate should sue for an accounting and audit back to 1973.

- The court direct the coexecutors to further obtain an audit of Factors or at least, in the alternative, a full and complete accounting.

On August 14, 1981, Judge Evans appeared in court to announce his decision concerning the Blanchard Tual report. The courtroom was full of Elvis fans, who were in town for the fourth anniversary of Elvis's death. The judge issued an order demanding the cessation of all payments to Colonel Parker. He further ordered the Presley estate to bring suit against Colonel Parker for improper activities related to his managerial service for both Elvis and his estate. RCA was to be named in the suit as Colonel Parker's accomplice.

★ ★ ★

On August 16, 1981, the fourth anniversary of Elvis's death, headlines in newspapers across the country questioned the integrity of Colonel Parker's management of Elvis. One headline read, "Former Manager of Presley Denies Cheating Entertainer." Another: "Did Colonel Parker Take the King for a Ride?"

The Colonel lashed back against the criticism from the press. He issued a statement to the *Memphis Commercial Appeal* saying Elvis and Vernon were always pleased with his services and that both had wanted to continue their relationship with him indefinitely. Parker also claimed that detailed explanations were always given to Elvis before he entered into any contract on his behalf.

And, for the first time, Parker publicly criticized Elvis. He referred to him as a moody and headstrong client with little motivation. Managing Elvis was not an easy job, Parker said, and he deserved the compensation he had received. The Colonel also declared that he was fully prepared to defend himself against all of the allegations made against him.

Parker didn't have to wait long for a chance to defend himself. Following Judge Evans's order, the Presley estate sued both Parker and RCA (an excerpt from the estate's complaint against Parker is contained in the appendix). RCA didn't want to be tied to Colonel Parker as a co-defendant, so it sued Parker and countersued the Presley estate.

Colonel Parker filed his countersuit in Nevada, alleging that he was entitled to half of Elvis's assets. The basis for his suit was the claim that he and Elvis had become partners over the years. But no one seriously believed that Parker and Elvis had ever been partners. Those close to Parker at the time say the suit was just part of his overall strategy to push the Presley estate to the edge of bankruptcy. The Colonel had the advantage of being able to afford to continue dancing in courtrooms for much longer than the estate. He knew he could keep the process going until his enemies became more reasonable.

For months and months the Colonel and his attorneys used every delaying tactic imaginable. Their favorite trick was to obtain changes of venue. Parker's lawyers successfully had the case moved from Memphis to New York to California and back again. The Presley estate found itself paying attorneys in three states.

Then, just when it seemed the estate finally had Parker on the ropes, the Colonel played his ace in the hole and revealed his deepest secret. In June, 1982, Colonel Thomas Parker, American showman, promoter, and entrepreneur extraordinaire, announced that he was, in reality, Andreas Cornelius Van Kuijk, a native of Holland who had emigrated to this country illegally in his youth. No soap opera writer in the world could have come up a more startling or unlikely plot twist! And it succeeded in throwing all of the legal battles into chaos.

Born in Breda, Holland, on June 26, 1909, the Colonel had stowed away on a freighter carrying a cargo of liquor to America when he was twenty years old. Once in the United States, he'd joined the army, where he served until 1931. In the fall of that same year, he took the name of a deceased army officer, Tom Parker.

After his discharge, Parker moved to Tampa, Florida, where he met and married Marie Ross. While living in Tampa, he embarked upon a career in the carnival. Over the next few years, he held a variety of positions in the Johnny J. Jones Exposition, from hot dog vendor to trainer of the Great Parker Pony Circus. Parker's most infamous "act" during that time was his dancing chickens exhibit, which most people credit him with inventing. The floor of the chickens' display cage was a sawdust-covered hot plate. To convince the birds to trip the light fantastic, Parker just turned up the heat.

Parker retired from the carnival in 1941 to run for elected office. He was successful in his campaign for dog catcher of the City of Tampa, but he quickly tired of public service. In 1942 he returned to show business as a manager of country music artists. Four years later, he acquired his well-known military title when his old friend Louisiana Governor Jimmy Davis, whom Parker had known during his carnival days, appointed him an honorary Southern Colonel.

At last Parker's reason for turning down all offers for tours outside of the United States was clear. He had no passport and couldn't get one without revealing his secret. Colonel Parker had cost Elvis Presley millions of dollars in earnings from foreign engagements because he was an illegal alien!

Parker's citizenship status was suddenly in doubt, as was the jurisdiction of the United States in the lawsuits pending. Sorting it all out would take months, maybe years, and the Presley estate was running out of resources. (It is presumably Parker's own fame that has protected him from going to prison.)

By the start of 1983, Parker's bleed-'em-white strategy was paying off. The Presley estate's attorneys informed the coexecutors that they were in a no-win situation. The estate had already spent over $2 million pursuing its lawsuit against Colonel Parker. To recover its legal expenses, plus the additional fees it would have to spend to win the suit, the estate would have to demand millions of dollars in damages from Parker. He could at that point declare bankruptcy and the estate would get nothing. Even if the Colonel did pay the estate, the IRS would claim the majority of the money in taxes, and the estate would end up with a net loss. If the estate pursued the case and lost, it would be bankrupt. The only economically viable solution was to settle with Parker.

The coexecutors agreed to pay Colonel Parker $2 million in exchange for his giving up all future claims on income from the estate. After twenty-eight years, Colonel Tom Parker was finally relieved of duty. RCA agreed to provide the $2 million in return for exclusive rights to release Elvis Presley recordings.

After the lawsuit was settled, the principals tried to put up a friendly front for the public. On June 16, 1983, the Presley estate, Colonel Parker, and RCA issued a joint announcement stating that they had "amicably resolved the various matters of controversy between them." The estate also paid tribute to the "significant contribution of Colonel Parker and RCA records in the unparalleled career of Elvis Presley." In reality there is still considerable resentment and dislike on all sides.

Today, the Presley estate seems to be embarrassed by the fact that it receives practically no royalties from the sale of Elvis's records. A Presley estate insider calls the $5.4 million RCA paid for Elvis's royalty rights "a figure so small it just makes your head ache." Representatives of Elvis Presley Enterprises (EPE) have said that a new deal has been reached with RCA by which the estate receives royalties on packaged anthologies of Elvis recordings. The estate will not comment on the size of the royalty payment, except to say that "the particulars are our business." In truth, EPE receives only token goodwill payments on any song Elvis recorded before March 1973.

★ ★ ★

Privately, those inside the Presley organization have varying opinions of Colonel Parker; publicly, they are unanimous in their praise of him. In fact, the estate now claims that Colonel Parker's management style and contract with Elvis were not unusual compared with other artist/manager relationships of the 1950s and 1960s, and they do have a point. Modern-day norms of management don't just make Colonel Parker look bad, they reflect poorly on the managers of that era in general.

After all the revelations and lawsuits, Priscilla Presley continues to defend Colonel Parker and is quick to praise him in the media. When a coffee table book about Graceland, produced with the cooperation of Elvis Presley Enterprises, turned out to contain a tirade by the author against Parker, Priscilla tried unsuccessfully to have the publisher pull all copies of the book from the stores. She even attended Parker's eighty-fifth birthday party. The event was held at the Las Vegas Hilton, and it was hosted by the Colonel's old friend Baron Hilton.

It is unclear why Priscilla continues to defend Parker, a man who clearly cost her ex-husband and her daughter many millions of dollars. Perhaps the settlement of the lawsuits included a provision that compels her to do so. Or maybe she's trying to preserve the myth that Elvis Presley and Colonel Parker were the greatest artist/manager team in the history of show business; the dark side of Parker conflicts with the Cinderella story she continues to sell to the public.

★ ★ ★

With all we know now, it's easy to blame Colonel Parker for everything that went wrong with Elvis's career, but Elvis must carry his share of the blame. He could have put professionals into the positions he reserved for friends and family. He could have toured Europe if he'd demanded to do so. He could have appeared in quality films instead of low-budget clunkers. He could have insisted on recording top-notch songs instead of the forgettable tunes for which the Colonel could get him a piece of the publishing rights. And, if he'd wanted to, he could have fired Colonel Parker.

In his final report, Blanchard Tual allowed that Elvis had contributed to his own financial difficulties. "I am sure Elvis never read any of the contracts," Tual wrote. "He went along with the Colonel because he was very unsophisticated and from a very young age had all of the money he could ever want. Elvis did not care whether the Colonel made 25 percent, 50 percent, or 80 percent. Elvis received tax advice and assistance from accountants and attorneys such as Joe Hanks, Charlie Davis, and Beecher Smith III. However, he did not seek their advice on a regular basis. Elvis never sought advice on any agreements with Colonel Parker and generally tended to ignore his lawyers unless and until he got into trouble."

★ ★ ★

In 1984, Colonel Parker made his first appearance at an Elvis Presley event since the court settlement. He was the guest of honor at a small celebration held in Tupelo on the anniversary of the death of that community's most famous scion. As of this writing, the Colonel has appeared at no other Elvis-related public event.

In 1990, the Presley estate bought Colonel Parker's collection of Elvis memorabilia in a multimillion-dollar transaction. Parker decided to sell to the estate even though it had been outbid by a Japanese group. He probably didn't want them to open a competing Elvis attraction. The items in Colonel Parker's collection will one day be displayed in their own museum at Graceland, which can now show only small portions of it at a time.

Today, Colonel Parker lives in Las Vegas. Every day, visitors to the Las Vegas Hilton pass by the most famous manager in show business history without realizing it. Few would recognize the old man pumping twenty-five-cent tokens into the slot machines.

Parker has said that he is working on a book, one that will finally tell the real story of his relationship with Elvis. To date, no such book appears to be forthcoming. He also says he misses Elvis, that he often cries when he thinks about him. Given the revelations of Blanchard Tual and others, one can't help but wonder whether it's Elvis he misses or the limelight and money.

4

PRISCILLA PRESLEY, CEO

ON THE AFTERNOON of August 16, 1977, Priscilla Presley was sitting in a Los Angeles beauty salon, having her hair done. No doubt she was thinking about last-minute preparations before she left the next morning for a vacation in New Guinea. When Priscilla left the shop, she was surprised to find her sister, Michelle, standing outside crying. Her first thought was that something had happened to Lisa Marie, who was visiting her father in Memphis. Michelle assured Priscilla that her daughter was fine. There was a problem, she said, with Elvis.

Before her sister finished telling her, Priscilla knew that Elvis was dead. She'd been expecting this day for some time. Elvis had always told her he would die young; it was in his family. His mother had passed away at forty-five. When Priscilla had seen her ex-husband a few months earlier, for what would be the last time, his condition had shocked her. She knew his prediction would come true unless he made drastic and immediate changes in his life. She also knew Elvis would never change.

When Priscilla called Graceland, Joe Esposito answered the phone. He told her that he would be sending Elvis's jet, the *Lisa Marie,* to Los Angeles right away to bring her to Memphis. He also said that Linda Thompson, Elvis's former live-in girlfriend, would be flying with her. Linda was Elvis's first long-term relationship after the divorce, and there was no love lost between the two women. That Lisa Marie and Linda had grown very close hadn't helped. Priscilla told Esposito that Thompson would most certainly *not* be flying with her; she could arrange her own transportation.

On the flight to Memphis, Priscilla was deep in thought. Her entire life played in her mind like a movie. She thought about Lisa Marie and worried about what would happen to her. She thought about Elvis; they had been apart for a long time now, and she had built a life and a successful career of her own away from Graceland. But what would the world be like without Elvis? She could barely remember what her life had been like before she met him. It was such a long time ago.

★ ★ ★

Priscilla Presley was born Priscilla Wagner on May 25, 1945. Her father, Navy Lieutenant James Wagner, died in a plane crash when Priscilla was six months old. Her mother later married another military man, Air Force Captain Joseph Beaulieu, who adopted Priscilla. When Priscilla was fourteen, Captain Beaulieu's unit was transferred to Germany. Priscilla was distraught at having to leave the United States. In an effort to cheer herself up, she joked with her friends that while she was away, she might get to meet Elvis Presley.

There is some disagreement about the events leading up to Priscilla's introduction to Elvis. In Priscilla's version of the story, Currie Grant, an Air Force Airman who knew Elvis, asked Priscilla if she would like to meet him. According to Grant, Priscilla approached him, asking for an introduction. However it was actually arranged, Priscilla went to visit Elvis at his home in Bad Nauheim, where—despite their age difference (Elvis was twenty-four)—they hit it off right away. It wasn't long before they were seeing each other every night.

The romance was interrupted when Elvis was shipped home in March 1960. Priscilla talked her parents into letting her go to Graceland to spend Christmas with the Presley family that year, but for the next two years her only contact with Elvis was by telephone. Then in October 1962, Elvis convinced Priscilla's parents to allow their seventeen-year-old daughter to move to Memphis to finish high school. At first, Priscilla lived with Vernon and Dee in their house down the street. Eventually, she moved into Graceland.

Elvis might have been content to date Priscilla forever had he not been pressured by Colonel Parker to marry her. The Colonel believed it would be bad for Elvis's image if it were known that they were "living in sin"—living together without being married. Colonel Parker insisted that Elvis marry Priscilla as soon as she turned twenty-one.

Following Colonel Parker's instructions, on May 1, 1967, Elvis and Priscilla were married at the Aladdin Hotel in Las Vegas. Exactly nine months later, Priscilla gave birth to Lisa Marie.

After the birth of her daughter, Priscilla gradually became disenchanted with her marriage. Elvis was away from home most of the time, working on a movie or an album. When he was performing, only the guys were allowed to accompany him on the road; the wives had to "keep the home fires burning." When Elvis finally did come home, he and Priscilla rarely spent time alone together. The Memphis Mafia was always around.

Perhaps Priscilla could have overlooked these difficulties of life with Elvis had it not been for his infidelity. Priscilla was forever hearing rumors about Elvis's extracurricular romances. For a while, she was able to pretend the rumors weren't true, but she found she couldn't pretend forever.

At her request, Elvis and Priscilla separated on February 23, 1972. Priscilla had already begun an affair of her own with her karate instructor, Mike Stone. Elvis had suggested that Priscilla take up karate to occupy her spare time while he was away. He arranged for Stone, with whom he had trained before, to give his wife lessons. Their student/teacher relationship soon grew into something more. Priscilla and Stone took Lisa Marie camping one weekend when Elvis was out of town. The two slept in the same sleeping bag and engaged in what four-year-old Lisa Marie reportedly thought was a night of "wrestling."

Several attempts to reconcile the marriage ended in failure; Priscilla was still dating Stone, and Elvis was still Elvis. On October 9, 1973, a Los Angeles court granted them a divorce.

They maintained a friendly relationship throughout the proceedings. They were even pictured kissing outside the courthouse. Priscilla and Elvis's relationship actually improved after the dissolution of their marriage. They were able to go back to being friends. Elvis's trust in Priscilla was so great that he would often ask her to talk with his girlfriends to educate them about his likes and dislikes. Priscilla was glad to give them the benefit of her experience.

Unfortunately, Priscilla had no one she could turn to with her own relationship problems. Her first two serious boyfriends after the divorce exploited her traitorously. Mike Stone sold the story of his experiences with Priscilla to a tabloid. After her seven-year affair ended with model Michael Edwards, he wrote a book, *Priscilla, Elvis and Me,* in which he revealed intimate details about Priscilla. He also revealed in the book that he was in love with thirteen-year-old Lisa Marie.

Disillusioned by these experiences, Priscilla went through a series of short-term liaisons. She dated the famous, including Richard Gere, and the not-so-famous, like Ellie Ezerzer, a Los Angeles hair stylist. It would be several years before she found a lasting relationship.

★ ★ ★

With a $2 million divorce settlement, Priscilla didn't need to work, but in the months following her departure from Graceland, she felt a growing need to accomplish something on her own. She wanted desperately to show the world that she was more than just Elvis Presley's ex-wife.

Priscilla first chose the fashion business to make her mark. In 1974, she introduced herself to a clothing designer she admired named Olivia Bis. The two hit it off and decided to become partners. Priscilla provided the financing, Bis the designs, and the two opened their own boutique at 9650 Santa Monica Boulevard in Los Angeles. They christened the store Bis and Beau.

Priscilla worked in the store every day. It gave her a sense of purpose and a source of pride. It made her feel as though she were finally emerging from the long shadow of Elvis Presley. Yet it quickly became clear that her Hollywood clientele were attracted to the store primarily because of the Elvis connection. Bis and Beau was a modest financial success, but Priscilla sold her share of the business to her partner in 1976.

Determined to succeed as a designer, Priscilla tried her hand at creating a line of children's clothing, and when that didn't work she designed a line of women's apparel specifically for a cable television shopping channel.

Priscilla's next career move surprised everyone: she decided to become an actress. She spent the next three years taking acting courses, working hard to develop real skills. She wanted to be more than just a novelty. Her drama coach had trained Tom Selleck, Cheryl Ladd, and several other stars of the day. She eventually signed with the William Morris Agency—her ex's theatrical rep.

In 1979, William Morris urged Priscilla to audition for a role on the television program *Charlie's Angels*. The show's producers had practically promised her agent that she would get the part. Priscilla declined because she didn't want to be tied to "fluff" so early in her career. She believed a better choice for her first acting job would be a television commercial. William Morris went to work and quickly landed Priscilla a three-year contract with Wella Balsam Shampoo.

Her first commercial aired on October 31, 1979, and she quickly fell in love with the limelight she had so despised when it was shining on Elvis.

Priscilla's first television role was to have been a guest spot on Tony Orlando's 1979 television special. However, at the last minute the program was changed and Priscilla's role was eliminated. Her acting career didn't begin in earnest until 1980, when she became the cohost of the television series, *Those Amazing Animals*. The ABC series was a kind of weekly televised zoo. When Priscilla got the role, she wanted to use her maiden name, but the producers insisted she use Presley. *Those Amazing Animals* received more attention for a promotional poster featuring Priscilla in a leopard skin loin cloth than it ever did for its content. After one season, the program was canceled.

After the cancellation, Priscilla resumed her acting classes. About the same time, her agent received a barrage of offers. In 1982, she starred in her first movie, *Come Back*. Priscilla's agent used a tape of *Come Back* as an audition for the producers of the popular television series *Dallas*. They liked what they saw and cast Priscilla in the role of Jenna Wade.

Priscilla became a regular on *Dallas* in 1983, and she stayed with the show for five years. In 1985, she was voted the most popular television star in Germany.

A year later, she met a television writer and producer named Marco Garibaldi on the set of *Dallas*. She was looking for a writer to help her with a script idea, and a friend suggested talking with Garibaldi. After two months of working together, they fell in love.

With Garibaldi, Priscilla was determined not to repeat her past mistakes. As the relationship grew more and more serious, she asked him to sign an agreement stating that he would not write a book about her if they ever broke up. He gladly complied.

Priscilla had wanted another child for years, but she hadn't found the right father—until she met Garibaldi. When rumors began to circulate that she was pregnant, Priscilla denied them in an effort to preserve the couple's privacy. After six months, denials became impossible. In March 1987, Priscilla delivered a baby boy. She and Garibaldi named him Navarone.

Lisa Marie was present for the delivery of her half brother, and she was reportedly very excited. By all accounts, Lisa Marie had—and still has—an excellent relationship with Garibaldi. While other men had looked at Priscilla's daughter as excess baggage, from the start Garibaldi treated Lisa Marie like a member of his family. In Elvis's absence, he has reportedly become something of a father figure.

Despite having had a child together, Priscilla and Garibaldi have so far chosen not to marry. Priscilla says she worked long and hard for her independence, and she's afraid a marriage license would turn her back into a piece of property.

The more cynical observers attribute Priscilla's refusal to marry to her desire to capitalize on the Presley name. Priscilla has said that the Presley name actually hurts her more than it helps.

After *Dallas,* Priscilla took some time off to write a book. In 1986 she wrote *Elvis & Me,* an autobiography focusing on her years at Graceland. She later produced the television adaptation of her book, as well as the short-lived series *Elvis, Good Rockin' Tonight.* The series was almost universally praised in the media, but it was very expensive to produce. It was a period piece shot on location. Unfortunately, the show never found its audience.

In 1988, Priscilla starred in her first comedy, *The Naked Gun,* which was a big hit, and Priscilla was widely praised for her role. She went on to appear in two equally successful *Naked Gun* sequels. To date, her only other film role was in the bomb *The Adventures of Ford Fairlane.*

In 1990, Priscilla came out with her own line of perfume, which she called "Moments." The perfume project was a big success, with annual sales of $70 million. Moments had a small advertising budget, which Priscilla bolstered with personal appearances in

J. C. Penney stores across the country. Moments eventually became one of the top-selling perfumes in Germany and Holland, but despite Priscilla's efforts, it never achieved a similar domestic success. Its phenomenal sales abroad was really a measure of Elvis's continuing fanatical following in Europe.

Priscilla had refused to use her name on her perfume, preferring to let it succeed or fail without the Presley imprimatur. But there was no escaping the effects of name recognition on the product's sales figures. According to Lawrence Pesin, president of the company that manufactures Moments, "Presley's image recognition value on a positive level is virtually unsurpassed in the minds of mainstream American female shoppers. The image is being sold, not the fragrance."

While Priscilla has proven herself to be a competent actress, the keys to her success continue to be her name and her good looks. Her beauty seems to grow as she gets older. In 1992, *People* magazine named Priscilla one of the fifty most beautiful people in the world.

Priscilla's success in television and movies improved her self-esteem and helped to distinguish her from her former husband. She was no longer Priscilla Presley, ex-wife of Elvis; she was now Priscilla Presley, actress/ex-wife of Elvis. A small distinction, perhaps, but to Priscilla it was progress.

Show business also changed Priscilla's spiritual life. In 1979 she met actor John Travolta at a Hollywood party. Travolta later introduced her to the Church of Scientology. Priscilla quickly joined the church and got Lisa Marie involved. She seldom publicly discusses her involvement with Scientology except to say that it is responsible for much of her success.

But back in 1977, when Priscilla got the phone call that Elvis had died, she was only just beginning to create this new, independent life. Standing by his grave on the day of the funeral, with her daughter and her former father-in-law beside her, she no doubt felt that this day marked the end of a strange, exciting, heartbreaking, and genuinely remarkable period. She had never known anyone quite like Elvis, and she never would again. She couldn't have imagined that in less than two years his legacy would draw her back to Graceland, and that she would be the one to save the estate from bankruptcy and recreate Elvis's image into the icon it is today.

★ ★ ★

Three days after Vernon Presley's death in June 1979, Priscilla met with Joseph Hanks, Elvis's former accountant and now coexecutor of his estate, in his downtown Memphis office. The purpose of the meeting was to bring Priscilla up to speed. As one of the three newly appointed coexecutors, she would now be privy to all the financial details of her former husband's estate. What she learned that day shocked her.

Since Elvis's death, the estate's income had fallen to around a million dollars a year. The expense of maintaining Graceland was over $500,000 a year (due, in the main, to the elaborate security system Vernon had established). With no new films or records being released, the estate's income would surely continue to fall until its expenses exceeded its revenues. Bankruptcy was a very real possibility, and Hanks predicted that, if something didn't change, it would occur by 1987. When Lisa Marie turned twenty-five, there might be nothing left for her to inherit.

The Presley estate would actually come to the brink of bankruptcy much sooner than Hank's prediction. Interest in Elvis was fading noticeably. The thousands of fans coming to visit Elvis's grave had dwindled to hundreds. Of themselves, visitors to the grave site were of no financial consequence, since they didn't pay admission. However, the decreased visitor traffic directly affected souvenir sales at the gift shops across the street, and that hurt. The Presley estate now depended for much of its income on royalties from souvenir sales. Even the issue of the *Memphis Commercial Appeal* announcing Elvis's death had dropped in price to 99 cents.

Priscilla couldn't believe the dismal condition of Elvis's estate. There were never any outward signs of money problems when Elvis was alive. Until she became an executor, she had known very little about the details of Elvis's financial situation. Until now, she had never known anything about Elvis's agreement with Colonel Parker.

"Everyone was publicly saying how much money that we had and how much money Elvis made," Priscilla told a reporter for the *Orange County Register* in 1988, "but no one knew how much money he spent. The estate was in bad shape, and how it got that way is amazing because when you look at it you say, Oh my God, why didn't somebody do something? Why weren't there any investments? Why wasn't there a trust or money put away?"

★ ★ ★

Of course, the coexecutors' first decision was to try to retain the services of Colonel Parker, the promotional wizard who had done so much to build the Elvis empire and who would certainly be needed to save it. At first, Priscilla was only too willing to be guided by more experienced hands, and in the beginning, the bank and Joseph Hanks made most of the day-to-day decisions. The press speculated endlessly about who was really calling the shots at the Presley estate, with opinions equally divided between Priscilla and the National Bank of Commerce. But Priscilla was only involved in the major decisions that came up during estate business meetings, for which she flew in from L.A. However, that changed when Priscilla and her coexecutors went before Probate Judge Joseph Evans with a motion to continue Colonel Parker's compensation arrangement. After that, Priscilla assumed the lead role in what became nothing short of a rescue mission.

Priscilla's nearly disastrous decision to retain the Colonel is understandable. She was inexperienced and the financial affairs of the estate were very complicated. Besides, she wasn't the only one who credited the Colonel with much of Elvis's success. At that time, there was no reason to suspect otherwise, despite his lucrative management contract. Her coexecutors hadn't questioned the Colonel's deal, and they were there day to day. Yet, to tell the story honestly, one must acknowledge Priscilla's early misstep.

Priscilla, however, doesn't readily admit to any shortcomings in her stewardship of the estate, and that myth has been perpetuated by the media. According to the press, Priscilla single-handedly saved Lisa Marie from the havoc wreaked on her father's finances by his uneducated father, the "evil" Colonel Parker, and even Elvis himself, the dumb country boy who had more money than he knew what to do with.

A more honest version of the story would give Judge Joseph Evans and Blanchard Tual equal billing with Priscilla as "saviors" of Elvis's estate. They stepped in when the estate's own executors were unwittingly setting themselves up for disaster.

★ ★ ★

To outsiders, Priscilla seemed totally unsuited to play anything but a figurehead role in the financial affairs of the estate. She had no experience managing a multimillion-dollar business. Her only qualification appeared to be that she bore the name Presley. She was even somewhat on the outs with Elvis fans at the time because she had walked out on her husband. What right did she have to come back and take over Graceland?

While she had little practical experience, Priscilla believed she had a natural aptitude for the position. She had been coming up with ideas to help Elvis improve his financial situation as far back as the early 1960s. One of her early ideas was to turn his money-losing Circle G Ranch into a working cattle ranch. This would have allowed Elvis to enjoy his newfound hobby and make a profit at the same time. Elvis never acted on this idea or any of Priscilla's other ideas. Priscilla attributed this to the fact that she was young and a woman.

During her years with Elvis, Priscilla says, she also closely followed the way in which Colonel Parker promoted her husband's career. She admired the contribution she believed the Colonel had made to his success. Despite later revelations about the Colonel's perfidy, she came to view him as something of a role model as she assumed more responsibility for the estate and, ultimately, as the keeper of Elvis's memory.

Whatever the fans thought or the press opined, Priscilla was the legally appointed coexecutor of the estate and Lisa Marie's mother. In the end, those were all the qualifications she needed.

When Priscilla began to lay the groundwork for rebuilding the Elvis empire, she decided to establish a separate business entity to work on the estate's behalf. She chose the name Elvis Presley Enterprises for her new company. The original EPE had been established by Colonel Parker back in 1956 to license Elvis products. Sales of Elvis novelties in the 1950s were phenomenal: EPE licensed everything from dolls to lipstick to record players, all bearing Elvis's name and picture, and it became a multimillion-dollar business almost overnight. Priscilla hoped the name would bring the same prosperity to the new company.

By far the most serious problem facing Priscilla and her fledgling empire was the estate's tax liability. In 1981, the IRS reappraised the Presley estate for the second time in order to reflect the royalties it had received since Elvis's death. When the reappraisal was complete, the estate owed an additional $10 million in inheritance taxes. There was simply nowhere near that kind of money in the estate's coffers. The estate's attorneys had to convince Judge Robert Brandt to issue a temporary order postponing collection procedures, buying the estate a little time. But, the lawyers argued, Graceland might very well have to be sold to pay off the IRS if something wasn't done soon.

Priscilla was desperate to find the money to keep the estate afloat and Graceland off the auction block. Her first idea was to try to recover some of the hundreds of thousands of dollars Elvis had given away over the years. When Elvis gave money away, it was usually in the form of a check. On the memo line he would often write "personal loan." Elvis probably never intended to be paid back, but he called the money a loan so the beneficiary of his generosity could maintain his or her dignity. According to the recipients of these "loans," Priscilla knew that Elvis never expected to be paid back.

Nevertheless, Priscilla decided to see what would happen if the estate sued for repayment. The first test case sought repayment of $10,000 Elvis had given to Marty Lacker, one of his employees. Elvis first met Lacker in high school. Along with Joe Esposito, he served as co–best man at Elvis and Priscilla's wedding. If the estate's lawyers prevailed against Lacker, they planned to go after everyone who had ever received money from Elvis.

EPE picked the wrong person for their test case. Lacker was not afraid of Priscilla or the Presley estate. He quickly filed a countersuit asserting that Elvis had promised him, and many others, an additional $50,000 for his participation in an unreleased karate film Elvis produced. The countersuit demanded payment of the $50,000. The estate quickly agreed to drop its suit, and the strategy.

By 1981, almost all the money accumulated in the twenty-six years since Elvis Presley began his career was gone. The estate's income had plummeted to $340,000, forcing the estate to begin dipping into its cash reserves to pay the annual $500,000 upkeep of Graceland. If the estate was to be saved from bankruptcy, new sources of income had to be developed. To generate that income, Priscilla turned to the only real asset the estate had: Elvis himself.

Her idea was simple, yet brilliant. Since Elvis was no longer around to make records, appear in movies, or perform in concert, the estate would have to rely on his memory to generate revenue. Elvis would be transformed into a symbol, a character that could be licensed to merchandisers. The estate would turn Elvis Presley into its own version of Mickey Mouse.

The problem with this idea was that, during the last years of his life, Elvis's image was not very Disneyesque. His weight had ballooned and he had been addicted to prescription medication. By the time of his death, Elvis Presley had become a grotesque caricature of the performer he once was. This Elvis would never do as the symbol of the new empire.

Priscilla's solution to this problem was also simple and brilliant: she would act as though the 1977 Elvis never existed. Only the young Elvis, the King in his prime, would be acknowledged. It was this Elvis that would adorn the T-shirts, plates, shot glasses, billboards, and promotional literature of Priscilla's new empire. In her sanitized version of Elvis's life, he died after his *1968 Comeback Special,* an idol in his prime, like James Dean. He would not become another Marlon Brando, an overweight mockery of what he had once been. In his book, *Dead Elvis,* author Greil Marcus claims that even the Elvis jumpsuits on display at Graceland have been altered to a smaller size than they were when Elvis actually wore them.

But, to make a long story short, her strategy worked. Not only did Priscilla successfully recreate the 1950s rock icon but the estate was saved from bankruptcy (and it has gone on to flourish). Elvis has once again galvanized our imaginations, in no small part because of the remarkable job Priscilla has done erasing the memory of Elvis as he was when he died. Priscilla has now assumed the lead role in the stewardship of Elvis's image, carefully guarding his name and reputation. She also guards against overexposure, just as Colonel Parker had done so carefully when Elvis was alive.

The image-conscious Elvis Presley Enterprises even feels compelled to explain why Elvis's estate was so small when he died. In a press release from Graceland, a slightly sanitized explanation is given: "Elvis Presley could have left one of the great fortunes in entertainment history had he been one to worry about financial planning rather than freely enjoying and sharing his wealth as he did." An associate of Priscilla's summed up Elvis's finances very simply, "Elvis was not a guy destined to die wealthy."

★ ★ ★

Today, Elvis Presley Enterprises is a well-run marketing machine, with Priscilla Presley and investment manager Jack Soden sharing the decision making. EPE has two offices, one in Los Angeles and one in Memphis. Priscilla runs the Los Angeles branch, and Soden works in Memphis. While the Memphis office is very public, the location of Priscilla's L.A. headquarters is a closely guarded secret. Even the phone number is unlisted.

Priscilla Presley is the creative force behind EPE, and she reviews all licensing agreements into which the Presley estate enters. Jack Soden is the financial expert of the organization. The pair is EPE's version of Walt and Roy Disney. Yet, conspicuously absent from Priscilla's Sunset Boulevard office is anything bearing Elvis's picture. When you step into offices of Disney CEO Michael Eisner, you are surrounded by Mickey Mouse. If it were not for a corporate name plate, visitors to Priscilla's office would never know where they were.

At the first of each year, Priscilla leads a planning meeting of EPE executives. At this meeting they review potential Elvis products, television programs, and video ideas for the upcoming year. The group also uses the meeting as a brainstorming session for making improvements at Graceland. At one such session the decision was made to upgrade the quality of merchandise being sold at the Graceland gift shops.

Initially, consultants were hired to help Priscilla manage the various lines of business conducted by EPE. EPE employed the same Los Angeles publicist used by Ford Motor Company and R.J. Reynolds Nabisco. The licensing and music publishing divisions were managed by independent contractors. Even Jack Soden was initially hired as a consultant to organize the opening of Graceland. As EPE expanded its licensing and music publishing divisions, it eliminated the consultants and hired in-house managers.

One of the first full-time managers hired by EPE was Joseph Rascoff. Rascoff, then the business manager, had previously held similar positions with the Rolling Stones and the Who.

Rascoff immediately saw the parallels between Disney and EPE. If Disney had built a whole industry around a mouse, he reasoned

EPE could do the same with Elvis. Rascoff's plan was to introduce Elvis to a new generation of fans. In his view, there was no reason Elvis couldn't be a hip, new recording artist in the eyes of a ten-year-old.

Rascoff went to work trying to market new Elvis records, television programs, and collectibles. A modernized video of "Blue Suede Shoes" was created to introduce Elvis to the MTV generation. Another plan of Rascoff's was to create a Broadway show based on Elvis's life, though that never materialized. Rascoff was responsible for dramatically increasing royalties to the Presley estate. Under his watch, licensing royalties more than tripled in one year. Rascoff's work generated the capital necessary to allow EPE to expand the scope of its operation.

* * *

EPE is now made up of three divisions. The flagship division is Graceland, which includes the mansion, shops, and restaurants (see Chapter 5). Then there is the licensing division and the music publishing division (described below).

The licensing division of EPE controls the licensing of Elvis's name and likeness for use on retail merchandise. In general, this division's role is the same as that previously filled by Factors. The licensing group allows manufacturers to use Elvis's name and picture on products in exchange for a royalty. However, instead of receiving a small portion of such royalties, as it did under the Factors agreement, the estate now receives 100 percent of the royalties.

After devoting most of its energy to Graceland during the 1980s, Elvis Presley Enterprises has focused on merchandising opportunities in the 1990s. Projects are now planned more than a year in advance. A video and documentary are already slated for the twentieth anniversary of Elvis's death in 1997. A deal has been made with Turner Broadcasting to license the use of Elvis's image from the thirteen Elvis movies that Turner owns. Turner and EPE have also worked together to release a number of videos. Future licensing plans include Elvis editions of Harley Davidson motorcycles and even Cadillacs.

The release of the Elvis stamp triggered a new wave of interest in licensing Elvis products. As many as forty ideas for new Elvis merchandise are presented to EPE each day by mail, telephone, and in person. Today, the calls to EPE with new product ideas are more frequent than they've ever been.

For a long time, EPE was too strict about the number of products it would license. Priscilla and company passed up lucrative opportunities in film and television out of fear of overexposing Elvis. On the other hand, they were very lax in controlling the quality of the items that they licensed. They soon realized that to be taken seriously they would have to improve their product lines.

"As long as we tended to license small operators and distributors selling inexpensive items," says Jack Soden, "that's the way we would be regarded. The marketplace would regard us as the licensor of trinkets and beads, of truck stop paraphernalia."

Not surprisingly, EPE has become extremely selective about the licenses it grants for Elvis products. Some 95 percent of the products pitched to EPE are immediately rejected. The company has made progress in improving the tastefulness of the Elvis merchandise on the market. You can no longer purchase Elvis sweat or genuine Graceland dirt. The plan to convert the Circle G Ranch into a cemetery for Elvis fans was scotched, as was the same eager entrepreneur's idea to sell space in the mausoleum in which Elvis and Gladys Presley were originally buried to spread·the ashes of cremated fans.

Those few ideas that do meet EPE's standards are subjected to a rigorous quality-control process. Once a license is granted, EPE must approve the image of Elvis that will be used on the product. The company will not approve the use of a picture of Elvis that portrays him as anything less than perfect. EPE absolutely refuses to license a product picturing an overweight Elvis. If the licensee cannot obtain a photograph on their own that meets EPE's approval, they can choose one from EPE's library of a hundred thousand photographs.

Anyone wishing to sell items bearing Elvis's image must pay a licensing fee and a royalty to EPE. Entering the Elvis business today can be costly. EPE collects fees as high as 15 percent of sales in return for conveying a license to use Elvis's name and likeness. To bring an Elvis product to market can require payments to the estate of as much as a million dollars.

Yet many manufacturers have found the fees to be well worth the cost. Elvis's face can sell the most mundane product in large quantities. For example, at forty dollars each, a set of Elvis collector's cards sold fifty thousand sets. Over one million Elvis postcards are sold each year. A short distance from Graceland, there are warehouses filled with some of the over twenty-five hundred Elvis products on the market today.

Elvis merchandise also has international appeal. There are more Elvis fans living outside of the United States than inside. In August 1994, EPE took a major step toward capitalizing on this largely untapped market by appointing Carol Butler to the position of director of worldwide merchandising. Ms. Butler previously served as manager of licensing for Anheuser-Busch.

EPE is following in the footsteps of Disney, Coca-Cola, and McDonald's in trying to establish itself as an international powerhouse. Under Butler, the licensing division has built a global network of agents who promote the licensing of Elvis's name and likeness around the world. Today, EPE has licensing agreements in every industrialized nation on earth.

Among the countries in which Elvis is most popular, Japan may rank first. He's so well loved in that country that a large statue of the King stands outside the Tokyo train station. To capitalize on this popularity, Japanese investors approached EPE with several ideas for constructing an Elvis attraction in their country. EPE took the investors seriously; after all, it worked with Tokyo Disneyland.

In 1991, EPE reached an agreement with its Japanese partners for the construction of a six-acre amusement park recreating an

American city of the 1950s. Financed by a Japanese bank, Elvis Town U.S.A. was to be constructed in Tokyo at a cost of $80 million. The plan for the park included an enclosed dome to facilitate year-round operation. The park was also to include stores, restaurants, night clubs, a car dealership selling antique vehicles, and a forty-thousand-square-foot Elvis museum.

In return for a percentage of ticket, food, and merchandise sales, EPE would license the use of Elvis's name and likeness to the park, and they would also contribute to its design and the management of the facilities.

Elvis Town U.S.A. was slated to open in 1994, but construction has still not begun. Since 1991, Japan has experienced a weak economy, a falling stock market, and a rash of banking difficulties. As of this writing, plans for the amusement park have been put on hold until a new commitment for financing can be arranged.

The worldwide recession has also postponed EPE's plan for a global traveling exhibition of Elvis Presley memorabilia. EPE had planned to transport the Elvis museum to Europe, Australia, and South America. The treasures of the King were to be put on display to draw the curious to his castle in Memphis. But as plans for the tour progressed, it became obvious that it would be very expensive, and EPE decided to postpone the exhibition until tourism around the world improved.

★ ★ ★

The third arm of EPE is its music publishing division, and potentially it's the most lucrative of them all. Unlike most recording artists, Elvis only recorded songs to which he held the publishing rights. As a result, his two publishing companies, Elvis Presley Music and Gladys Music, own the copyrights to over a thousand songs recorded by Elvis and others. While Elvis sold his artist royalty rights to RCA in 1973, he still retained his publishing rights. In other words, anytime an Elvis song is sold or broadcast, RCA receives artist royalties because they hold the rights to his recordings prior to 1973, and Elvis's publishing companies get publishing royalties because Elvis owned the songs themselves, either completely or partially.

EPE's music publishing division oversees the collection of royalties on those songs Elvis owned. Each time one of these songs is sold or played on the radio, in a movie, or on television, a royalty must be paid to EPE. These royalties have contributed a sizable income to EPE, and they will continue to do so as long as Elvis's records sell.

EPE's music publishing division maintains branches all over the world. Under the direction of Gary Hovey, Priscilla's brother-in-law, EPE renegotiated its foreign subpublishing agreements to obtain more favorable terms. Also, a new royalty rate was agreed upon that will generate millions of additional dollars for EPE.

Today, music publishing royalties earn EPE around $1.5 million per year, and the division is the company's fastest growing segment. Through continuing acquisitions, the number of songs controlled by EPE increases each year.

★ ★ ★

Within the first five years of its operation, EPE transformed an estate nearing bankruptcy into a high-powered, money-making machine. National magazines soon began to recognize the financial success of EPE. In 1984, *Life* magazine reported that licensed Elvis products promised to gross $50 million in the next three years. Two years later *Forbes* magazine valued the estate at $100 million. During subsequent years, the estate's value has multiplied at a phenomenal rate, approaching a value today of $200 million.

Annual revenues generated by Elvis merchandising, movies, record sales, and Graceland currently exceed $100 million. EPE's share of the Elvis market has been estimated to be as high as $50 million per year, but the company will only confirm that its annual gross exceeds $15 million. Its actual yearly receipts are probably somewhere between these two numbers.

There is no question that EPE has achieved a remarkable level of success. The organization has multiplied the net worth of the Presley estate by twenty times in the last fifteen years. If a Fortune 500 company were able to achieve results like this, it would be considered one of the greatest success stories in the history of Wall Street.

And, indeed, Priscilla's success has been admired and applauded in the press. She has frequently appeared on the covers of several women's magazines, each singing her praises as the savior of the Presley estate. The September 1993 issue of *Working Woman* featured an article about Priscilla's management of EPE, crediting her for the restoration of the Presley fortune. Priscilla was credited for taking the business further than Elvis ever could have taken it himself. *Working Woman* recognized that Priscilla had created a tightly run and aggressive company to exploit Elvis's image. She began as the keeper of Elvis's flame and became the chairwoman of an enterprise that has made Elvis Presley one of the highest-earning entertainers in history.

In an October 1994 interview in *McCall's* magazine, Priscilla said, "It has taken a while to find out what I like and what I don't like. It feels so good not to have someone dictate to you." Clearly, being in charge suits Priscilla, and she's made the most of the opportunity—without having to answer to the Colonel, Vernon, or Elvis.

To those who assume that she is just a beautiful woman who had the good fortune to marry Elvis Presley, Jack Soden says you don't know Priscilla. He credits the success of EPE directly to her personal vision and will. Another associate agrees: "If Priscilla had remained on the sidelines as just Lisa Marie's mom, this operation would not be nearly what it is today. She deserves the credit for making the Elvis phenomenon happen."

Soden says Priscilla never had anything but a long-term view. She could have panicked when she realized the difficult situation facing the estate, but Priscilla refused to listen to the lawyers and accountants who urged her to sell everything. According to Soden, "People said to us, 'Why are you doing this? Elvis is dead. It's over. He will soon be forgotten.'" Instead, he says, Priscilla kept her cool and made the right decisions. Priscilla started EPE from scratch and succeeded against all odds. Soden says he'd rather undertake a business deal with Priscilla than anyone with a Harvard MBA.

However, other members of EPE attribute their success to "the hottest entertainment property in the world, plus a lot of luck." Even Soden admits that it would have been difficult for EPE to have failed. "We like to think that we know what we're doing here," he says, "but we also know it could be [that] the interest in Elvis is so strong that this place could be managed by idiots for seventy years—and the idiots wouldn't be able to mess it up."

Priscilla has often been perceived as the King's "ice princess." People who knew both Elvis and Priscilla say that she is much tougher than he ever was. But Lisa Marie says that beneath this façade Priscilla is very emotional and vulnerable. She pulls the tough-guy routine out of her acting bag when a business situation becomes particularly difficult. However, Lisa Marie cautions, her mother has a strong sense of loyalty, and if you betray her, watch out.

Priscilla has always been very congenial to her coexecutors and the executives at EPE. They respect her opinions and she respects theirs. She lets the executives she hires do their jobs with very little interference. She rarely second-guesses the people who work for her. As a result, EPE has almost no turnover at the managerial level.

Priscilla is not afraid to sing her own praises either. In an interview with *Working Woman* magazine, she mentioned that she didn't go to college and she didn't have a business degree. What she did have was a tremendous drive to succeed and improve herself. If it wasn't for this drive, she said, the financial miracle that has taken place probably would never have happened.

Priscilla also says that she fought against taking the lead in the affairs of Elvis's estate because she was trying to make it on her own. "When I was first named executor," she said in an interview with *U.S.A. Weekend* magazine, "I thought it was a curse." Later she would publicly admit that, while at first she had taken the job to protect

Lisa Marie, her motivation and interest in the business changed. "It just grew and grew with all of the planning and goals," she says. "Lisa Marie became secondary and business itself became important."

Not everyone shares this glowing public image of Priscilla. According to a former longtime employee of Elvis's, Priscilla changed when she was named executor of the estate. "She was in control," the employee says, "and she came on pretty strong. She has blown off all of the friends she had. She is rude to everybody, but that is her style. There is not a lot of warmth in Priscilla. She has more plastic than a Corvette."

Vernon Presley's second wife, Dee Stanley, has also complained of Priscilla giving her the cold shoulder. Dee tells of times when she has come face-to-face with the woman who, as a girl, had lived in her house, only to be ignored. She says that Priscilla has totally excluded her from the family and Elvis-related events.

Dee's sons, Billy and David Stanley, also paint an unflattering picture of Priscilla. They cite an incident involving some home movies taken of Billy, David, and Elvis, which became quite valuable after Elvis's death. When Priscilla found a buyer for her collection of home movies, she persuaded several people who were in them to sign over their commercial rights, including the Stanley brothers. She received $250,000 for the rights to the movies and paid nothing to the others.

"When Vernon died," Billy Stanley recalls of the incident, "Priscilla came to Memphis and told us we needed to sign our movie rights over to her." She added that if anything was ever done with the movies she would make sure the boys were taken care of, Stanley says. "We never heard anything from her." David Stanley is much more blunt about the incident: "You might say she screwed us."

Priscilla was not understanding when Joe Esposito, Elvis's long-time friend, tried to sell his own home movies. EPE sued Esposito to stop the sale. Apparently selling home movies of Elvis—even your own—is the exclusive domain of Priscilla Presley.

Another member of the Stanley family makes a more sinister charge against Priscilla. He alleges that she made an insulting remark about Vernon Presley on the day before Vernon's funeral. He claims that she said, "I am glad that greedy son-of-a-bitch is dead."

There's also considerable debate over how Priscilla came to be chosen as Vernon Presley's successor. Priscilla publicly claims that she reluctantly assumed leadership of the Presley estate out of respect for the Presley family and her desire to protect Lisa Marie's inheritance. Insiders claim she plotted and campaigned for the job.

A friend of the Presley family recalls a conversation she had with Vernon about what would happen to the Presley estate when he died. Vernon was worried about what would happen to Lisa Marie, the friend says, with Elvis gone and Vernon's mother, Minnie Presley, too old to manage the affairs of the estate. Vernon said he really did not want to name Priscilla as executor of the estate, but he felt he had no other choice. If nothing else, Priscilla would look out for Lisa Marie's best interest.

Whatever the details of her ascension, there is no denying the success of the organization Priscilla created. Still, there have been a few blemishes on EPE's record.

One of the organization's few failures was the short-lived, 1990 television series *Elvis, Good Rockin' Tonight*. The subject of the series was Elvis's life from the time of his first record release for Sun Records in 1954 until his career skyrocketed in 1956.

Priscilla Presley served as the show's producer. The pilot was shot on location in Memphis at a cost of $1.5 million. Despite being well written and having an excellent cast (including Michael St. Girard as Elvis), the ratings of the series were low. After thirteen episodes *Elvis, Good Rockin' Tonight* was canceled.

Another of EPE's rare disappointments involved the organization's attempt to branch out into the world of professional sports. In 1993, Memphis was trying to land a National Football League expansion team. A group of investors had pooled their assets in an attempt to acquire ownership of the team. In September 1993, the surprising announcement was made that the group had welcomed a new partner: EPE.

EPE was, in fact, a natural addition to the Memphis partnership. All of the groups competing for the team had fortunes to offer, but the Memphis group would be the only one that could offer Elvis. NFL Properties, the multimillion-dollar operation that licenses all products bearing NFL logos, could add Elvis to their lineup. The estate would gain another outlet for licensing Elvis products, as well as part ownership of an NFL franchise. This ownership share would be of considerable value: the market price of NFL teams has approached $200 million dollars.

The cash contribution of EPE was not revealed; however, both the lead investor, William Durrant, and Jack Soden termed EPE's involvement as "significant." It is unclear if this significant involvement was to include a substantial cash investment. Sources close to the situation revealed later that the primary contribution of EPE would have been Elvis, with the cash component remaining relatively small.

Ultimately Memphis was passed over by the NFL. There will be no Memphis Hound Dogs—at least not until the next round of NFL expansion.

Just as surprising as EPE's foray into the NFL is their recent willingness to share Elvis with other organizations. EPE has gradually begun to work with groups it previously viewed as competitors. At first, when the Rock 'n' Roll Hall of Fame and Museum in Cleveland, Ohio, approached EPE about lending their museum some Elvis items, EPE was reluctant to do so. After lengthy discussions, EPE was finally convinced that the Hall of Fame could be an advertisement for Graceland rather than competition. Visitors to the Hall of Fame would see a small collection of Elvis items and have their appetites whetted for more. EPE reached an agreement with the Hall of Fame under which it would lend items from Graceland on a rotating basis.

Even though they have reached an agreement, all is not well between EPE and the Hall of Fame. When the Hall of Fame held its grand opening concert, the only performer of any importance not acknowledged by a film clip or a performance was Elvis Presley. Either the Hall of Fame continues to hold a grudge against EPE or EPE refused to license the use of Elvis in the event. When asked for an explanation, both parties refused to comment.

EPE has also recently agreed to allow and support an annual celebration of Elvis's birthday at Walt Disney World's Pleasure Island entertainment complex. The party for Elvis will be called "Night of 1,000 Elvises." EPE hopes that the Disney event will generate favorable publicity and help keep Elvis's name in the news. As the management of the Presley organization has matured, it has realized that events like this can help generate demand for Elvis products.

Still, EPE has proven to be more adept at taking than giving. A case in point: when the Smithsonian Institute wanted to put up a display devoted to Elvis, it asked the estate to donate one of Elvis's stage costumes, as well as a few other personal items. EPE never responded to the request. If the estate had loaned the Smithsonian one of Elvis's jumpsuits, it would have had 299 left, only a small fraction of which are ever on display at Graceland.

Another example: an organization dedicated to encouraging children to read approached the estate about using Elvis on a poster. Permission was granted—for a ten-dollar fee.

After turning down so many charities, it was becoming embarrassing Priscilla and Jack Soden decided to set up their own charitable organization. The Elvis Presley Memorial Foundation was established by EPE in 1987. The foundation serves as a fund-raising vehicle for a number of charitable causes. One promising project involved the establishment of a scholarship in Elvis's name at the University of Memphis College of Communication and Fine Arts. The scholarships are designed to benefit needy students pursuing careers in acting or music. Several entertainers have made donations to the fund as a sign of appreciation for Elvis's influence on their careers.

Unfortunately, EPE seems to have devoted little of the energy and attention that turned the estate around to making the foundation a success. Most of the foundation's funds are derived from a licensing deal with Mastercard for the use of Elvis's image on "theme" credit cards. In the beginning, the Mastercard deal produced $90,000 a year in revenues. As interest in theme credit cards has slowed, revenues have fallen to less than $30,000 a year.

The focus of Priscilla and EPE clearly is the production of revenue and the expansion of the Elvis empire. In that, they have succeeded beyond all predictions or expectations—except perhaps Priscilla's.

5

GRACELAND

ONE OF PRISCILLA PRESLEY'S most conspicuous accomplishments as the leader of Elvis Presley Enterprises was the establishment of Graceland as the capital of the new Elvis empire. Priscilla's vision and determination transformed Graceland from a life-threatening drain on the Presley estate into the most visible sign of its tremendous wealth.

In March 1957, Elvis purchased Graceland mansion in his hometown of Memphis, Tennessee, for $102,500. He outbid the Memphis YMCA, which had offered $35,000. The real estate agent in charge of the sale was shocked at the size of the offer, but happy to accept. Elvis would reside at Graceland for the remainder of his life.

The property was a farm during the Civil War. The original owner was S.E. Toof, publisher of the *Memphis Commercial Appeal.* Toof named the farm Graceland after his daughter. The mansion was built in 1939 by Grace Toof's niece, Ruth Moore. When Elvis bought the property, it was the home of the Graceland Christian Church.

At the time of Elvis's death in 1977, the cost of maintaining Graceland was half a million dollars a year. Of that amount, $100,000 went for upkeep and repair of the mansion and grounds, and $400,000 went for salaries of staff and security. Unexpected expenses were incurred in 1981 when the grounds of Graceland were vandalized. This incident prompted Priscilla to upgrade their system: she replaced Elvis's uncle Vester, then head of security, with a professional security service.

Not only did the new security service add to the cost of maintaining Graceland, it also angered many fans. Vester Presley had guarded the front gate at Graceland for over twenty years. Though he was entrusted with keeping people out, Vester had allowed, at his discretion, considerable access to the grounds while Elvis was alive, and he continued to do so after Elvis's death. Priscilla felt compelled to explain her position to the angry fans in a letter published in the *Memphis Commercial Appeal*. This was just the first of many changes Priscilla would make that would upset Elvis's fans, but she had more important things to worry about. She had to find a way to save Graceland.

★ ★ ★

Each year after Elvis's death the estate came closer to bankruptcy. The money coming in was dwindling, public interest in Elvis was waning, and the expenses did nothing but go up. Almost immediately upon becoming an executor, Priscilla was forced to consider the unthinkable: the sale of Graceland.

Elvis's will allowed his estate's executors to take any action they felt to be in the best interest of his heir, Lisa Marie—including selling Graceland. Selling Graceland would accomplish two things. First, a sale would raise several million dollars of much-needed cash. Second, by eliminating Graceland, the executors would do away with almost all of the estate's expenses.

When Priscilla began to consider potential buyers, she first thought of the City of Memphis and the Grand Ole Opry. She believed that either of these entities might be interested in opening the mansion and grounds for tours. The Grand Ole Opry expressed no interest, but the City of Memphis was a serious bidder.

Before his death, Vernon Presley had been working with the city on plans for an Elvis Presley Memorial Museum. The city was still committed to making the project a reality and planned to continue discussions with Vernon's successor. They were eager to talk to Priscilla when they learned that she had placed Graceland back on the block.

Wyeth Chandler, then mayor of Memphis, hired a consulting firm to project the cost and revenues that could result from turning Graceland itself into a museum. To finance the purchase of the property, city officials came up with the idea of issuing special municipal bonds. They felt certain the bonds would be snapped up by Elvis fans.

In August 1980, stories once again began to surface about the city's bid for Graceland. The fans were not in universal agreement that this was a good idea. One determined Elvis admirer decided to take matters into his own hands, and he organized a group of like-minded fans to buy Graceland. John Berry formed the Graceland Preservation Society and installed himself as president. The group sent a mass mailing soliciting donations to finance their cause, but their efforts yielded only $2,400 in contributions.

The City of Memphis was able to make a slightly more serious offer. On behalf of the city, the mayor submitted a bid of $10 million for Graceland. The terms called for a portion of the purchase price to be paid up front, with the remainder to be paid over a number of years from the profits of the operation.

Despite the estate's dire need, Priscilla decided to turn down the city's offer. What the estate needed was an immediate influx of cash; the installment payments suggested by the city were unacceptable. Also, the total compensation package of $10 million was felt to be too low.

In February of 1981, the city increased its offer to $12 million. The Presley estate once again declined. Priscilla had decided that Lisa Marie should be the one to choose whether to sell Graceland when she came of age. She felt uncomfortable selling what was now Lisa Marie's strongest link to her childhood. It just wasn't Priscilla's to sell, she felt. There was also the small problem of Elvis, Vernon, and Grandma Presley lying out in the backyard. Priscilla couldn't very well sell the cemetery containing most of Lisa Marie's family. Of course, that meant she had to save it.

Secretly, Priscilla began to think about another way to capitalize upon the fans' eagerness to come beyond the gates of Graceland. She became convinced that Graceland had to be opened to the public if it were to be saved. It was the only way the estate could afford the cost of maintaining the mansion.

Visitors came to Graceland by the thousands after Elvis died. They viewed his grave and paid no admission for the privilege. They bought Elvis souvenirs in the gift shops in the mall across the street from Graceland. Thousands of dollars were being spent, with very little of it going to the Presley estate. The best way for the estate to get a piece of all that action was to turn these visitors into paying customers.

Although the motivation for opening Graceland to the public was clearly financial, representatives of the estate present the story in a more humanitarian light. In its version, the estate had been deluged with requests to open the house since Elvis's death. The family and executors decided to open Graceland as a memorial to Elvis and a gift to the fans. The estate is also quick to point out that Elvis himself enjoyed giving tours of Graceland. In a way, they were just carrying on a family tradition—now with a five-dollar admission fee.

But there were obstacles. Priscilla was surprised to learn that a Memphis law prohibited the charging of a fee to visit a private home. So it turned out that Vernon had been *unable* to charge admission to the thousands of fans who came to visit Elvis's grave. The estate asked for and was granted an exception to the law. (No one seems to know why Vernon didn't do the same thing.)

In early 1982, rumors began to circulate in the media that portions of Graceland were going to be opened to the public. It was thought that a small fee would be charged to enter the grounds, and an additional five dollars to enter the trophy room and racquetball court. It was still not known if the home itself would be open for tours. In fact, Priscilla did not initially intend to open any of the mansion's living quarters.

Originally, as rumored, Priscilla had planned to open only Elvis's racquetball court and his trophy room. She was reluctant to open the mansion—her former home—because it was the only part of her relationship with Elvis that had been kept private. Her advisors argued that a tour consisting of only the racquetball court and the trophy room wouldn't be enough to draw large crowds. The fans would come only if they could tour Graceland itself. Eventually, financial concerns won over sentimentality, and she agreed to open the majority of the mansion to tours.

The estate confirmed the rumors with an announcement that Graceland would be open in June 1982. The entire first floor of the mansion with the exception of the kitchen and a bedroom would be included in the tour. The trophy room was already being reworked to allow for heavy traffic flow. The remainder of the mansion would remain structurally unaltered. Admission prices were set at five dollars for adults and one dollar for children.

Priscilla knew she was going to need some managerial help with both Graceland and the estate's other businesses. After interviewing several candidates she chose Jack Soden, a Kansas City investment manager. Previously, Soden had been an associate of Priscilla's close friend and investment advisor, Morgan Maxfield. He worked with Priscilla on her personal financial affairs after Maxfield died. Soden was hired at a salary of $60,000 a year plus a bonus.

Priscilla was impressed with Soden because his vision of the potential of Graceland was similar to hers. She was also impressed that he was completely detached from the worship of Elvis. In fact, Soden wasn't even a casual Elvis fan. "It indicated that all of the BS would be out of the way," she said later. She believed that a fan

would not be able to make decisions about what was best for
Graceland from a business standpoint. Questions about how Elvis
would have liked things done would not become an issue. In Soden,
Priscilla found someone whose only concern would be the maxi-
mization of profits.

Priscilla and Soden began their preparation for the Graceland
opening by meeting with consultants who devised elaborate plans
for the project. These plans would have cost $3 million to put into
place. There was no way the estate could afford such a plan. The
consultants also recommended a year-long survey to learn what the
tourists would want to see on a tour of Graceland. With the bleak
financial condition of the Presley estate, a year was too long to wait.
In the end, Priscilla and Soden abandoned the consultants and
decided to open Graceland on their own.

Their plan was to make Graceland into a piece of Americana.
They envisioned a place that a broad spectrum of tourists would
want to visit, not just the die-hard Elvis fans. Instead of turning to
high-priced consultants, Priscilla and Soden would look to those
operating other attractions for advice. They visited several famous-
home tour operations across the country, including Mount Vernon,
Monticello, the Getty Museum, and Hearst Castle, always looking
for free advice and ideas. Priscilla and Soden also consulted with
Disney and the National Park Service, which manages many historical homes.

Of all of the homes and museums she visited, Priscilla was
most impressed with Hearst Castle. Though it is open to tourists, it
has been maintained exactly as it was when the Hearst family lived
there. Priscilla wanted Graceland to be maintained in the same way.
She wanted the mansion to be available if Lisa Marie ever decided
to move back in.

Originally, plans for opening Graceland included the construction of souvenir stands near the racquetball building. However,
after speaking with representatives from Hearst Castle, Priscilla and

Soden decided that the presentation would be more dignified if no money changed hands on the grounds. Ticket and souvenir sales were confined to an area across the street. Today, a reminder is given during the mansion tour that no money changes hands on the grounds of Graceland.

The Vanderbilt family's Biltmore estate contributed the idea that items of a personal nature should be included in the narration of the tours. They would give visitors a better sense of what it was like when Elvis lived there. Also, the idea of busing tourists from the ticket center to the front door of Graceland in designated-time tour groups came from Biltmore management.

Priscilla and Soden visited Disneyland several times for advice about the utilization and selection of Graceland tour guides. According to Jack Soden, after visiting Disneyland, they settled on guides with the same all-American look as Disney's personnel. The training program Graceland employees go through is also modeled after Disney's.

Tour guides at Graceland get well schooled in "Elvisology." They must be prepared for any question a guest might come up with. The standard tour is definitely scripted, but the guides can deviate from the script when prompted by a visitor's question. However, when they are asked questions about Elvis's private life, they dummy up. The guides have been instructed not to respond to questions about Elvis's drug use or his sex life. Their scripted answer to the more delicate questions is simply, "I don't know. I wasn't there."

Once Priscilla and Soden knew how they wanted to present Graceland, they set about physically preparing the mansion for its opening. Financing the work necessary to open the mansion and grounds was no simple matter. Cash on hand was limited to about $500,000. Using the mansion as collateral for a loan was out of the question, since Graceland had already been pledged as security for a loan Elvis had taken out in 1977.

An alternate source of funds had to be devised. Ken Brixey, the newly hired public relations director for Graceland, was charged with finding a way to raise capital. Brixey had previously served as the director of entertainment for the Memphis amusement park Libertyland. He quickly went to work arranging group tours in advance of opening day. Revenues from advanced ticket sales went to finance the opening.

Priscilla wanted Graceland to be maintained as closely as possible to the way it was when Elvis lived there. Absolutely no additions were to be made to the grounds of Graceland. She felt that leaving the mansion as it was would maximize its appeal to tourists. Also, the house still held sentimental value to Priscilla.

However, returning Graceland to its "original" state required some remodeling. According to Priscilla, in the years after she divorced Elvis, Graceland had been turned into a house full of crimes against good taste. Much of the tacky decor she credited to Linda Thompson. Linda seemed to have a fixation on a single color: red. The "red Graceland," as it was known among insiders, featured red velvet curtains and furniture, peacock feathers, tear-drop light fixtures, leopard skin pillows, and a menagerie of fake-fur throw rugs. Most who saw it thought it looked like a brothel.

Priscilla returned Graceland to its old decor, the way it looked when she had lived there, the way it had been for eighteen or twenty years. The reds were replaced with white carpeting, blue drapes, and gold furnishings. The restored version of Graceland was more in line with the dignified, conservative presentation Priscilla and Jack Soden were looking for.

Elvis probably would not have minded Priscilla's decision to return Graceland to its pre-Linda decor. Elvis had grown to hate the red Graceland. In the last year of his life, he was often seen entering from the rear of the home and going up the back stairs to avoid having to look at his fur-covered living room.

Since its opening in 1982, the decorations at Graceland have changed several times. In 1991, the gold piano was removed from the music room where it had stood since Graceland opened to the public. The piano was owned by a group of investors, and they decided to move it the Country Music Hall of Fame. Another piano owned by Elvis replaced it.

After the mansion was re-redecorated, the only other noteworthy construction was the addition of a parking lot across the street. Fortunately, some years earlier Elvis had purchased the eleven acres on which the parking lot would be built. Priscilla considered constructing a building to house Elvis's car collection, but there wasn't enough money to pay for the project. Elvis's cars and motorcycles would have to go on display in the carport.

Just before the opening, a group of three hundred tour bus operators were given a preview of the tour. This preview was designed to prepare the drivers to answer questions their passengers might ask during their journey to Memphis. The drivers' familiarity with the Graceland operation would enhance the total experience of the visitors. The tour of Graceland would actually begin the moment a guest stepped on the bus.

Graceland opened its gates to the public on June 7, 1982, just in time for the fifth anniversary of Elvis's death. The tour was an immediate success. It gave the fans something to get excited about. And it did something else: it allowed them to focus on Elvis's triumphs rather than his failures.

Jack Soden is fond of telling the story of how he and Priscilla took $500,000 in cash plus $60,000 in advance ticket sales and used every penny to open Graceland. But best of all, it took only thirty-eight days for the $560,000 investment to be returned. Before the grand opening, Soden had decided to limit the number of tourists to two thousand per day, but that limit was quickly abandoned. In its first year of operation, Graceland attracted over five hundred thousand visitors. First-year revenues were $4.5 million dollars.

Visitors to Graceland begin their tour at the ticket center across the street from the mansion. After purchasing their tickets, they're shuttled in small buses to the front door in groups of twenty.

A tour guide greets visitors as they step off the bus. As the guests move through different areas of the tour, they are greeted by different tour guides. Each tour guide relates particular information and anecdotes.

Originally those touring the mansion were shown the living room, music room, dining room, television room, the den—nicknamed the "jungle room" in honor of its furnishings—the pool room, and the trophy room, which displays Elvis's gold records and his stage costumes. Also included in the tour was a building in the backyard of Graceland that had served as Vernon Presley's office. Elvis's personal racquetball building was also part of the original tour. The final stop was the Meditation Garden, where Elvis, Vernon, Gladys, and Minnie Mae Presley are buried.

Conspicuously absent from the first tours was the second floor of Graceland, which includes Elvis's bedroom. The tour guides told visitors that the second floor was off-limits by request of the Presley family. Actually, it was Priscilla who placed Elvis's bedroom off-limits. She couldn't bear the thought of thousands of tourists parading through the room where Elvis died.

But if you couldn't see Graceland in person, the next best thing was to watch it on television. The Showtime cable network featured a special in honor of Elvis's fiftieth birthday called *Elvis Presley's Graceland*. The estate received $850,000 for allowing the program to be produced. The special was simply a tour of the mansion hosted by Priscilla Presley. As she walked through the house, Priscilla related significant events that had occurred in various rooms when Elvis was living at Graceland. She also included personal stories about her life with Elvis. The inspiration for *Elvis Presley's Graceland* was a televised tour of the White House given by Jackie Kennedy while she was first lady.

Priscilla had a difficult time controlling her emotions when filming the program. Several times she began to cry and filming had to be stopped.

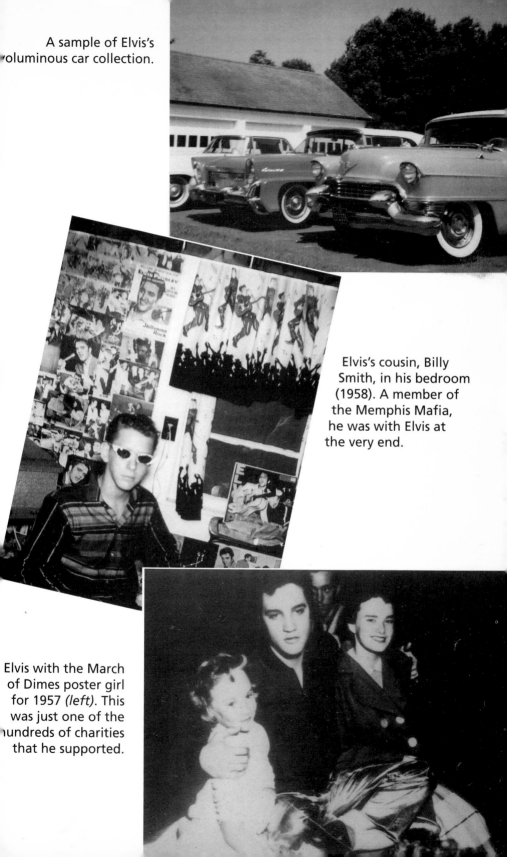

A sample of Elvis's voluminous car collection.

Elvis's cousin, Billy Smith, in his bedroom (1958). A member of the Memphis Mafia, he was with Elvis at the very end.

Elvis with the March of Dimes poster girl for 1957 *(left)*. This was just one of the hundreds of charities that he supported.

Vernon and Gladys answer fan mail sent to G.I. Presley (1958).

Elvis signs an autograph in Germany around the time he met Priscilla (1959).

Elvis in a Jeep in Germany.

Colonel Parker offers Elvis a fruit basket on the train carrying Elvis to Memphis after his discharge from the Army (1960).

Elvis and Red West, who was Elvis's first bodyguard, even in high school.

Elvis with Memphis Mafia member and high school class president George Klein.

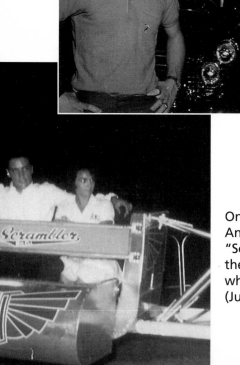

On again, off again girlfriend Anita Wood with Elvis on the "Scrambler." Elvis rented out the entire amusement park when he wanted to use it (July 12, 1960).

One of Jack Soden's first goals when he went to work for the Presley estate was to shut down the tacky souvenir stands across the street from Graceland. Built in the 1960s, the mall had operated like any other shopping center—until Elvis's death. Then, almost overnight, the mall became, in the words of the Presley estate, "An unsightly blemish of tacky Elvis souvenir shops which carried mostly bootleg items not licensed by the estate." Soden envisioned the strip mall filled with shops and attractions that would complement Graceland rather than detract from it.

In 1983, he put together a group of investors and bought the mall. Investors were necessary because the Presley estate didn't have the cash. The Presley estate was given managerial rights over the mall, as well as a master lease.

The estate began to police the mall's tenants looking for unlicensed Elvis products. As the merchant's leases expired, the estate did not renew them, gradually converting the shops to its own uses. The distasteful souvenir stands were soon replaced with estate-owned souvenir stores selling equally tacky products.

By 1987, all of the tenants were out and the estate initiated a major remodel of the mall. This remodeling included the addition of small museums, shops, and restaurants. Included in the expansion was Sincerely Elvis, a small museum housing items associated with Elvis's personal life. The museum features items of Elvis's personal clothing, Lisa Marie's baby bed, and various objects taken from the off-limits second story of Graceland. A small theater was installed in the mall that continuously plays a twenty-two-minute film recapping Elvis's career. This film is the only free attraction at Graceland.

In 1993, the estate bought the mall back from the investor group. Today, all land and attractions at Graceland are entirely owned by the estate.

Visitors to Graceland will find several gift shops devoted entirely to Elvis. Good Rockin' Tonight sells his records, compact discs, and videos. Elvis Threads stocks T-shirts, jackets, hats, and other clothing. Other gift shops offer shot glasses, beer steins, coffee mugs, snow globes, erasers, clocks, plates, and spoons—all, it need not be added, featuring Elvis's picture. Priscilla's perfume is featured in the gift shops. The hungry visitor can stop at the Heart Break Hotel Restaurant, Rockabilly's Diner, or an ice cream parlor. Graceland even has a branch of the U.S. post office where letters can be stamped with a souvenir Graceland cancellation.

Despite all efforts to date, most of the Elvis souvenirs are still hilariously tacky—and Graceland has been well chided over the years because of it. Perhaps it's Elvis, or it's the relentless concentration of so much Elvis in one place, but in a country known for tacky tourist souvenirs, Graceland is the stuff of comedy routines. And the ribbing of stand-up comedians is not without effect either. When David Letterman, on national TV, made fun of some bedroom slippers with Elvis's head on the toes, they were taken out of the stores.

According to Jack Soden, a plan is under way to upgrade the quality of the merchandise in the Graceland shops. For example, many of the stores now offer products featuring reproductions of the Elvis stamp (probably the classiest Elvis product). But how far this "upgrade" will go is questionable (if even advisable, to the relief of comedians and tourists everywhere). Another spokesman for Graceland said he did not consider the paperweight containing Graceland soil to be of dubious taste. After all, it had been one of the biggest sellers on the Home Shopping Club.

Priscilla personally dislikes much of what is sold at Graceland. When asked if the merchandise reflects her taste, Priscilla puts her hand over her mouth and makes gagging sounds. But apparently not everyone feels that way. "The thing my staff tries to convince me of," Priscilla says, "is that the stuff is selling, and we certainly don't want to put a stop to that."

So, as Jack Soden sees it, what the public wants, the public will continue to get. Though he would prefer to license only "dignified" products, he's not going to refuse to license items the public clearly wants to buy. Otherwise, he wouldn't be doing his job—maximizing profits for Elvis Presley Enterprises.

To keep the tourists coming, Graceland is constantly adding attractions, which also allows EPE to gradually increase the admission price. This is a another lesson Priscilla and Soden learned during their time with the Disney organization.

But at first, before attractions could be added, EPE had to procure more Elvis artifacts to display. Unfortunately, some of the best items had been sold by Vernon Presley during his desperate two years at the estate's helm. EPE has been forced to buy these items back or work out agreements with their owners to borrow them.

Two of Elvis's priciest toys came home in 1984 when the *Lisa Marie* and the *Hound Dog II* were brought back to Graceland. Vernon had sold both of the jet planes in his panic to raise cash for the troubled Presley estate. An arrangement was made with the planes' current owners to put the items on display as part of a joint venture with the Presley estate.

The return of the planes was marketed to the hilt. A parade was organized to lead the *Lisa Marie* from the airport to its destination across the street from Graceland. The jet's wings had to be temporarily removed so that it could be towed down Elvis Presley Boulevard. Two men rode on top of the plane to lift low-hanging stop lights as it passed underneath.

A replica of an airport terminal was created to serve as the entrance to the new airplane attraction. A map display illustrates each flight Elvis took on the *Lisa Marie*. A bank of video monitors in the terminal constantly plays a short film featuring the jet's pilot. The pilot tells the story of the time Elvis flew to Denver to pick up a delivery of peanut butter sandwiches.

In 1989, the estate undertook its most extensive addition to the mall, which by then had been renamed Graceland Plaza. In June, a new museum dedicated to housing Elvis's complete car collection was opened. Since the beginning, Graceland had needed someplace more suitable to display his cars than the Graceland carport, someplace that would do justice to Elvis's famous passion for automobiles.

The thirteen-thousand-square-foot museum was built at a cost of $1.5 million dollars. Visitors walk along a tree-lined reproduction of a highway lined with over twenty of Elvis's cars, motorcycles, and golf carts. The collection includes the 1955 pink Cadillac Elvis bought for his mother. (Gladys never learned to drive it.) Priscilla has donated a Mercedes convertible Elvis gave her. There is also a small-scale drive-in theater that continuously plays Elvis movies. Viewers sit in 1957 Chevrolet seats and listen to the sound through authentic drive-in movie speakers.

On March 13, 1995, the public was admitted to the kitchen at Graceland for the first time. The decor, a mix of gold and avocado, was still the same as when it served as Elvis's peanut-butter-and-banana-sandwich factory. The kitchen had been off-limits because Elvis's Aunt Delta was still living at Graceland after it had been opened to the public.

It's hard to say why Elvis's Aunt Delta was allowed to continue living at Graceland for ten years after the mansion had been converted to a tourist destination, or why she would want to. Aunt Delta was the last in a long line of relatives who were totally dependent on Elvis. Her sense of propriety was obscured by her difficult-to-comprehend belief that she deserved the "pension" she was drawing from her nephew. Aunt Delta lived at Graceland until she died in 1993. By then, over seven million people had filed past her bedroom on the Graceland tour.

But parts of Graceland continue to remain closed. Despite occasional hints that the site of Elvis's death will be opened, Priscilla has not yet relented.

In 1990, several million dollars were spent to buy Colonel Parker's collection of Elvis memorabilia—thirty-five tons of it. Plans are under way to expand the museums across the street from

Graceland to house this collection. Until they can be built, items from the Colonel's collection are displayed in small quantities in some of the existing attractions.

In February 1994, the year he turned eighty-five, a year-long tribute to Colonel Parker was begun at Graceland. A special exhibit devoted to Parker was put on display for a year at one of the Graceland museums. Special commemorative merchandise was created for the occasion.

Jack Soden released a statement explaining why the same organization that had sued Colonel Parker to sever its business relationship with him was now paying him such a tribute. "Elvis and Colonel Parker made history together," the statement read. "They also shared an abiding friendship that is often overlooked and misunderstood by the press and the public. We see his eighty-fifth birthday year as a perfect occasion to recognize his contribution to the Elvis phenomenon and to thank him for his friendship."

The Presley estate even published a commemorative magazine devoted to Colonel Parker and Elvis's relationship. The magazine was called *Elvis and the Colonel: The Partnership Behind the Legend.* It portrayed their relationship as a kind of fairy tale, as if the lawsuit never happened.

The elegant museums at Graceland today stand in stark contrast to the simple displays that were originally presented. When Graceland was first opened, the Elvis artifacts were displayed with no glass cases surrounding them. But harsh lighting damaged many of the items—for instance, they turned Elvis's black wedding tuxedo a chocolate brown. As it became obvious the collection was withering away, EPE hired conservation experts to redesign the displays. Temperature- and humidity-controlled cases were subsequently constructed to house Elvis's treasures.

In 1995, the monologues delivered by Graceland tour guides were replaced by cassette tapes. Lance LeGault, who provides the narration for the audio tour of Graceland, was a movie stand-in for Elvis during the 1960s. On the tape, LeGualt describes each room with occasional anecdotes from Priscilla and songs from Elvis mixed in.

While the tapes didn't eliminate the tour guides altogether, their numbers were reduced from one hundred to seventy-five, significantly cutting the estate's costs while enhancing the experience of the visitors.

When Graceland was first opened, there were almost no references to Priscilla Presley on the tour. At the time, the average Elvis fan still disliked her. Priscilla and Elvis's divorce was felt to be the event that had started Elvis's downfall. Over the years, public sentiment has changed and Priscilla is no longer viewed as the villain. She is now prominently featured on the Graceland tour via her commentary on the audiotapes.

Ticket prices have also changed. When Graceland opened in 1982, the admission fee was five dollars. With the addition of the *Lisa Marie* in 1984, the admission price was raised to ten dollars. Today a "platinum tour," good for admission to all of the attractions at Graceland, runs seventeen dollars.

★ ★ ★

Higher ticket prices seem not to have affected attendance, which has increased every year since Graceland's 1982 opening. Today, about seven hundred thousand people a year line up to take the tour. Graceland is the second most visited home in the United States, trailing only the White House. The peak season for visitors is the summer months, when five thousand visitors arrive each day. In the busy summer months, every two minutes groups of twenty board the shuttle bus that begins their tour of Graceland. The mansion and grounds are open every day of the year except Christmas, Thanksgiving, and New Year's Day.

As soon as Graceland opened, local groups began asking to hold private parties in the mansion. The mansion was out of the question, but the car museum and the restaurants were soon made available for banquets and parties. Today, Graceland hosts two to three private parties a week. At first these events were loosely struc-tured; now a variety of Elvis theme parties can be arranged for groups of as many as five hundred.

In 1984, Graceland's annual gross income was $5 million. That figure has grown to exceed $15 million. Of this total, $5 million is spent in the Graceland gift shops on Elvis memorabilia. In addition to its $15 million gross, EPE continues to receive licensing fees and royalties on Elvis products sold in the gift shops.

Contrary to popular belief, average visitors at Graceland are very much like average visitors at any other tourist attraction in America. They're not rednecks trying to look like Elvis. In fact, a majority of visitors are only casual Elvis fans. Only 2 percent belong to an Elvis fan club.

Visitors come from considerable distances to see Graceland. Approximately 93 percent come from outside the state of Tennessee. Some 15 percent of the visitors come from overseas, making Graceland a major international tourist destination.

There are over three hundred Elvis fan clubs around the world. The largest fan club with twenty thousand members is in England. Each year these clubs organize trips to Graceland for their members.

Graceland has been visited by celebrities, politicians, rock stars, religious leaders, and even the entire cast of a Broadway show. Singers have been particularly interested in making the pilgrimage to the mecca of rock 'n' roll. Performers as diverse as Phil Collins, Boy George, Sting, and the members of U2 and Guns and Roses have taken the tour. What unites them all is their love of Elvis.

The busiest time of year at Graceland is the week surrounding August 16, the anniversary of Elvis's death. It has come to be known as "Elvis International Tribute Week"—"Elvis Week" for short. During these few days in August, fifty thousand people visit Graceland. The faithful come from all over the world. Some plan and save the entire year to be able to attend. One lady from Little Rock, Arkansas, parlayed her savings from grocery coupons to finance the trip.

Elvis Week festivities feature several special events, including a trivia contest, a sock hop, autograph sessions with those who were close to Elvis, and a laser light show set to Elvis's music. One year the Memphis Hyatt Hotel featured a banquet with Elvis's favorite foods prepared by one of his cooks, Nancy Rooks.

The highlight of the year at Graceland is the candlelight vigil held on the anniversary of Elvis's death. Over twenty thousand fans carrying candles silently make their way up the driveway of Graceland and file past Elvis's grave. The line begins to form six hours before the ceremony, as the faithful brave the heat to lead the precession. After passing Elvis's grave they stop to look at the dozens of floral arrangements sent from around the world. Some of these arrangements cost as much as $350. Attendance at the candlelight vigil increases every year. Each year the procession has to start a little earlier to accommodate all of the visitors.

★ ★ ★

The Presley estate is not the sole beneficiary of the remarkable success of Graceland. It has also had a tremendous impact on the economy of Memphis. The United States Travel Data Center estimates that visitors to Graceland generate $150 million dollars per year for the economy of the city. Graceland has also become one of the largest local employers. Over 250 full- and part-time workers are employed year-round by the estate. In the summer months the staff swells to 500.

Before Graceland was opened, there was very little tourism in Memphis. A number of new tourist attractions have developed to take advantage of the crowds coming to see Elvis's home. These included the restoration of Sun Studios, where Elvis's recording career began. Also Beale Street, the center of the Memphis music scene when Elvis was getting started, has been revitalized. With the addition of blues clubs, restaurants, and shops, Beale Street has become its own attraction.

By 1991, the tour of Graceland became an established American institution. Graceland took its place among the historic homes of America, such as George Washington's Mount Vernon and Thomas Jefferson's Monticello, when it was placed on the National Register of Historic Places.

A college student was responsible for securing a spot for Graceland on the register. She visited Graceland and was surprised to find there was no plaque designating Elvis's home as a historic spot. The managers of the Presley estate were reluctant to lobby for this kind of recognition, fearing that their motives would be misunderstood or, worse, that they would be turned down. She filed an application with the National Park Service herself, nominating Graceland for the honor.

It's extremely unusual for the Park Service to bestow that honor on the home of an individual who has been dead for less than fifty years. Furthermore, no rock 'n' roll musician had ever been granted such an honor. Yet the Park Service made an exception for Elvis.

When Priscilla and Jack Soden began planning Graceland, they had no idea how big it would become. Jack Soden gives Priscilla a great deal of credit for the project's success. Part of his praise is, of course, an employee paying tribute to his boss, but Soden seems to have genuine respect for Priscilla. "Priscilla, most of all, had a very strong sense of how Graceland should be done," he said at the 1995 Conference on Elvis at the University of Mississippi. "There was a great desire to open Graceland with a lot of dignity and, to a certain extent, that meant not catering to the current whims that might exist. The safe thing to do would have been to sell Graceland and buy stocks and bonds with the money. Priscilla had a strong feeling that she wanted to give Lisa Marie both financial security and Graceland."

6

ELVIS PRESLEY™

BESIDES GRACELAND, the most valuable asset the Presley
estate possesses is Elvis's name and likeness. During his lifetime that
asset was too often taken for granted; in the years following his
death, it was the subject of controversy and litigation. The question
of who owns and controls Elvis's image wasn't settled until the
1980s. The struggle of the Presley estate to protect its most valuable
asset tested existing legal precedent, fueled the passage of new laws,
and gave judges and legislators something to argue about for years.

The right of individuals to control the use of their names and
likenesses during their lifetimes was originally known as the "right
of privacy." This legal principle was not established with the commercialization of an individual's image in mind. Its purpose, and
hence its title, was to protect an individual's right to maintain his or
her privacy.

The right of privacy was subsequently used as the basis for
lawsuits by individuals seeking to block the unauthorized use of
their famous ancestors' names and likenesses. The heirs of Jesse
James and Al Capone both brought suits against film studios who
had made movies based on the lives of their infamous ancestors. The

heirs lost their cases because the courts decided there was no invasion of privacy, that these rights had, in fact, ceased to exist when the people themselves had died.

The right of celebrities to control the commercial use of their names and likenesses during their lifetimes was established in the 1953 court case *Haelen Laboratories v. Topps Chewing Gum Inc.* Haelen and Topps were rival baseball card manufacturers. Their dispute was over what Haelen Laboratories alleged to be its exclusive right to use certain players' pictures on its baseball cards.

In its decision, the court upheld Haelen's claim. The court recognized for the first time that the right of an individual to profit from his or her image was separate from the right of privacy. The judge called this right to control the commercial use of one's image the "right of publicity." In its statement, the court said, "This Right of Publicity would usually yield them [the baseball players] no money unless it could be made the subject of an exclusive grant that barred another advertiser from using their pictures." With this decision, the legal right to profit from the commercial use of one's likeness was established.

This idea of an individual having the exclusive right to use his or her name and likeness was soon challenged in the 1956 court case, *Zacchini v. Scripp Howard Broadcasting Company.* Zacchini was a circus performer billed as "The Human Cannonball." The act consisted of Zacchini being launched from a cannon into a net two hundred feet away.

A Scripp Howard reporter came to one of Zacchini's performances and asked to film it. Zacchini refused to grant permission, but the reporter filmed his act anyway. The film was then broadcast in its entirety, again without Zacchini's consent.

Zacchini subsequently sued Scripp Howard, charging that it had improperly appropriated his professional property by broadcasting his act without his permission. The case went all the way to the U.S. Supreme Court, with Zacchini prevailing. This Supreme Court decision firmly established the exclusive right of an individual to commercially exploit his or her name and likeness.

While the Supreme Court decision made it clear that celebrities held the exclusive right to their names and likenesses, it was unclear what happened to that right when the individual died. Did the right pass down to his or her heirs, or did the right die with the individual? The first case to address this inheritability question involved the heirs of character actor Bela Lugosi.

In 1931, Lugosi starred in the Universal Pictures film *Dracula*. The film was an instant classic, and the actor's identity became virtually inseparable from the character he portrayed. However, Lugosi never again portrayed Dracula, nor did he make any attempts to license his image for the production of merchandise.

Bela Lugosi died in 1956. Four years later, Universal began entering into licensing agreements that authorized the use of the likeness of Lugosi as Count Dracula in the production of commercial merchandise. Universal granted licenses to fifty different manufacturers for the production of T-shirts, lunch boxes, Halloween costumes, models, and various other items bearing the likeness of Lugosi's Dracula. The licenses specifically allowed the use of the Dracula character, but prohibited the use of Lugosi's name.

In 1966, in a California court, Lugosi's wife and son sued Universal, claiming that the licensing agreements had violated their right to the late actor's name and likeness. The judge in the Lugosi case had two issues before him to consider. First, had Lugosi, as Universal Pictures claimed, granted them the right to his likeness as Dracula for any purpose when he signed the contract to portray the character in the movie? Second, if Lugosi had not assigned that right to Universal, had it been passed on to his heirs upon his death?

Concerning the first issue, the court found that Lugosi's contract with Universal only permitted the use of his name and likeness in conjunction with the promotion of the movie *Dracula*. Lugosi had not assigned the right to Universal to license the use of his image for the production of merchandise. On the issue of whether Lugosi's heirs had inherited the right to use his name and likeness, the court ruled that they, indeed, had inherited that right, and it ordered Universal to discontinue licensing Lugosi's image without his heir's consent.

As might be expected, Universal appealed the court's decision, focusing on the issue of the survivability of the right of publicity. The appeals court decided in favor of Universal, declaring that Lugosi's name and likeness had entered the public domain upon his death. The court held that "the right to exploit one's name is personal to the artist and must be exercised if at all during his lifetime." The judges reasoned that if name and likeness were inheritable, the ancestors of all public figures could obtain damages for the unauthorized use of their ancestors' images. The descendants of presidents, for example, could seek royalty payments for the use of their forebears' pictures on stamps or money.

Several years later, another attempt was made to establish the inheritability of name and likeness. In 1975, the heirs of Stan Laurel and Oliver Hardy sued Hal Roach Studios, the producer of the classic Laurel and Hardy films of the 1930s. The studio was licensing merchandisers to use images of the characters played by the deceased actors in those films. The heirs were suing to recover a share of the profits from the licensing deals.

The attorneys for Hal Roach Studios argued that the heirs of Stan Laurel and Oliver Hardy had no right to control the licensing of the names and images of the dead actors, and he cited the Lugosi case to support his case. Since Laurel and Hardy had never acted to protect their rights to exploit their images during their lifetime, the opportunity to do so had ended with their deaths.

This time, the New York court that heard the case found in favor of the heirs. The court ruled that the right of publicity did not have to be exercised during the actors' lifetimes to have been established. The judges saw no logical reason why an individual should forfeit a right just because he or she had never used it. They also saw no reason why heirs should not be able to inherit the right to control the use of name and likeness as they would any other form of property.

The debate over the inheritability of a person's name and likeness exploded after Elvis's death. During the period immediately following his passing, the estate found it had very little control over the use of Elvis's name and picture. When Elvis died, merchandisers of all shapes and descriptions lunged at the chance to put the King's picture on every imaginable novelty item with no royalty consideration going to the estate. A scourge of unlicensed Elvis products hit the streets overnight. Posters, calendars, videos, T-shirts, you name it—all were produced and sold without the estate's approval. Many of the tackiest items were being sold in stores right across the street from Graceland.

As the Presley estate's newly appointed licensing agent, Factors Etc. Inc. faced a significant roadblock in its efforts to stop unlicensed manufacturers of Elvis-related merchandise. The Lugosi and Laurel and Hardy decisions contradicted each other, so there was no clearcut answer to the question of image and name inheritability. The licensing agent would have to clarify the issue in court.

Factors didn't have to wait long for its first case. Immediately after Elvis's death, Pro Arts Inc., an Ohio-based company, purchased a photograph of Elvis from a staff photographer at the *Atlanta Journal.* The photographer had taken the picture of Elvis some years earlier and owned the copyright to it. Pro Arts used the photograph to create a "memorial" Elvis poster. It was titled "In Memory," and the years of Elvis's birth and death were printed along the bottom. On August 19, 1977, Pro Arts began to sell the poster. On August 24, Pro Arts sent a letter to Colonel Parker's Boxcar Enterprises, which had contracted with Factors, stating that it was selling "a memorial Elvis poster to meet the public demand."

Factors responded by informing Pro Arts that it owned the exclusive right to manufacture and distribute Elvis merchandise, and that if Pro Arts continued to produce and sell its Elvis poster, Factors would sue. But Pro Arts was making a bundle on the poster (a million dollars in profits, by some estimates). It had no intention of stopping.

On September 26, 1977, Factors filed suit against Pro Arts in the Federal District Court of Northern Ohio. In that case, the court found that the right to Elvis's name and likeness had, in fact, passed to his heirs upon his death. Pro Arts was ordered to cease production of the Elvis poster.

In its appeal to the court's decision, Pro Arts argued that since it had purchased the copyright to the photograph from which the poster was created, the company was within its legal rights to sell it. Pro Arts also objected to the notion that the Presley estate had inherited the right to control Elvis's image. And even if that right did exist, the Pro Arts attorney's asserted, Pro Arts was within its right to produce the poster because it was the commemoration of a newsworthy event. Producing the poster, therefore, was a First Amendment right.

The appeals court found in favor of Factors, rejecting Pro Arts's claim that the poster was simply a record of a newsworthy event. In the court's opinion, Elvis had validly assigned the right to merchandise his name and likeness to Boxcar during his lifetime. Boxcar had, in turn, assigned this right to Factors after Elvis's death. The court did not believe that death should affect this arrangement.

In its decision, the court said, "The right of publicity is not a new concept, but to the detriment of legal clarity it has often been discussed only under the rubric 'right of privacy.' When a 'persona' is a product, and that product has already been marketed to good advantage, the appropriation by another of that valuable property has more to do with unfair competition than it does with the right to be left alone. There is no reason why the valuable Right of Publicity clearly exercised by and financially benefiting Elvis Presley in life should not descend at death like any other intangible property right."

Factors had won its first battle, but the war was still raging. When it learned that the Memphis Development Foundation was planning to produce and distribute miniature replicas of a statue of Elvis it had erected in downtown Memphis, Factors took the organization to court.

The Memphis Development Foundation is a nonprofit group dedicated to improving both the economic and social situation in Memphis. In 1979 the foundation decided that, as part of its civic efforts, it would honor Elvis by placing a bronze statue of him on Beale Street in downtown Memphis. A plan was developed to pay for the statue through donations from the public. As an incentive, anyone who donated twenty-five dollars or more would receive an eight-inch replica of the statue.

When Factors learned of the plan, it brought suit against the foundation. Factors objected to what it perceived to be an offer to sell a statue of Elvis Presley for twenty-five dollars. It seemed to make no difference to Factors that the foundation saw the transaction as a donation. In Factors's opinion, it infringed on its "exclusive right to reap commercial value from the name and likeness of Elvis Presley."

Factors opposed the use of Elvis in fundraising because it infringed upon their exclusive right to market his image. It was concerned that if Elvis memorabilia were given away it would reduce the market for other merchandise.

The district court decided the statue could be built in downtown Memphis. However, the court upheld Factors's exclusive right to Elvis's name and likeness. It prohibited the use of miniature statues as inducements for contributions toward the cost of the statue. The fact that the aim of the fundraising effort was a civic project had no bearing on the question of the legality of using Elvis's image without permission from Factors. Elvis had developed good will that his heirs were entitled to inherit.

In his opinion, Memphis District Judge Harry Welford stated, "The well-reasoned cases, it is believed, set out a clear distinction between the valuable 'Right of Publicity' of public figures such as Presley and the 'Right of Privacy' in the sense of being left alone, free from harassment or humiliation in a tortious claim. Elvis Presley himself, through Parker and Boxcar, fully pursued this exclusive right of publicity during his lifetime. The party holding this exclusive right during his lifetime and the personal representative of Elvis Presley after his death unequivocally attempted to assign exclusive rights to his name and image as it related to the kind of statuary involved in this proceeding."

The victory for the estate, and its ownership of Elvis's name and likeness, was quickly challenged when the Memphis Development Foundation appealed the court's decision. The Sixth Circuit Court of Appeals overturned the district court's decision, and denied that the right to exploit Elvis's name and likeness had been passed on to his heirs. The court held that the heirs could not legally assign a right to Factors that they did not have. The court also voiced concern about the extremes to which heirs of famous individuals could go if allowed to inherit the rights to the names and likenesses of their ancestors: "Does the right apply to elected officials as well as to movie stars, singers, and athletes? Does the right include a football stadium 'RFK,' utilities 'Edison,' a pastry 'Napoleon,' and insurance 'John Hancock'? Would we then allow George Washington's family to demand payment for the use of his picture on the dollar bill and his name for our capital?"

In their unanimous decision, the judges said, "After death the opportunity to gain shifts to the public domain where it is equally open to all. . . . The memory, name, and picture of famous individuals should be recognized as a common asset to be shared, an economic opportunity available in a free market system. Fame is a benefit from which others may benefit but may not own."

In 1994, another round of controversy started over the Elvis statue (this time not legal in nature). A combination of Memphis's hot summers and cold winters had severely damaged the statue, and it was removed from its home on Beale Street for a $15,000 restoration job. After the repairs were finished, the statue was moved to a new tourist information center where Memphis attractions, including Graceland, would be promoted.

The merchants of Beale Street were quite upset at the loss of the Elvis statue. It had been a big draw for the area. Tourists would come to see the statue and then visit the shops nearby. The Beale Street merchants met with Elvis Presley Enterprises and asked for the loan of an Elvis artifact, such as a car, to replace the statue. Despite the merchants offer to provide twenty-four-hour security, EPE declined.

Rather than resolving the issue of whether Elvis's estate had inherited his name and likeness, Factors's lawsuits only added to the confusion. At one point in 1983, Factors had exclusive control over the use of Elvis's name and likeness in New York, while in California and Elvis's home state of Tennessee, the name and likeness were public domain.

For a period of time, the California courts had ruled that Elvis Presley's right of publicity had survived his death. The courts relied heavily on the original decision in the Bela Lugosi case, which had indicated that name and likeness should be inheritable. Later, when the Lugosi decision was reversed by the California Supreme Court, Elvis's heirs lost their rights in the Golden State.

The Court of Appeals in Tennessee used the decision of the California Supreme Court as the basis for rejecting the estate's claim at home.

The New York judges also based their decision on the original Lugosi verdict. But when the California Supreme Court overturned that verdict, New York ignored it in its consideration of subsequent cases involving name and likeness issues.

In declining to recognize inheritability of name and likeness rights, the California and Tennessee courts raised several troubling questions about the issue. How long would the right last? Forever, or a few years? Copyright and patents both have a finite life. Should name and likeness also have such limitations? At what point does the right of the celebrity's heirs contradict the right of free expression as guaranteed by the First Amendment?

Other courts approached the question from a different perspective, recognizing a celebrity's expectation that he or she is creating a valuable capital asset that will benefit his or her heirs after death. That asset should be passed on just like a house or stocks and bonds.

Some courts were recognizing that an image is property, and therefore inheritable; others were finding that an individual's image was a personal attribute, like a title, an office, friendship, or an employment contract, and therefore *not* inheritable.

After mixed and confusing results in the courts, the Presley estate decided to try the Tennessee State Legislature. If the estate could convince the legislature to pass a law establishing once and for all the inheritability of name and likeness, it would finally have what it needed to police the market. The estate hired a lobbyist to deliver its message to the Tennessee lawmakers. In 1984, the State of Tennessee enacted the Personal Rights Protection Act.

The Personal Rights Protection Act of 1984 states, in part, "(a) Every individual has a property right in the use of his name, photograph, or likeness in any medium in any manner. (b) The individual right provided for in subsection (a) shall constitute property rights and shall be freely assignable and licensable and shall not expire upon the death of the individual so protected, whether or not such rights were commercially exploited by the individual during the individual's lifetime, but shall be descendible to the executors, assigns, heirs or devices of the individuals so protected by this part."

The new law granted an individual the rights to his or her name and likeness for his or her lifetime, plus ten years after death. To maintain their rights, the individual's heirs need only use the image for commercial purposes within two years subsequent to the initial ten-year period. Exceptions to the law were made for the use of name and likeness in connection with news, public affairs, or sports broadcasts. In other words, the Personal Rights Protection Act would not supersede the First Amendment of the Constitution.

Soon after the Tennessee law was enacted, California passed legislation protecting the heirs of celebrities. (No doubt the large number of famous persons residing in California had something to do with the legislature's quick action.) Very similar to the Tennessee law, the California Celebrity Rights Act prohibits the unauthorized use of the name, signature, voice, photograph, or likeness of any person for fifty years after his or her death. Estates are required to register with the Secretary of State of California if they wish protection to control a celebrity's image. Once they have registered with the state, violators of the estate's rights can be sued for any profits received, plus punitive damages. The California law exempts plays, books, and musical compositions from the right of publicity, since they are recognized as protected First Amendment expressions.

Several other states followed the lead of Tennessee and California. Virginia, Kentucky, Florida, Nebraska, Oklahoma, and Utah all enacted their own legislation establishing name and likeness inheritance rights. Court decisions in New York, New Jersey, and Georgia established the inheritability of name and likeness in these states.

April 20, 1987, was a watershed in the history of the Presley estate's fight for control of Elvis's image. On that day, a Tennessee court of appeals ruled that the right of publicity is inheritable intangible property under Tennessee law. Therefore, the Presley estate owns Elvis's name and likeness and could prevent others from using them. The court said, "Investment in a career deserves no less recognition and protection than investments celebrities might make in the stock market or other tangible assets."

This decision was the first of its kind in an appellate court in Tennessee. Subsequently, courts across the country began to recognize the inheritability of a celebrity's name and likeness. The conflicting court decisions that had plagued the Presley estate came to an end. The estate's legal right to its most valuable asset was now firmly established.

The Presley estate effectively created a monopoly. A photographer with copyrighted pictures of Elvis could not even release a poster of the picture without the consent of his estate. The name Elvis Presley could not be used in any commercial venture without explicit permission. A museum of Elvis artifacts could not even be called "The Elvis Museum" without the estate's okay.

By 1988, EPE's dominion over the memory of Elvis Presley was all but undisputed. Wherever they fell, the earthly shadows of the King of Rock 'n' Roll belonged to the estate, and any who would use them paid tribute—and any who didn't found themselves in court. Once its rights were legally settled, the Presley estate was ruthless about protecting them. The lengths to which EPE has gone to protect its rights is as remarkable as its struggle to gain those rights.

7

SUE ME TENDER

ELVIS PRESLEY IS PROBABLY the best-protected brand name in the history of show business. Since it was established in 1979, EPE has filed more than a hundred lawsuits to assert the estate's exclusive right to Elvis's name and likeness. No venture is too small to escape the eagle eyes of the estate's attorneys; no product is too cheap to be beneath their notice. They have pursued anyone and everyone who has violated their territory, from big-time TV producers mentioning Elvis in their shows to a small-timer peddling copies of Elvis's will; from college students setting up an unauthorized Elvis page on the World Wide Web to a purveyor of Elvis's "sweat." (The company's slogan was "His Perspiration Is Your Inspiration.") Anyone who wants to reprint even the epitaph on Elvis's grave—the first thing ever copyrighted by the estate—had better ask for permission if they want to stay out of a courtroom.

So protective are EPE lawyers that they have even pursued creators of the supreme symbol of pop culture kitsch: the velvet Elvis painting. Once flourishing at flea markets and roadside stands across America, these paintings are now an endangered species (which may or may not be such a bad thing).

Anytime Elvis Presley's name or picture is used in a commercial television program or a movie, EPE attacks. The producers of the television comedy *Cheers* had to obtain permission from EPE for an episode in which one of the stars has a dream about Elvis. Both the script and the actor who played Elvis had to be approved. When the producers of the movie *True Romance* wanted to use the ghost of Elvis as a character, they first sought the permission of EPE. In 1989, EPE considered suing producers of another television program, *Designing Women,* for an unauthorized episode in which it believed Elvis was portrayed inappropriately.

Even noncommercial, amateur "producers" have to watch their steps. Visitors to Graceland are notified that video and audiotaping is prohibited inside any museum, attraction, or gift shop. Licensed videos are available at the gift shop.

EPE has gone to considerable trouble to protect its claim on Elvis's name and likeness outside the United States. Sales of Elvis-related products outside the country are just as strong as they are inside, so controlling the global market for Elvis goods is very important to the estate's profitability. EPE actually brought suit in a Japanese court against a Japanese firm that filed for trademark protection on the word "Elvis" written in Japanese. The suit was settled with the company giving up its Japanese trademark. Since that time, EPE has registered its trademarks throughout Europe and the Far East.

Elvis Presley didn't become the most protected brand name in the history of show business overnight. In fact, during Elvis's lifetime, Colonel Parker kept only loose controls over the production of unlicensed Elvis products. After the initial 1950s boom, sales of Elvis memorabilia slowed dramatically, and since they were not significant enough to warrant the Colonel's attention, bootleggers produced Elvis products with considerable freedom.

Elvis's death set off another boom. Between 1977 and 1980, the Presley estate probably lost millions of dollars in licensing fees due to the production of bootleg Elvis products. Instigated by

Factors, which had signed the exclusive licensing contract, somewhat more serious legal attempts were made to stop the sale of unauthorized Elvis merchandise, with mixed success (see Chapter 6).

Then, in 1981, the estate contacted an attorney to help copyright the inscription on grandma Minnie Mae Presley's tombstone. (The estate successfully secured that copyright, so we couldn't print the inscription here without first getting their permission.) Memphis attorney Barry Ward was surprised to learn that the estate was worried about grandma Presley's epitaph but had never bothered to establish trademark protection for Elvis's name. In a way, this was one of the most direct and obvious strategies for controlling the production of Elvis-related products.

EPE followed Ward's advice and registered "Elvis," "Elvis Presley," "Elvis in Concert," and "Graceland" as trademarks. "The King" was applied for but denied. (Commonly used terms, such as "king" or "light," are not often granted trademark protection.) Once EPE tasted of the power of the brand name, it became ravenous.

EPE has since charged Barry Ward with tracking down companies releasing unauthorized Elvis Presley products and stopping them. Ward's law firm, Glankler-Brown, had provided legal services to the estate for a number of years, including drawing up Elvis's will. After the estate's lawsuit was settled with Colonel Parker, Ward was engaged as its general counsel.

An autographed picture of his two most famous clients, Priscilla and Lisa Marie Presley, hangs on a wall in Mr. Ward's office, and he keeps a black notebook full of favorable EPE court rulings out on his desk.

Ward is understandably proud of his firm's record of wins in the fight to control the use of Elvis's name and likeness. According to Ward, the estate's claim is now so well established that a letter from him is generally all it takes to stop any unauthorized or unlicensed use. When his warnings are ignored, he says, EPE fights and usually wins. The black book is a testament to the estate's victories in court. But when given a choice, Ward says, the estate would much rather collect a licensing fee than litigate.

Ward relies on a variety of resources to aid him in his surveillance of the Elvis market. His people make regular checks on a computer database that tracks all Elvis products currently being sold. He employs a clipping service that subscribes to sixteen thousand newspapers and magazines, as well as a service that monitors all television commercials aired in the United States. EPE also employs a network of private informants, who report any Elvis products they believe to be unauthorized.

Within ten years of Elvis's death, EPE had established an iron grip on the name and likeness of its namesake—a feat Colonel Parker hadn't managed in twenty-two years. Ward and company have been so successful that very little unauthorized Elvis merchandise even exists today. A high-ranking member of the EPE staff admits that bootleg Elvis merchandise no longer poses much of a threat to the estate's bottom line. In fact, if there were *no* bootleggers, the estate would worry that Elvis's popularity was slipping.

★ ★ ★

In the years following its first tentative steps into the courtroom, EPE emerged as a genuine trailblazer in establishing and protecting the rights of celebrities to control the use of their names and images. Court decisions in EPE-initiated lawsuits have been precedent-setting. Today, almost any court case involving a name and likeness issue will cite a Presley case in its decision. EPE's actions started a veritable avalanche of lawsuits in this area.

Johnny Carson, the former *Tonight Show* host, sued a company in Michigan for advertising "Here's Johnny" portable toilets. The novelty items were advertised as "The world's foremost commodian." Jacqueline Kennedy Onassis sued Dior when the company used a look-alike actress in one of its clothing advertisements. Vanna White sued the producers of a commercial that featured a robot flipping letters in a parody of what Ms. White does on the game show *Wheel of Fortune*.

While the courts have tended to give celebrities broad authority to control the use of their names and images, they have ruled against them when constitutional freedoms were involved. In 1991, the estate of Janis Joplin sued to stop production of a play based on Ms. Joplin's life. The U.S. District Court in Seattle ruled that use of Joplin in the play was protected under the First Amendment right of freedom of speech. The production continued without permission of Joplin's estate.

Under the precedent established by this ruling, a play was produced about Elvis without the sanction of EPE. The Janis Joplin case has also been widely used as a defense by Elvis impersonators, who have argued—so far successfully—that they may perform without the approval of the estate.

Today, the commercial use of Elvis Presley's name and image in plays, books, and movies is protected under the Constitution. (Which may explain why so many books have been written on this subject.) Nonetheless, EPE occasionally approaches a screenwriter, playwright, or author about securing a license. When the writer points out that the Constitution has already granted the license, the issue is dropped.

Still, book authors must be careful when using Elvis as their subject matter. An author may not sell an unlicensed book that contains only photographs of Elvis. Words must be included in the book or it is not considered protected speech.

EPE considered taking action against the author of *Is Elvis Alive?*, which claimed to show evidence that he is still alive. While the book itself didn't need a license from the estate, the cassette tape included with the book did. The tape contained a conversation with Elvis that supposedly took place several years after his death. The estate considered using the unlicensed tape as a means of stopping the book. When the book proved to be unpopular, the estate decided against taking legal action.

★ ★ ★

EPE's aggressive legal campaign has not been confined to stopping improper use of Elvis's name and likeness. It has occasionally been forced to sue to collect its licensing royalties. In 1995, Egdon Heath Inc. obtained a license from the estate to produce T-shirts and jackets bearing Elvis's image. The agreement called for a minimum royalty payment of $50,000. When Egdon Heath was able to come up with only $25,000, EPE went to court.

The cancellation of the twelve-city concert tour Elvis was scheduled to begin the day he died also drew the estate into court. Over a million dollars in advance tickets had been sold. When the concerts were canceled, refunds were offered, but many ticket holders held on to their tickets, which had become instant collectibles valued at much more than their purchase price. Inevitably, a dispute over the unclaimed refund money ensued.

The Presley estate asserted that it was entitled to the money. It contacted all of the concert halls and demanded to be paid immediately. The estate agreed to be financially responsible in the event any tickets were later presented for refunds. The concert halls were not anxious to turn over hundreds of thousands of dollars without a fight. Many venues considered the money to have been abandoned, and therefore, their property. They saw no reason to pay for a performance that Elvis never gave.

The estate spent many years litigating in several states to recover this money. Its success in court was mixed. After holding funds for twelve years, a Nassau County, New York, arena was forced to hand over $86,000 in unclaimed ticket money to the Presley estate. The judge hearing the case held that the estate was required to pay only the $5,000 cancellation fee called for in Elvis's appearance contract with the arena; the rest of the money, the judge ruled, it could keep.

In December 1988, a Memphis court ruled that holders of tickets for two canceled local concerts were the only parties who deserved the opportunity to recover the unclaimed refunds. Any money left after the refund claims were processed would go to the state. By the time the court reached its decision, the unclaimed money had grown to $411,000 with interest.

A few die-hard Elvis fans are still holding onto their unused concert tickets—more than a few because they believe he might return to perform the shows someday. Among the believers is a Fort Worth, Texas, man who filed suit against EPE alleging that Elvis had faked his death and is in hiding. The man said he knows that Elvis is still alive because he frequently receives telephone calls from him.

D'Etta Leach and Billy James thought they had hit upon a perfect way to profit from the debate over whether Elvis is really dead. James, a disc jockey from Charlotte, North Carolina, came up with the idea of creating "Elvis on Tour" T-shirts. The back of the shirt would list locations where Elvis had been spotted, including a Burger King in Michigan and a convenience store in Texas.

James brought his idea to Leach, the owner of a novelty T-shirt company. Leach's company had produced a highly successful T-shirt that poked fun at Tammy Faye Bakker, ex-wife of the then-jailed televangelist Jim Bakker. The shirts featured large, spidery mascara smears over the caption "I ran into Tammy Faye at the mall."

Leach liked James's idea and put the T-shirt into production. The "Elvis on Tour" T-shirt was a big hit, selling over $100,000 worth almost overnight. Sales came to a grinding halt, however, when EPE got wind of the product. EPE's legal reps sent a letter to Leach demanding that she cease production immediately. Leach, in turn, contacted her own attorney, who advised her that, while he believed she was within her constitutional rights to produce the T-shirts, she could never beat EPE. Going to court against EPE would be like "David taking on Goliath." Leach subsequently removed the shirts from the market.

The continuing debate over whether Elvis is really dead is the theme of the Elvis Is Alive Museum in Wright City, Missouri. Included among the museum's exhibits is Elvis's funeral room, complete with a casket and a wax replica of Elvis; the tomb room, which recreates Elvis's grave at Graceland; and the Elvis tape room, which continuously plays a telephone conversation with Elvis that supposedly took place in 1984, seven years after his death.

According to Graceland's director of communications, Todd Morgan, small, unlicensed Elvis museums spring up on a regular basis. EPE's lawyers just contact them with the usual warnings, and either call for the operation's shutdown or a licensing fee, depending on the quality of the museum. Ironically, the estate had learned about the museum when its owner, Beanie Smith, contacted them about buying items to sell in his gift shop.

In this case, Smith declined Morgan's invitation to apply for a license. (Morgan says the estate would also have required a name change.) In response, EPE sent out a cease-and-desist notice.

Smith chose not to respond to EPE's threats. No stranger to the public arena, Smith's résumé includes unsuccessful campaigns for governor and lieutenant-governor, a stint as the organizer of an anti-Communist group, and a job conducting seminars that showed homeowners how to protect themselves in the event of race riots. He is also a Baptist minister.

Two years later, the Elvis Is Alive Museum is still in operation, and Smith has yet to find himself in court. The museum gift shop is fully stocked with Elvis merchandise; Smith found himself another vendor.

This failure to follow through on the part of EPE's attorneys is not particularly unusual. It's likely that EPE has no intention of suing every small operator it threatens. Sending a cease-and-desist letter is a very inexpensive ploy that usually does the trick. Most people who receive the letter either withdraw or agree to pay for a license. For the most part, EPE pursues only those cases involving big money.

★ ★ ★

Despite the seemingly endless reports of "Elvis sightings" in the tabloid press, most Elvis fans aren't expecting him to emerge from hiding anytime soon. His continuing popularity, however, has created a surprisingly robust business for the next best thing to his return: Elvis impersonators. The sheer number of working Elvis impersonators is a testament to the commercial power of his image: an estimated fifteen hundred pseudo-Elvises perform regularly today. Elvis impersonations began while he was still alive, but after Elvis died, public demand for performers "doing" Elvis increased sharply. Soon, the better impersonators were able to command as much as $10,000 for a single appearance. Over $3 million a year was suddenly being generated by what had been a novelty act. With so much money involved, it's not surprising that at least one impersonator is known to have had plastic surgery to make himself look more like Elvis.

In the wake of Elvis's death, Colonel Parker was the first to try to establish control over the fake Elvises. In 1978, he worked with BMI (Broadcast Music Inc.) to come up with a tricky license enforcement strategy. In February of that year, BMI sent out a notice to performers and theater owners stating that the organization would license a maximum of three vocal performances of Elvis Presley songs. Anyone wanting to sing more than three Elvis songs would have to obtain a "special license" from BMI. This special license would serve as the means by which Colonel Parker would get his cut.

Fortunately for the impersonators, BMI does not control every song Elvis recorded or performed in his lifetime. Also, the BMI restriction only applied to the Elvis portion of its catalog, leaving the Elvises free to sing any other BMI song they wanted.

It quickly became obvious that the BMI scheme wasn't going to work. The impersonators filled their acts with the hits of the day, performed as Elvis would have sung them. Audiences found it entertaining to hear them performing songs Elvis had never recorded. With no other means to control them, the Colonel gave up trying.

When Priscilla and company came to power, EPE decided to try its hand at reigning in the burgeoning ranks of ersatz Elvises. In 1980, it identified over two hundred individuals who were making their living impersonating Elvis. EPE claimed its motivation for requiring the Elvises to pay licensing fees was concern for their namesake's image. However, EPE only seriously contemplated pursuing legal action against the most successful impostors, which suggests that EPE's motivation was primarily financial.

At first, EPE tried sending letters to the impersonators, demanding that they cease to portray Elvis Presley without official sanction. In general, the Elvises ignored this letter.

One of the first impersonators EPE pursued seriously was Johnny "Elvis" Spence. EPE threatened to sue Spence if he followed through with his plans to perform a concert at a 12,500-seat hall on the tenth anniversary of Elvis's death. Spence had applied for a license from EPE but had been turned down. Fortunately for Spence, he was able to settle his differences with EPE outside of court.

What EPE really wanted was a case that would establish its rights in court over all Elvis impersonators. As its test case, the estate chose Rod Russen, producer of *The Big El Show*, which was advertised as a tribute to Elvis. Russen had engaged Larry Seth to impersonate Elvis in the show. For sale at *The Big El Show* were albums, pennants, and buttons, all bearing an image very similar to Elvis's. Russen caught EPE's attention when he filed for trademarks on the show's name and logo.

In its lawsuit, EPE charged that Russen had infringed on the estate's trademark, engaged in unfair competition, damaged its ability to license Elvis, and caused the public to believe that EPE had sanctioned the show. EPE asked for damages equal to three times the profits from *The Big El Show* and that the show be stopped.

Russen's attorney claimed that Colonel Parker had been aware of the show from its beginning. Russen had spoken to the Colonel in 1975, the attorney said, and Parker assured him that neither he nor

Elvis objected. Russen's attorney argued that Parker had, through his words, licensed the show.

The court gave no weight to Russen's claims that Colonel Parker had sanctioned *The Big El Show.* EPE was the owner of the property in question, not Colonel Parker. Elvis Presley Enterprises had filed a timely notice of opposition to Russen's application to register a trademark and logo. EPE also had filed a timely suit objecting to the performance of *The Big El Show.*

In the Russen case, the court reaffirmed that Elvis Presley's name and likeness had been inherited as a part of his estate. However, the court found that *The Big El Show* was not unfair competition. In its decision, the court further wrote that there was no likelihood that Larry Seth would be confused with Elvis Presley. He disagreed with EPE's argument that *The Big El Show* diminished EPE's ability to license Elvis. In the judge's opinion, an Elvis impersonator did not need a license from Elvis Presley Enterprises to perform. An impersonation is an exercise of freedom of speech.

The judge did find that the merchandise being sold at the concert was a violation of EPE's trademark. He was particularly concerned with the similarity between actual photographs of Elvis Presley and *The Big El Show's* promotional material. The judge issued a restraining order prohibiting Russen from using the Presley logo, sketch, likeness, or picture.

Despite this early loss, EPE continued to sue the most successful impersonators. *Legends in Concert,* a very successful Las Vegas show featuring impersonators of several musicians, including Elvis, has tangled with Elvis Presley Enterprises on several occasions. Ironically, Mark Trator, the attorney who represents *Legends in Concert,* was instrumental in getting a name and likeness rights law passed in Nevada. However, the Nevada law specifically allows impersonators to perform without permission from heirs of the individual being impersonated. Because of this provision, Trator has prevailed against EPE in court, and *Legends in Concert* continues to include Elvis impersonators.

Mr. Trator has stated that the Presley estate ignores 99 percent of the Elvis impersonators working today, focusing their efforts on the most financially successful ones. This suggests to Mr. Trator that EPE is more concerned with making money than protecting Elvis's image. While he does not object to EPE's pursuit of profit, he says he does not admire their hypocrisy.

Probably the most unusual Elvis impersonator lawsuit to date, however, did *not* involve the Presley estate. The plaintiffs in the suit were members of a group of skydiving Elvis impersonators called the Flying Elvi. The defendants were members of a competing group, called the Flying Elvises. Both groups formed after seeing *Honeymoon in Vegas,* a feature film in which a fictitious group of skydiving Elvis impersonators performed over the skies of Las Vegas. Taking a page out of the EPE book, the Flying Elvi claimed copyright infringement, unfair competition, deceptive trade practices, and interference with business opportunity. The Flying Elvises claimed that they had received permission from Elvis Presley Enterprises to operate. To this, the Flying Elvi responded that EPE did not own the rights to Elvis as a skydiver because Elvis never performed that way. (The case is still pending.)

On the whole, EPE has been only slightly more successful than Colonel Parker in controlling Elvis impersonators. Of the over fifteen hundred Elvis impersonators working today, some are licensed by EPE, but most are not. Those that aren't have formed the Elvis Presley Impersonators Association of America to represent their interests. EPE seems to have given up pursuing unlicensed impersonators unless they sell illegal merchandise at their shows. According to a spokesperson for EPE, the estate now treats the pseudo-Elvises "with benign neglect."

Notwithstanding all efforts to quell or control this strange phenomenon, impersonating Elvis continues to be a thriving, lucrative business.

★ ★ ★

Despite the estate's consistent courtroom successes, there continue to emerge a few brave souls willing to test EPE's resolve. The estate has, thus far, been quick to challenge these heretics, whenever and wherever they appear. In 1991, EPE brought suit against British businessman Sid Shaw and his company, Elvisly Yours, which marketed a variety of items bearing Elvis's picture. Before founding his company in the 1960s, Shaw's claim to fame was his unsuccessful campaign for the British parliament as a member of the Elvis Presley party.

Shaw never bothered to license his products through EPE. The suit the estate filed against him charged that Elvisly Yours was selling, among other things, unauthorized women's underwear adorned with Elvis's face.

Rather than acquiescing immediately to the estate's demands, Shaw countersued, claiming that the laws and the licensing fees were unfair. His objection was based primarily on the fact that the current name and likeness laws hadn't existed when Elvis had died, and that EPE shouldn't be allowed to apply them retroactively.

Shaw's attorneys also argued that EPE had actually purchased Elvis products from Elvisly Yours to sell in Graceland's gift shops. Attorney Peter Brown said his client "has seen others doing it, not only before this but after the lawsuit commenced. They were buying from him, leading him to think that it was all right. So, what kinds of policing activities were they undertaking? What were they doing when they knew that he was out there selling goods?"

EPE argued that it had repeatedly told Elvisly Yours that the company was violating EPE's trademarks. Shaw's response to their warnings had been that he was going to continue to sell Elvis merchandise until they stopped him. At which point, EPE decided it had no choice but to file suit against Shaw.

The Cincinnati court hearing the case ruled in favor of EPE, prohibiting Elvisly Yours from selling Elvis Presley products in the United States. Sid Shaw wasn't completely driven out of the Elvis market, however. He continues to peddle his wares in England through his Elvisly Yours Ltd. company.

Moreover, it seems that EPE wants control not only of who gets to manufacture Elvis merchandise but *where* that merchandise is sold. Some of the most successful sellers of Elvis-related products are located in a tiny strip mall separated from the EPE-owned Graceland Plaza by a fence. These stores, which by their very existence cut into the Presley estate's profits, are thorns in EPE's side. The estate has tangled with the owners on several occasions.

Their most recent confrontation was in September 1994, when EPE brought suit against most of the stores in the mall. Included in the suits were The Wooden Indian, Souvenirs of Elvis, and Memories of Elvis, all of which deal exclusively in various types of Elvis memorabilia. EPE claimed that, in 1993, it had become aware that the stores named in the suit were selling unlicensed Elvis merchandise. EPE also claimed that the store owners knew they were selling unlicensed merchandise and refused to stop, even after the estate had notified them. When the store owners refused to pull the offending merchandise from their shelves, EPE was forced to enforce its rights in court.

The suits against the stores all alleged violation of EPE's right of publicity, as well as trademark infringement and violation of the Tennessee Personal Rights Protection Act of 1984. EPE sought to have the stores permanently enjoined from selling merchandise bearing the name and likeness of Elvis Presley, unless such items were licensed or otherwise approved by EPE. The estate also requested a full accounting of all profits from the sale of unlicensed Elvis memorabilia. The suits asked for three times the amount of these profits to be awarded to EPE as compensation. The estate also asked for $250,000 in punitive damages from each store for reckless violation of EPE's rights. Finally, the suits requested that all unlicensed merchandise be seized by the court from the stores and destroyed.

In their response to the suits, the store owners categorically denied EPE's allegations. They didn't argue with the estate's contention that it was the exclusive owner of the name and likeness of Elvis Presley. Two of the stores admitted selling items not licensed by the Presley estate. However, these items were books and magazines, which did not require licenses. The store owners all denied that they had made substantial profits from the sale of these items. Finally, they argued that EPE selectively enforces violations of its trademarks and commercial property rights.

At the time, Elena Tubbs, co-owner of Souvenirs of Elvis, said of the Presley estate, "They want to have their thumb on everybody." (The suit is still unsettled.)

★ ★ ★

The diligence with which EPE controls the use of Elvis has become legendary in Memphis. Residents refer to the licensing department of EPE as "the Elvis Police." If you talk to two people in Memphis, at least one of them will have an Elvis Police story to tell. A Memphis man tells of the time he tried to sell a photograph of eighteen-year-old Elvis, taken at Memphis's Mid-South Fair in 1953. Believing the picture would be perfect for promoting the 1993 Mid-South Fair, he called the fair's marketing department. The man described the picture to the assistant director of marketing, who was quite excited about the possibility of using it. She told the man that she would discuss the picture with her boss and call him back the next day.

The next morning, when the assistant marketing director called, the man knew immediately that something was wrong. She regretfully informed him that the fair would not be using his Elvis picture after all. She had spoken with her boss and he was afraid to use the picture because he didn't think EPE would like it. The Mid-South Fair had no desire to be sued by EPE.

One of the by-products of the tourist explosion brought on by the development of Graceland has been the opening of several casinos in tiny Tunica, Mississippi, some thirty miles to the south. There twelve casinos have replaced the decades-old cotton fields. One of them was bound to include Elvis in its decor.

When EPE discovered that Tunica's Lady Luck Casino had included Elvis in a mural of local singers painted on one of its walls, it demanded that the casino remove the image or pay a licensing fee. Reportedly, that fee was a million dollars a year.

The Lady Luck's owners decided it could do without Elvis. When guests arrived for the casino's grand opening, a black cloth was covering the King's face in the mural. Eventually, Elvis was painted over with another singer closely associated with casinos: Frank Sinatra.

Part of the reason EPE demanded such an outrageous fee from the Lady Luck was undoubtedly because it was considering lending Elvis's name to a casino of its own. EPE is notoriously phobic about others using Elvis in a business that it might want to get into someday.

★ ★ ★

You might assume that EPE would not require a license fee for products that are given away. You would be wrong, however, as the creator of an Elvis Web site on the Internet recently learned.

In the summer of 1994, Andrea Berman, who was then a graduate student at Texas A&M University and a longtime denizen of the Internet, created the Elvis Home Page. She had been wanting to establish a site on the World Wide Web for some time, but none of her ideas seemed interesting enough. Then, while on a trip to Memphis, Berman came up with the idea of using Elvis, and Graceland, as her subject matter.

The stated purpose of the Elvis Home Page was "the posting of information about Elvis Presley." The Web site featured a "Cyber Graceland Tour," which consisted of twelve photographs of Graceland, taken from postcards and brochures copyrighted by EPE. Also included in the tour were sound clips of Elvis singing some of his hit songs. As is currently typical of most Web sites, there was no charge to take the Cyber Graceland Tour or for access to the Elvis Home Page.

When EPE learned of Berman's Web site, it sent her a letter demanding that the Cyber Graceland Tour be removed. This was EPE's first major copyright complaint filed in response to an item on the Internet. EPE's main complaint was the copyright infringement of the pictures and the songs Berman was using. But the letter—from Manatt, Phelps, and Phillips, attorneys at law—also read, in part:

> [The Cyber Graceland Tour] engages in unfair competition in violation of 15 U.S.C. Section 1125 and state law, in that, inter alia, it improperly infringes on EPE's proprietary rights to create a supposed "tour" of Graceland that will lessen the demand for an authorized electronic Graceland tour by either satisfying the demand of potential consumers for such a tour or alienating potential consumers by providing them with an inferior, low-quality product.
>
> We have noted the disclaimers in the Elvis Home Page, as well as your claim that you didn't "intend" the Graceland tour to infringe EPE's rights. Please be advised that said disclaimers do not excuse the above-described infringement of EPE's rights.
>
> On behalf of EPE, we demand that you immediately withdraw the "Cyber Graceland Tour" from the Elvis Home Page on the Internet, and that you agree in writing: 1) that you will not in the future reproduce or make publicly available the "Cyber Graceland Tour," or any portion thereof by computer database or otherwise, and 2) that you will engage in no further actions that infringe EPE's rights.

Berman immediately removed the copyrighted images and songs from the Web site, closed down the "cyber tour," and signed the agreement. She posted a note at the site explaining what had happened and asked for help "rebuilding" it with public domain images and sounds. As might be expected, she received a flood of support from others on the Internet, and the site is now back to its former glory. In fact, the Cyber Graceland Tour is back as well, but this time someone else has created it using his own personal photographs (which, as far as Berman is concerned, makes her legally safe). To visit the Elvis Home Page, go to: http://sunsite.unc.edu/elvis/elvishom.html.

Berman has not had contact with EPE since the original incident, and it remains to be seen whether EPE will follow up on its threat to remove any and all "cyber tours" of Graceland, even if they contain public domain images. EPE has plans to create its own site at some point in the future, which will feature Elvis trivia as well as plenty of Elvis merchandise for sale. Obviously, EPE also wants the exclusive right to create its own electronic tour of Graceland, one that may not be accessible for free.

★ ★ ★

Many of EPE's cease-and-desist demands contain both elements that are beyond debate (such as copyright infringement) and assertions that are questionable. Usually, the more doubtful demands hinge on whether EPE is violating someone's First Amendment rights. In one such case, the estate went after a small performing arts center that was planning to open a play titled *Miracle at Graceland*. The play was to include images of Elvis as well as some of his songs.

When EPE learned of the production, it sent a notice to the play's organizers, demanding that "Graceland" be removed from the title. EPE also informed the producers that Elvis's songs could not be used without its permission, which EPE was not willing to grant in this case. EPE also strongly suggested that all images of Elvis be removed from the play's sets.

Without question EPE was within its rights to demand that no Elvis songs be used in this little play. However, whether EPE could prevail in court with its demand that images of Elvis be kept out of the play is in serious doubt, and the producers could almost certainly have won the right to use "Graceland" in the title. Both the use of Elvis's image and the use of Graceland in the title of the play would probably be found by a judge to fall under First Amendment rights.

However strong their case might have been, the producers of the play chose not to fight. They didn't have sufficient funds to pursue a lengthy court battle with EPE. Elvis's songs and images were dropped from the play, and the title was changed to *Miracle in Memphis.*

★ ★ ★

EPE's attempts to control all things Elvis have even extended to Elvis fan clubs. Fan clubs are typically promoted by artists. Even Colonel Parker recognized the value of Elvis fan clubs. He gave them pictures of Elvis to distribute to their members, as well as supplying other novelty items at no charge.

Instead of viewing fan clubs as promotional tools, EPE has looked at them as potential licensees. If a fan club wants to go to Graceland and participate in Elvis-related activities, it has to conduct its affairs according to EPE's wishes. Many fan clubs grudgingly go along with the estate; others make no attempt to do so.

EPE's licensing policy has created a lot of enemies among fan club presidents. Probably the most virulently anti-EPE group is the Burning Love Fan Club. Headquartered in Streamwood, Illinois, the club's motto is "Just taking up where Elvis left off." Bill DeNight, the club's president, uses his group's newsletter to rail against the evils of EPE. (He refers to Graceland as "Greedland.") His complaints revolve around what he sees as the contrast between Elvis's generosity and EPE's anything-for-money attitude. A favorite expression of DeNight's is "EPE spells Elvis M-O-N-E-Y." DeNight's furor reached a peak when he heard that there was a plan to require all Elvis fan clubs to purchase a license.

In response to the licensing plan, DeNight sent a résumé to Priscilla Presley, offering to replace Jack Soden. DeNight promised that if he were given the job he would run things as Elvis would have wanted. Needless to say, DeNight was ignored. However, he succeeded in getting EPE to drop the idea of licensing fan clubs.

Despite the elimination of the fan club licensing plan, DeNight is still not at peace with the Presley estate. In response to what he sees as EPE's continued exploitation of Elvis's memory for money,

DeNight stages an annual protest at Graceland. He has also painted an anti-Graceland slogan on the side of his van, which reads "Graceland spells Elvis M-O-N-E-Y." Each time there is a major Elvis event in Memphis, he drives his van back and forth in front of Graceland, from sun up to sun down.

EPE has a simple response to DeNight's charges, and to anyone else who would decry their commercialization of Elvis Presley. The day Elvis walked into Sun Studios, EPE representatives say, he chose to be a business. When he died, that business went on without him.

At times, the disputes EPE becomes involved in are almost comical. In 1985, a Nashville man claimed that he was the illegitimate son of Elvis Presley. Ron Dale Lieberdane Bachett Jr. claimed that Elvis fathered him in 1949, at age fourteen. Bachett later had his name legally changed to Elvis Presley Jr.

In 1987 EPE's attorneys wrote a letter to this gentleman informing him that it would take legal action if he attempted to commercialize his new name. Bachett/Presley's wife wrote a letter in response to EPE's demand, stating that her husband had no plans to use the name commercially. He simply changed it in recognition of his late father.

Either the man's wife was misinformed or her husband had a change of heart. Three years later, Bachett/Presley formed a corporation called Elvis Aaron Presley Jr. Inc. In December 1990, EPE filed a suit demanding that the corporation be disbanded. EPE also asked that the court order Bachett/Presley not to use the name "Elvis" or "Elvis Presley" for commercial purposes.

In January 1991 the court ruled that Bachett/Presley could keep the corporation he had named after himself. The judge didn't feel that the mere formation of a corporation bearing Elvis's name was a violation of EPE's trademark. Elvis Aaron Presley Jr. Inc. was formed as an advertising business, not an Elvis business. However, the judge also ruled that EPE could enforce its rights if Bachett/Presley attempted to use the name commercially.

After the court's verdict, Mr. Elvis Presley Jr. ran an unsuccessful campaign for the Nashville City Council, disproving the adage that name recognition means everything in politics.

★ ★ ★

While EPE has filed numerous lawsuits, very few have been filed against EPE. Of those, only a handful have been successful.

In 1988, Betty Gloyd of Memphis scored one of the few successes. Late one night, in August 1988, Ms. Gloyd took a group of visitors to see Graceland. The tours had ended for the day, so the group had to be content with viewing the mansion from outside the fence. One member of Ms. Gloyd's party was a German student visiting the United States. The student noticed that the gates of Graceland were open and walked onto the grounds. Once inside the gates, he was immediately apprehended by Graceland security.

When Ms. Gloyd went to the guardhouse inside the gate to explain that the student was German and didn't understand he had done anything wrong, she was also taken into custody. The police were called, and Ms. Gloyd and the German student were taken to the Shelby County jail, where they were charged with criminal trespassing. After spending six hours in jail, the charges were dropped.

When Ms. Gloyd learned that the guards had told the press that she and the student had forced their way onto the Graceland grounds, she became very angry, hired a lawyer, and brought suit against the two security guards, EPE, and two Graceland employees. The suit charged that Gloyd had suffered mental anguish and a diminished reputation as a result of her arrest. The suit sought damages of $5 million.

During the trial, it was revealed that the guards were afraid they would lose their jobs if they admitted the gates were open, and they lied to justify the arrest. The jury subsequently found that Ms. Gloyd had been falsely arrested and awarded her $65,000 in damages.

★ ★ ★

EPE has instigated the majority of lawsuits involving Elvis Presley, but there have been a handful of suits brought by other parties. In April 1987, the Elvis Presley International Memorial Foundation sued the Elvis Presley Memorial Foundation, claiming that the former organization had the exclusive right to use Elvis's name. Both plaintiff and defendant were charitable organizations whose mission was to raise money for hospitals in Elvis's name.

The Elvis Presley International Memorial Foundation had formed in 1980 without requesting permission from EPE. However, the International Foundation and EPE had developed a good relationship in the ensuing years. In fact, EPE encouraged the foundation's use of Elvis's name.

In May 1985, the Elvis Presley Memorial Foundation was formed in conjunction with EPE. The International Foundation filed suit the following year. The lawsuit demanded that the Memorial Foundation be disbanded and prevented from using Elvis's name.

The court ruled that the International Foundation didn't own the exclusive right to establish a fundraising group named after Elvis, and it allowed the continuation of the Memorial Foundation. The judge also suggested that perhaps both groups could be a little more charitable toward each other.

Surely the most sinister charge against EPE to date was lodged by a Texas man who claims that the Presley estate conspired to devalue his rare film of Elvis. In late 1994, the man was looking through a trunk in his parent's attic when he discovered a home movie dating back to his parents' honeymoon in 1955. On the film was a portion of a concert performance at the resort where the young couple had stayed. As he watched the film, he recognized one of the performers: a young singer named Elvis Presley.

The man thought the film should be valuable, and he began to investigate how best to go about selling it. First, he contacted EPE for the estate's advice, and he later sent them a copy of the film. His suspicion about the value of the film was confirmed when EPE reported that what he had was now the earliest known film of Elvis Presley. The man from Texas was impressed with how friendly and helpful EPE was being.

When he began to actively market his film, the most promising offer came from one of the cable shopping channels. The channel's representatives wanted to license the film for the production of videocassettes. The potential revenues from these licensing fees were projected at over a million dollars.

The man from Texas and the shopping channel reached a handshake agreement, with only a few details to iron out. All seemed well until a representative from the shopping channel called back to say that the deal was off. According to the man, the shopping channel had received a letter from EPE warning that it didn't have the right to sell a videocassette of Elvis Presley without the consent of his estate. If the channel persisted with offering the proposed video, EPE would sue.

Neither the film's discoverer nor the shopping channel was willing to challenge EPE, and the deal was canceled. The man from Texas began looking for ways to sell the film without incurring the wrath of EPE. Eventually, he decided to put the film up for auction at Guernsey's, an auction house in New York City. Guernsey's was holding what it billed as the largest offering ever of rock 'n' roll memorabilia.

Guernsey's placed an estimated selling price of $100,000 on the film. However, no minimum bid was established for it. The auction house convinced the man that selling the film without establishing a minimum would encourage more bidders. Drawing more people into the bidding would create a bidding frenzy that would result in a higher selling price. This scheme was a highly questionable strategy. It is almost unheard-of for an item of this value to be offered with no minimum bid. The seller was unaware of this fact, however, and trusted the advice of the auction house.

Before the auction, Guernsey's received a letter from the licensing division of EPE. The letter stated that, while the auction house was free to sell the Elvis film, the sale could not legally include the rights to commercially release the film. EPE suggested that a disclaimer be placed in the auction catalog stating that EPE owned the exclusive right to exploit the name and likeness of Elvis Presley. Furthermore, the disclaimer should state that the film was being sold as a collector's item only, with no commercial rights attached. Guernsey's saw nothing wrong with the request and inserted the disclaimer.

When it was finally held in January 1995, "The World's Greatest Auction of Rock-n-Roll Memorabilia" turned out to be one of the world's greatest failures. Most of the items offered with a minimum asking price failed to sell. Many of the items listed without minimums sold at a fraction of their pre-auction estimated value—including the Texan's film. The earliest known film of Elvis Presley sold for only $12,000!

The buyer of the film was a Los Angeles–based production company with close ties to the Presley estate. The company had produced Elvis videos in the past in conjunction with EPE. One of the company's employees had been a longtime friend and employee of Elvis. He remained close to the Presley family after Elvis's death.

After the now-former owner of the film got over the shock of the auction debacle, he began to smell a conspiracy. In his opinion, EPE had sabotaged the auction so that the L.A. production company could buy the film for the least amount of money possible. The catalog disclaimer had frightened away all potential buyers with a commercial interest. With commercial buyers eliminated, the only bidders would be collectors, and it was doubtful that a collector would be able to bid very high. EPE would then get a piece of the action through a joint venture when the film was released on video.

The film's discoverer believes that EPE began to hatch this plan when he first called the estate. As of this writing, the man from Texas has contacted a lawyer and is considering filing suit against EPE and the production company.

8

RETURN TO SENDER

IN 1992, ELVIS PRESLEY achieved an unprecedented level of recognition when his image appeared for the first time on a United States postage stamp. Never before had a rock 'n' roll artist been honored with a stamp. To no one's surprise, it would become the most successful—and controversial—commemorative release in the history of the U.S. Postal Service. Elvis was now an officially recognized national icon.

The release of the Elvis stamp was a national event unparalleled in the annals of the U.S. Postal Service. The selection process itself was unlike anything seen before. It involved years of lobbying, internal struggles at the Postal Service, and a nationwide vote.

To be considered for this kind of philatelic honor, an individual must be dead for at least ten years, so Elvis's first year of eligibility was 1987. Beginning in that year, his name began coming up in meetings of the Citizens Stamp Advisory Committee, the body responsible for choosing stamp honorees.

In July 1988, Postmaster General Anthony Frank endorsed the Elvis stamp idea. While this was far from a final decision, it did legitimize the notion. Frank explained why he believed Elvis deserved stamp recognition: "[I am] asked often, Why Elvis? and I think the outpouring of interest is a pretty good answer to that. The American people really have deep feelings for him and he is a part of our pop culture. He made a real difference in the way people look at and enjoy music."

The stamp committee, however, did not agree with Postmaster Frank. Each time Elvis's name was placed in nomination before the committee, it faced considerable opposition. Many of the committee's members believed that Elvis's drug problems made him an unsuitable candidate. His name was always rejected. After one rejection, Belmont Farris, chairman of the stamp committee, was asked for an explanation. His answer was vague at best: "The committee chooses people who have stood the test of time."

By then, one would have thought Elvis Presley would have passed a longevity test with flying colors. After all, while he was alive, he had been the most popular entertainer in the world for twenty years, and there was a strong argument to be made that he was still the most popular entertainer in the world. How could the Postal Service justify selecting other entertainers with only a small fraction of the public support Elvis received?

The stamp committee was not alone in its opposition to the Elvis stamp. Edward Roibal, chairman of the House of Representatives Appropriations Subcommittee, the legislative group that approves postal subsidies, was very vocal in his opposition. He believed Elvis didn't deserve a stamp because of his personal habits, namely his abuse of prescription medications. In Representative Roibal's opinion, issuing a stamp honoring Elvis would send a bad message to the youth of the nation.

The suggestion of honoring Elvis with a stamp also brought a response from the religious community. A Jewish clergyman penned an editorial published in the *New York Times* that was typical of the opposition. In his editorial, Rabbi Ben Kamin wrote, "The news that the Postal Service is considering a new stamp recalling Elvis

Presley sent shivers down my spine. The government has been using its 'Just Say No to Drugs' campaign. For the sake of our kids, the Postal Service should just say no to the Elvis stamp."

Many collectors were also opposed to the idea of an Elvis stamp. The specific reasons for the dissent from this quarter are hazy. Traditional stamp collectors in general tend to be rather conservative. Perhaps the idea of recognizing a rock star like Elvis Presley would cheapen their pastime. They also objected to the commercialization of such a stamp by licensing its reproduction on T-shirts, coffee mugs, and various other novelty items.

Even the American Civil Liberties Union got into the act when it issued a press release intended as a joke. The ACLU announced that it was prepared to go to court to block release of the stamp on the grounds that it was unconstitutional. To put the "King" of rock 'n' roll on a stamp, the release stated, would violate Article 1, Section 9, Clause 8 of the U.S. Constitution: "No title of nobility shall be granted by the United States." It's not clear whether anyone laughed.

Meanwhile, other countries were not nearly so hesitant to honor Elvis with a stamp. The Caribbean nation of Grenada has the distinction of being the first country to issue an Elvis stamp. By 1991, eleven countries had released Elvis stamps. Only the Queen of England has appeared on the postage of this many nations.

Die-hard Elvis fans persisted in their quest for the stamp. The most determined lobbyist was Pat Geiger, a seventy-two-year-old Elvis admirer from North Springfield, Vermont. For a while, Ms. Geiger dedicated her life to convincing the Postal Service to issue an Elvis stamp. In 1987, she began a massive letter-writing campaign to further her cause. She encouraged others to contact the postmaster general on Elvis's behalf. Some sixty thousand people followed her suggestion and wrote letters to Mr. Frank. She also gathered ten thousand signatures on a petition for an Elvis stamp.

Ms. Geiger's activities on Elvis's behalf quickly caught the attention of the media, who found that Pat was not camera- or microphone-shy. She used television and radio interviews to publicize her cause, and she turned out to be an articulate spokesperson. "If you are going to wait for a perfect man, you will never issue a stamp," she said. "Elvis had one failing and a million good qualities."

Her most persuasive argument in favor of the Elvis stamp centered around the revenue the stamp was sure to generate. Ms. Geiger wrote to Frank asking how he could turn his back on such a guaranteed cash cow when the Postal Service was facing a $1.6 billion deficit.

Ms. Geiger received her answer in 1992 when the Postal Service announced that Elvis Presley would, indeed, appear on a commemorative stamp. "People have been lobbying us for years to put Elvis on a stamp," Frank said at the time. "Some people actually think he should never be honored because of his alleged drug problems. But, even if he had such problems, he was a genuine American musical giant and for sure he won't be the first flawed American to show up on a stamp." Economic need seems to have triumphed over public accusations of amorality.

Commemorative stamps are, of course, an important source of income for the Postal Service. Stamp collectors buy them to keep, not to use for postage. The Postal Service profits enormously by selling stamps that will never be used to mail a letter; it could hardly pass up the much-needed revenues the Elvis stamp would surely generate. Albert Einstein and Wernher von Braun were important historical figures worthy of stamp recognition, but Elvis was going to bring home the bacon.

Once the committee approved Elvis, one important question remained to be resolved: which Elvis would be used? In the public's mind, there were really two Elvises: the young, fresh-faced rock 'n' roller of the 1950s and the more mature Las Vegas entertainer of the 1970s. In other words, there was the skinny Elvis and the fat Elvis.

The Postal Service commissioned thirty drawings for consideration. There were several artists involved. None of them claimed to be Elvis fans; they just wanted their drawing chosen for the stamp. EPE determined the poses of Elvis that they could depict. From these thirty, the field was narrowed to two. One was an image of Elvis circa 1956, the other was a likeness captured as he appeared at his 1973 *Aloha from Hawaii* concert.

On February 24, 1992, Frank unveiled the two final stamp designs at the Las Vegas Hilton. The ceremony was broadcast via satellite to television stations across the country. Frank was joined in the ceremony by Milton Berle, Kathy Westmoreland—one of Elvis's backup singers—and Barbara Eden and Nicky Blair, who both appeared in movies with Elvis.

Postmaster Frank joked about the two images under consideration: "We want to be honest in our rendition but, well, don't be cruel. Younger Elvis would be fifty stamps to a sheet. The older, larger Elvis would be forty to a sheet. A big man takes a big stamp."

In a brilliant stroke of marketing, the final choice was left to the fans. Never before had there been an honoree that excited public interest enough to warrant such a vote. The election was conducted from April 6 to 24. Postcards depicting the competing designs served as ballots. These ballots were made available at every post office in the country and in an insert in *People* magazine. Over 1.2 million people cast their votes. The election cost the Postal Service $300,000, but Elvis fans spent $214,000 on postage to mail their ballots.

A ceremony was held at Graceland to reveal which stamp had prevailed in the balloting. The ceremony was coordinated to allow live coverage of the event on early morning television news programs. The postmaster general and Priscilla Presley officiated at the unveiling of the winning design. At 7:36 A.M., Priscilla made the announcement: the 1950s Elvis had won. The final vote was 851,200 for the skinny Elvis and 277,723 for the chubby one. Pat Geiger was on hand for the unveiling of the chosen design. As a sign of its gratitude for all her hard work, Elvis Presley Enterprises paid for her trip.

The vote on the Elvis stamp design was just the first step in a massive marketing campaign. An 800-number was established to provide information about the Elvis stamp. There were also television and magazine advertisements and mass mailings. In all, over a million dollars was spent on promotion. The Postal Service was heavily criticized for spending so much to promote the Elvis stamp, but the investment would return a profit of more than twenty times that amount. A spokesperson for the Postal Service called the Elvis stamp "as close as we can come to printing money."

At 12:01 A.M. on January 8, 1993, the Elvis stamp was officially released for sale at a ceremony held at Graceland. The release date was selected to coincide with Elvis's fifty-eighth birthday. Some fifteen hundred people stood in the rain for hours to get tickets to the ceremony. The event was carried live on television. In a rare appearance, Lisa Marie Presley gave a short speech about her father and the stamp. She appeared very nervous speaking before such an audience.

On the day of the release, Elvis impersonators were on hand at post offices around the country to promote the stamp.

From the start, sales of the stamp where phenomenal. People lined up for hours before post offices opened to be among the first to buy the Elvis stamp. In many areas of the country, signs were quickly posted saying, "Elvis stamps, sold out."

The Elvis stamp would actually be released on two separate occasions. Six months after the stamp's original release, it was released again as part of a series of stamps honoring America's music legends. In addition to Elvis, Buddy Holly and Otis Redding were featured.

The planned print run for the Elvis stamp was 300 million, twice the amount of a normal run, but sales of the stamp would surpass even the Postal Service's optimistic expectations. The net profit from sales of the stamp exceeded $25 million, making it far and away the top-selling commemorative stamp of all time. The profits were disproportionately high because, as postal officials had predicted, huge numbers of the Elvis stamps went unused. Postal officials said that the phenomenal success of the Elvis stamp helped them delay a postage rate increase for a year!

From the beginning, controversy was never far from the Elvis stamp. Shortly after its release, a rumor circulated that the Postal Service would use the stamp ballots to generate mailing lists for direct-marketing Elvis stamp products. The Postal Service was quick to deny this rumor. Only those who had marked on their ballot that they were interested in learning more about the stamp would receive promotional literature. The resultant mailing list, officials said, would only be used by the Postal Service and would never be sold to direct marketers of Elvis stamp products.

Some eight hundred thousand stamp voters were sent brochures created by Chapman Direct, a New York–based direct marketing agency. Chapman had worked with the Postal Service to market commemorative stamps since 1978. The brochure offered a variety of stamp-related products, including "limited edition," exclusive, first-day ceremony programs and sheets of Elvis stamps in souvenir saver sleeves. The items ranged from $5.95 to $19.95. Selling souvenir products was considerably more profitable than selling twenty-nine-cent stamps.

Another advertising blitz was conducted to promote the non-philatelic Elvis stamp merchandise. Over thirty companies were licensed to manufacture more than a hundred products bearing the image of the Elvis stamp. Licensed stamp products included clocks, blankets, music boxes, belt boxes, hats, and jewelry. So popular were these products that one manufacturer called the Elvis Presley stamp merchandising concept more successful than the hula hoop, the pet rock, and the mood ring combined.

The first product bearing an image of the Elvis stamp actually went on sale six months prior to the release of the stamp itself. In July 1992, the Home Shopping Network began to sell a nightgown adorned with an image of the stamp. By the time the stamp was released in January, there were hundreds of Elvis stamp products on the market.

Almost overnight and across the country, stores like K-mart and Walmart were swimming in Elvis stamp merchandise. And the cash registers were ringing! Revenues from the sale of Elvis stamp beer steins alone exceeded $3 million.

One clever stamp collector came up with a novelty product idea that was to cause a headache for the Postal Service. He would mail a letter with an Elvis stamp to an address that did not exist, causing the letter to come back marked "return to sender, address unknown," creating an instant collectible. When this prank was discovered, hundreds of people followed suit.

The release of the Elvis stamp brought about yet another disagreement over an unauthorized use of Elvis's name and likeness. And Iowa utility company used the Elvis stamp in an advertisement to promote the payment of electric bills through automatic bank withdrawals instead of by mail. The ad featured a picture of the Elvis stamp, followed by the slogan "Now Elvis never has to leave the building."

The utility company had secured permission to use the Elvis stamp from its local post office, but since 1982, when stamps began to be copyrighted, it has been necessary to secure permission from the Postal Service before a stamp can be reproduced for commercial purposes. The Elvis stamp carried the added burden of requiring the permission of Elvis Presley Enterprises as well. Neither EPE nor the Postal Service consented to the use of the stamp in the advertisement, and it was withdrawn.

Even after the Elvis stamp seemed to have proven itself, the controversy continued. Consumer advocate Ralph Nader jumped into the debate in 1992, with charges that the "costly ballyhoo" surrounding the Elvis stamp was a waste of government money and a diversion of the Postal Service's main purpose. Nader was critical of the stamp balloting, which he called "the final zany pirouette of Postmaster

General Anthony Frank." He also complained loudly about the amount of time top management at the Postal Service had spent on what he called "a costly trivialization and diversion of the post office's main purpose, the dependable and reliable delivery of the mail." He also objected to the $4,000 that had been spent to fly postal officials and celebrities to the unveiling of the final two stamp designs in Las Vegas. Nader attributed their devotion to the Elvis stamp to boredom with their regular jobs.

Postal officials did not dispute Nader's claim that significant amounts of money had been spent publicizing the Elvis stamp. However, they believed it was money well spent. The Postal Service makes $175 million a year from selling stamps to collectors. It expected the Elvis stamp to be the biggest moneymaker ever. In the end, the costs associated with the Elvis stamp were trivial compared with the profits it generated.

Ralph Nader was especially interested in looking at the agreement the Postal Service had signed with Elvis Presley Enterprises for the estate's permission to use Elvis on a stamp. The Postal Service refused Nader's request for a copy of the contract. Postal Service officials claimed that it was privileged information, but they went on to explain that they had not paid anything for the right to use Elvis on a stamp. EPE had waived its usual licensing fee, granting the post office a hundred-year license for a dollar.

What's that? he seemed to ask. Were we to believe that EPE was simply content with the honor of seeing Elvis on a stamp? Had Scrooge suddenly had a change of heart? Surely, Nader and others reasoned, there had to be something more to the contract, something the Postal Service was reluctant to share with the public. In fact, there was. Elvis Presley Enterprises, as usual, had negotiated for a piece of the action—not on the stamp itself but on all merchandising of the stamp's image.

EPE was not the first group to negotiate with the Postal Service over stamp rights. The first stamp honoree whose family bargained for a share of the profits from other merchandise was W. C. Fields. When the Fields family learned of the Postal Service plan to issue a stamp in honor of their famous predecessor's hundredth anniversary, they contacted an attorney to protect their rights to his image. Ultimately, though the Postal Service paid nothing for the use of Fields's image on the stamp, and no additional royalties, it coughed up $2,000 for the rights to put the comic legend's picture on T-shirts and other products.

The contract negotiated by EPE was considerably more demanding than the one signed by the Fields family.

Obtaining a copy of the agreement between the Postal Service and EPE has been a daunting task for all who've tried. In addition to denying Ralph Nader, the Postal Service denied the requests of several members of the press. It was later learned that EPE had insisted that the agreement be kept secret. Notwithstanding any such understanding between them, there's a little law known as the Freedom of Information Act, which was designed to make documents such as this one available to the public. There are exceptions to the act when national security is involved, but the deal between EPE and the Postal Service over a commemorative stamp was hardly a security matter!

The Postal Service continued to deny all requests for copies of the Elvis stamp agreement. On September 12, 1994, I requested a copy of the contract myself, citing my rights under the Freedom of Information Act. Here's the letter I received on October 17, 1994, in response to my request:

Dear Mr. O'Neal:

This is in response to your Freedom of Information Act request of September 12, for information relating to the agreement with the estate of Elvis Presley for the use of his likeness on a postage stamp.

The search of our records has been completed. After careful review, we have determined that the agreement contains confidential commercial information that is exempt under section 352.42C of the Postal Service's administrative support manual. This section protects "commercial information including trade secrets whether obtained from a person outside the Postal Service which under good business practice would not be publicly disclosed." Material withheld as protected by this exemption includes the terms of the agreement to use the image of Elvis Presley on postage stamps or other items. Disclosure of such terms would generally be viewed in the commercial world as a hindrance to an entity's ability to command the most advantageous terms in future agreements.

You have the right to appeal this denial of your request in writing to the General Counsel, U.S. Postal Service within thirty days of the date of this letter.

Sincerely,

James C. Tolbert Jr.
Manager Stamp Management

I appealed Mr. Tolbert's decision on October 25, 1994. In my appeal, I asserted that the justification given for refusing to release the contract was not applicable to an agreement for the production of a postage stamp. The appeal read, in part:

I reject your claim that an agreement between the U.S. Postal Service and a private individual for the use of an individual's likeness on a stamp is a violation of a trade secret. The Postal Service is a governmental organization, not a private corporation. How can an organization that has no competition have trade secrets? The U.S. Postal Service holds a monopoly on first-class mail, for which the Elvis stamp serves as payment. Furthermore, the placement of an individual on a stamp is done to honor the individual. It is not a business negotiation. The Presley stamp was unique. The information in the agreement will not hinder future agreements because in all probability there will never be anything substantially equivalent to the Presley transaction for you to negotiate.

I am determined to receive this information as it is my right as a citizen of the United States. If I am not successful in this appeal I will contact both my Senators and Representatives as well as other appropriate government officials outside your agency to ask that they intervene.

Sincerely,

Sean O'Neal

My appeal also refuted the claim that section 352.42C applied to the contract for the Elvis stamp. The referenced section of the Postal Service's Administrative Support Manual reads as follows:

> Records not subject to mandatory disclosure.
> This class includes:
> 1) Information about methods of handling valuable registered mail. 2) Money order records. 3) Technical information on postage meters and prototypes submitted for Postal Service approval before leasing to mailers. 4) Market surveys conducted by or under contract for the Postal Service. 5) Records indicating rural carrier lines of travel. 6) Records compiled within the Postal Service that would be of potential benefit to persons or firms in economic competition with the Postal Service. 7) Information that if publicly disclosed could materially increase procurement cost. 8) Information within records that might compromise testing or examination materials.

The only item in this section that could, by any stretch of the imagination, be applied to a request for the stamp contract is number six. And yet, even this item can be rebutted by pointing to the Postal Service's monopoly on first-class mail. Obviously, Frank, Tolbert, and company were grasping at straws for a reason to keep the contract secret.

Fred Eggleston, attorney for the Postal Service, to whom my appeal was made, realized that the Postal Service's bluff had been called. He agreed to release to me a copy of the contract, thus ending a four-month process. I received my copy on January 13, 1995.

Once I had the document in hand, I decided to see whether the Postal Service was generally this reluctant to provide copies of stamp agreements. To make it a fair test, I selected another entertainment industry icon: Marilyn Monroe. Since her death, Ms. Monroe's estate has earned million of dollars licensing her name and likeness. Her stamp was issued in 1995. When I contacted the Postal Service and requested a copy of its contract with the Monroe estate, I received the document in one week with no objections.

The Monroe estate received considerably less control over the release of her stamp than the Presley estate. Perhaps the Monroe representatives would have struck a harder bargain if they'd known the details of the Presley agreement. Of course, they almost certainly would not have been allowed to see it.

The agreement between the Postal Service and Elvis Presley Enterprises that both parties wanted so desperately to keep secret is only two pages long. Most of the document is devoted to dividing the spoils from selling the Elvis stamp and its related merchandise. When all of the legal jargon is sifted through, the contact contains three meaningful subsections, which read:

1) The Postal Service may use the likeness, name, and signature of Elvis Presley on U.S. postage stamps and stationery and related philatelic products commemorating him and advertising thereof.

2) Grantor agrees not to assert any claim against nor seek any compensation from the Postal Service relating to the commemoration of or any philatelic activity including the Postal Services customary licensing of reproduction rights and its philatelic design. This privilege should only extend to those Postal Service licensees who are licensed for the production of said philatelic items and to cachet manufacturers. In the event producers of philatelic items such as first-day covers wish to use art work rather than or in addition to the stamp itself, then said producers must obtain the prior written approval of Elvis Presley Enterprises for said art work.

3) The Postal Service will not license to third parties the reproduction of its philatelic design for use on nonphilatelic items unless said parties have previously obtained from grantor a license for the commercial use of the name, image, or likeness of Elvis Presley. Elvis Presley Enterprises is aware of the Postal Service's practice in this area and agrees not to unreasonably withhold such license.

The contract can be boiled down to a differentiation between stamp and nonstamp revenue. The Postal Service is free to receive all proceeds from sales of the stamp. EPE receives no compensation for allowing Elvis to be used on the stamp. But EPE controls the production of merchandise that contains reproductions of the stamp.

The contract goes on to state that revenues from merchandise sales will be divided between the EPE and the Postal Service. The exact percentages each party receives was blacked out in the copy the Postal Service sent to me. One can only assume that this means EPE is receiving the greater percentage of the merchandising revenue. This is the only plausible explanation for the extreme reluctance on the part of the Postal Service to release any information about its arrangement with EPE. If there is nothing to hide, why treat the contract like the plans to the D-Day invasion?

Apparently, the Postal Service was troubled by having to compromise its principles in exchange for the right to use Elvis. A memorandum from EPE's attorney, Barry Ward, to the Manager of Stamp Development for the Postal Service provides some insight into the philosophical differences between the parties. The memorandum reads, in part: "We have advised you of EPE's prior practice to require front-end payments with large guarantees. You have advised that this is not the custom utilized by the U.S. Postal Service, but that due to the uniqueness of the stamp design involving Elvis, it is agreed a royalty rate of 15 percent per license will be used on all licenses granted hereunder."

Ultimately, the Postal Service seems to have caved in to EPE's demands. The money was probably just too good to pass up. Given the financial troubles of the Post Office and the amount of money generated by the Elvis stamp, it's difficult to criticize the Postal Service's decision. One would hope, however, that as a government agency accountable to the taxpayers, the Postal Service would be more forthcoming about the details of its business arrangements.

9

HEIR TO THE THRONE

ELVIS PRESLEY ENTERPRISES was originally created to perform a kind of rescue mission and, in that, it succeeded beyond all expectations. An estate left in trust was saved from bankruptcy, and a family home was preserved, albeit in a radically altered form. Beyond its original mandate, EPE defined an industry and created an economic empire with amazingly far-reaching—even worldwide—influence.

And at the end of the day, it all belongs to Lisa Marie.

★ ★ ★

On the afternoon of August 16, 1977, nine-year-old Lisa Marie Presley was visiting her father at Graceland. She was in the mansion when Ginger Alden discovered Elvis's lifeless body. When the paramedics arrived, she rushed into Elvis's bedroom to see what was going on, but was ushered out just as quickly, so she never saw her father lying on the floor of his bathroom.

When Priscilla arrived at Graceland, she found her daughter in a surprisingly untroubled mood. To those around her, the girl seemed not to understand what had happened to her father. She behaved as though he had simply gone away on tour. Lisa Marie began to cry only when she saw her mother's tears.

Later, when mother and daughter went into Elvis's room, Lisa Marie inexplicably took Elvis's electric razor and baseball cap as keepsakes. She then went outside and raced her golf cart around the grounds of Graceland. To anyone watching, she would have seemed almost happy.

★ ★ ★

The only child of Elvis and Priscilla Presley was born on February 1, 1968, exactly nine months after their Las Vegas wedding. Lisa Marie's middle name was chosen to honor Colonel Parker's wife, Marie.

Elvis rehearsed the birth of his daughter as carefully as he did a Las Vegas opening. He and the Memphis Mafia made several trial runs to the hospital. They even traveled in a two-car motorcade just in case Priscilla's car would break down.

His fans immediately adopted Lisa Marie as their princess. They were no less excited than the British when an heir to the throne is born. Little Lisa Marie received hundreds of teddy bears from Elvis's fans. They loved her almost as much as they loved him.

Almost from the beginning, Elvis and Priscilla disagreed about the way in which their daughter should be raised. Mostly, their disagreements centered around Elvis's tendency to pamper the girl. Though both Priscilla and Elvis wanted their child to have the best, Elvis seemed unable to set *any* limits. Priscilla's desire to raise Lisa Marie like a normal little girl was constantly thwarted by Elvis's inexhaustible bankbook and virtual addiction to gift giving. Priscilla was forced to assume the job of moderating Elvis's excesses.

When Lisa Marie was three years old, Elvis bought her a mink coat and a diamond ring; Priscilla made him take them back. When the girl lost a tooth at her mother's house, the tooth fairy brought fifty cents; when she lost a tooth at Graceland, the tooth fairy brought five dollars. For Christmas, instead of a tricycle, Elvis bought then-eight-year-old Lisa Marie her own golf cart, which she would drive around the grounds of Graceland, stopping occasionally at the front gate to sign autographs. When she wanted to ride a merry-go-round, Elvis rented the entire amusement park. The guest of honor at her seventh birthday party was her favorite singer, Elton John. When Lisa Marie called her father from Los Angeles and told him she wanted to see it snow, he sent his personal jet right over to whisk her to Utah, where it was reportedly coming down hard. After twenty minutes of snow romping, the jet returned her to L.A.—and it only cost her dad $30,000. Despite her mother's efforts, Lisa Marie Presley would never be treated like a "normal" child by her father.

Elvis had always been extremely proud of both Lisa Marie and Priscilla. When he was a guest at the White House in 1970, he made a point of showing President Nixon pictures of his wife and daughter. After their divorce, Elvis and Priscilla agreed to share custody of their daughter. Both believed the girl should spend time with both her parents, and their continued good feelings facilitated an amicable joint-custody arrangement.

Those who knew her in those days say that, as a child, Lisa Marie was very sensitive about her parents' relationship. Priscilla and Elvis did their best after the divorce to put aside their differences when they were together with Lisa Marie. Whenever her father and mother were together, Lisa Marie saw two people with a great deal of affection and mutual respect for each other. By some accounts, Lisa Marie could scarcely tell that her mother and father were no longer married.

Elvis continued to pamper his little girl to the very end of his life. On August 8, 1977, he rented the entire Memphis amusement park Libertyland for Lisa Marie. The day before he died, Elvis had one of his people try to find a print of *Star Wars* for his daughter. (The distributor was unable to obtain a copy of the film.)

★ ★ ★

After Elvis's funeral, Priscilla and Vernon were seen arguing about where Lisa Marie should live now that her father was gone. Vernon reportedly wanted his granddaughter to move back to Graceland. He insisted that she would be safer on the grounds of the estate, with its twenty-four-hour security. He also wanted to make sure Lisa Marie continued to be part of the Presley family. But Priscilla wanted her daughter with her in Beverly Hills. She promised Vernon that Lisa Marie would visit often, but her home was with her mother in California.

After Lisa Marie and Priscilla returned to Los Angeles, Priscilla sent her daughter to a summer camp in Northern California for two weeks, hoping to shelter her from the impending media blitz. Her father's life was about to be opened up like an overripe melon, the salacious details of which would be splattered everywhere. This was not the time to expose a nine-year-old girl to her dad's dark side. Joe Esposito's daughters, Debbie and Cindy, went along to keep Lisa Marie company.

But the other kids at the camp knew all about Lisa Marie's recent loss, and there was no hiding from them. By the time Lisa Marie returned home, friends say, she had given up her denial and was ready to grieve for her father.

Priscilla reportedly began to take Vernon's concerns about her daughter's safety more seriously at this time. In fact, for reasons that remain unclear she became convinced that her daughter was in danger of being kidnapped if she stayed in the United States. During the mid-1970s, kidnapping was a concern of the very rich in this country. (It started as a terrorist tactic; then others began to copycat for money. Kidnapping has largely stopped today, probably due to the greater security measures in practice.) Lisa Marie would have been an ideal target for anyone looking to commit a high-profile crime to publicize a radical cause, or for ransom money—especially since most people believed she'd just inherited about $150 million.

Priscilla decided that her daughter would be safer in Europe. No one can say for certain whether she was aware that kidnapping was actually a much more common crime overseas than in the United States. She would remain in Europe for three months, but never for long in one place.

Lisa Marie in her golf cart two days before Elvis died.

Vernon at the wheel of the Cadillac that Elvis bought him (1978).

Priscilla, Vernon, and a Hilton Hotel official at the
Always Elvis Convention, Las Vegas (1978).

Priscilla and Lisa Marie flew first by themselves to London, where they attracted the immediate attention of the notoriously rabid British media. It quickly became obvious that the famous mother and daughter would find no safe haven in the United Kingdom. They next fled to Nice, France, under assumed names. After ten days in that city, Priscilla reportedly learned that it was home to several members of the Mafia, and she quickly departed with her daughter. Priscilla's next choice was probably her worst: she took her daughter to Rome, which at the time was headquarters to most of the kidnapping operations in Europe. Forty-eight hours later, their identities were discovered and they fled to Madrid, Spain.

During their sojourn in Europe, Priscilla decided her daughter should spend an extended period of time away from the United States. She visited several boarding schools in an effort to find a suitable place to hide Lisa Marie from the American press and would-be kidnappers. Some skeptical Presley insiders have suggested that Priscilla's true motivation was to get Lisa Marie out of the house so she could pursue her current relationship with Mike Stone.

Whatever her motivation may have been, Priscilla was unable to find a European boarding school willing to accept her famous daughter. Ironically, Lisa Marie was rejected because the schools believed she would pose too great a security risk.

When mother and daughter returned to Beverly Hills, Priscilla turned her home into a security compound. She installed a new alarm system and placed a closed-circuit television camera at the gate. As an added security measure, guard dogs were set to patrol the grounds. Priscilla's fear of kidnappers became so great that she seldom left her daughter home alone, even after she reached her teen years. Lisa Marie was known as Hollywood's most closely guarded child.

Priscilla's fears were not entirely unjustified. Several threats of kidnapping—and even occasional death threats—were made against Lisa Marie until the early 1980s. For several years, all phone calls coming into their home were tape recorded to document the threats being made against both of them.

Priscilla rarely allowed Lisa Marie to be seen in public. She permitted no news photographs or interviews of her daughter until she reached adulthood. The idea was to keep the public uncertain of Lisa Marie's exact appearance, and it worked. Priscilla did such an excellent job of keeping her daughter's face out of the media that it was possible for her to go out in public and not be recognized.

Even Priscilla's choice of Lisa Marie's school was driven by her fear for her daughter's safety. Lisa Marie attended Lycée Française, an exclusive Los Angeles private school. Because celebrity children comprised a large part of the student body, the school had a number of systems in place to safeguard its high-profile charges. Priscilla reportedly also felt that Lisa Marie would fit in better there than she would have in a public school.

Yet Priscilla discouraged her daughter from developing friendships with other "rich kids." She detested their phoniness and arrogance. She wanted her daughter to learn right from wrong and to develop character and a solid sense of values. She didn't want her to become another spoiled Beverly Hills brat.

At her mother's suggestion, Lisa Marie deliberately avoided dating celebrities. She briefly saw a child actor named Mieno Peluce, but they were really just friends. Dating "regular people" was part of the plan to give Lisa Marie a normal life as much as possible.

Despite Priscilla's efforts, Lisa Marie would never lead what anyone could call a "normal life." It was impossible for the daughter of the most famous entertainer in the world to pretend that she was ordinary. A public that would line up for autographs from Elvis Presley's hairdresser and buy books written by his nurse would certainly not ignore his only child.

Lisa Marie was finding it difficult to live the life her father left her. For years, her movements were almost as restricted as Elvis's had been. She was under intense and constant scrutiny, both by the public and Priscilla. She yearned to be able to go to the mall or to a movie without a bodyguard. When she was fifteen, she got her wish when Priscilla allowed her to travel to Spain with a group of kids her own age. Lisa Marie traveled under an assumed identity, which she successfully maintained throughout the trip. For one of the few times in her life, she was able to live like a normal teenager, free of the weight of being Elvis's daughter.

When Lisa Marie returned home from her trip, she wanted to preserve her newfound freedom. She begged her mother to allow her to walk to school like the other kids, instead of being driven by a chauffeur. Reluctantly, Priscilla relented, but Lisa Marie's new freedom was short-lived. After only a few days, she began to notice a man following her home, stalking her from a distance. After a week of this behavior, the man approached and asked if she was Lisa Marie. Well trained to handle such situations, Lisa Marie denied her identity, but the man responded that he knew who she was. He then handed her his business card and told her to have Priscilla call him.

When the police investigated the incident, they found that the man was a mentally disturbed individual who blamed Priscilla for Elvis's death. Thereafter, Priscilla insisted that her daughter ride to school with an escort.

★ ★ ★

While Priscilla effectively provided for Lisa Marie's physical security in the years after Elvis died, in many ways she fared less well helping her daughter maintain her emotional security. Lisa Marie's problems intensified, some said, when she found herself competing for her mother's affections with Priscilla's boyfriend, Mike Edwards. Increasingly, she began escaping to the one place where she always felt at home: Graceland.

During the first few years after Elvis's death, Graceland remained unchanged. Grandpa Vernon was there, as was great-grandma Minnie Mae. Elvis's cook Mary Jenkins still prepared dinner every night. Even

Lisa Marie's pets—three cats and a Great Dane named Snoopy—were still there.

Life at Graceland stood in stark contrast to the rigidity of her life in Beverly Hills. At Graceland, Lisa Marie was the center of attention. She could give orders to the household staff, much as her father had done. There were no rules. She could eat whenever she wanted to, sleep when she liked, wake when it suited her. She could give her pets the run of the house. It's little wonder Priscilla had to fight with her daughter to get her to come home.

After Vernon and Minnie Mae died, Priscilla kept Lisa Marie away from Graceland and, for reasons that aren't clear, the remaining members of Elvis's family. Perhaps she feared they would exploit her daughter, as so many of Elvis's relatives had exploited him. Today, Lisa Marie has virtually no contact with the Presleys.

Priscilla also did her best to protect Lisa Marie's own image and memory of Elvis. Though she had seen her father taking pills, she was too young to understand what he was doing. Priscilla wanted Lisa Marie to remember Elvis in a positive light, and to protect her from the negative publicity that proliferated after his death. Those who knew Priscilla say that she wouldn't even take her daughter to the grocery store for fear that she would see Elvis's face on the cover of the latest tabloid rag at the checkout counter. For years, she managed to shield Lisa Marie from the details of Elvis's death, from speculation about his drug addiction, and from the sordid tales of his womanizing. But Priscilla couldn't keep the truth from her daughter forever.

In the early 1980s, a sensationalistic book about Elvis hit the best-seller list. Titled *Elvis,* it unleashed another flood of unflattering remembrances of Elvis in the media. At the time of the book's publication, Lisa Marie was fourteen, and her mother simply could no longer hide the stories from her.

According to Priscilla, after the book was published, Lisa Marie went through a period of disliking her father. The stories she heard about him angered and disgusted her. Those close to the family believe that her anger was really a manifestation of Lisa Marie's pent-up feelings of abandonment, her feeling that her father had deserted her when he died. As she has grown older, Lisa Marie's anger seems to have been replaced by understanding and a renewed appreciation of the good times she spent with her father.

Accepting her father's whole story—the good and the bad—also freed Lisa Marie from the need to pretend that Elvis was perfect. While many in the Presley circle continue to deny that Elvis's death was drug-related, Lisa Marie readily admits it. She seems to have made peace with Elvis.

Today, Lisa Marie has grown to closely resemble her father. She has the same eyes and trademark pouting lips. She has even enhanced their resemblance by coloring her naturally blonde hair jet black. "Dark hair really suits my personality," she says.

★ ★ ★

Between the ages of thirteen and seventeen, Lisa Marie grew increasingly difficult for Priscilla to control. Lisa Marie began to mix with a bad crowd. At times, Priscilla had to hunt from house to house to find her and bring her home. Mother and daughter found themselves engaged in a battle of wills.

Lisa Marie was constantly at risk of being exploited by her friends. Then, as now, the tabloid press regularly approached people known to have contact with Lisa Marie and offered to buy their "stories." While most of her friends have been above such temptations, some have not. When she was young, her mother interrogated Lisa Marie's peers to make sure they were not interested in her because of Elvis. However, as she grew older, Priscilla could no longer control her daughter's choice of friends.

During this time, Lisa Marie developed a fondness for older men. When Priscilla objected to the age differences between Lisa Marie and her boyfriends, her daughter reminded her that she was only fourteen when she started dating Elvis. At age fifteen, Lisa Marie began dating her first serious boyfriend, who was twenty-one. At first, Priscilla was not happy about the relationship. But she is said to have warmed to the young man and eventually developed a genuine affection for him. She even praised him in a magazine interview.

They tried to carry on as a normal couple would, going on dates to normal places. On one particular date, they went to a public park for a picnic. All at once, a man appeared and began taking pictures of the couple. The pictures later appeared in a tabloid newspaper. Lisa Marie was very upset about this violation of her privacy. She was afraid that she and her boyfriend would no longer be able to go out in public and have a normal relationship.

Also, both Priscilla and Lisa Marie were baffled at how their tight web of security had been breached by this photographer. Further investigation revealed that it was Lisa Marie's boyfriend who had tipped off the photographer. He had sold exclusive access to their relationship to the highest bidder. Lisa Marie was devastated by this betrayal. It was years before she was able to trust a boyfriend again.

When Lisa Marie reached the eleventh grade, she dropped out of school. Priscilla strongly opposed this, and friends recall her trying to convince Lisa Marie that she was making a big mistake. But the girl's mind was made up and no amount of lecturing from her mother would change it. She apparently had no desire to continue her education, to go to college, or even to get a job. She was a young lady of considerable means who found it unnecessary to concern herself about such things.

★ ★ ★

Eventually—some might say, inevitably—Lisa Marie sought relief from her complicated life in the same place her father had: she began to abuse drugs. She began in her very early teen years, thirteen or fourteen. The extent of her drug use is a closely guarded secret. I am told that she had a fairly mild problem. Others have written that her drugs were sedatives and marijuana.

In 1983, Lisa Marie hit rock-bottom. She decided she had a drug problem and turned to her mother for help. At Priscilla's urging, she became involved with the Church of Scientology. She enrolled in a Scientology-based school and was also placed in the Scientology Celebrity Center's detoxification center in Los Angeles.

The center was successful in helping Lisa Marie break her drug dependency, and she became an ardent Scientologist. She has been reluctant to speak publicly about her association with the church. In a rare statement about the controversial religion, Lisa Marie said, "I am pretty levelheaded, and I see it as the most incredible thing I have ever been involved in." She credits Scientology with helping her resolve personal issues surrounding the death of her father and being his only child. "I had a lot of questions," she says. "Living and existing didn't answer them, but only upset me more. Scientology has answered those questions."

Since her conversion, rumors have circulated that all of Lisa Marie's money goes to Scientology in the form of donations and payments for church study programs. While the church's programs are expensive, Lisa Marie does not pay any more for attending them than anyone else would. A portion of the revenue from EPE does go to the Church of Scientology in the form of donations. However, Lisa Marie's contributions are insignificant compared to her income.

Rumors have also circulated that Lisa Marie's long-term plan is to turn Elvis Presley Enterprises over to the Church of Scientology. Nothing could be further from the truth. Lisa Marie has no intention of giving the family business away. Priscilla has assured anyone who asks that Lisa Marie has no intention of giving her money away to Scientology or anyone else.

After becoming a Scientologist, Lisa Marie's relationship with Priscilla improved dramatically. Lisa Marie encouraged her mother when she was trying to start her acting career. She has even written rebuttals to Elvis fans who send hate letters to Priscilla. Lisa Marie has said that she is awed by the way Priscilla's skills as a business-woman have grown as Elvis Presley Enterprises has grown, and that she has developed a profound respect for her mother's abilities.

Priscilla and Lisa Marie became such good friends that, after years of going their separate ways, they began to socialize together. They started making an annual trip to Graceland, spending a few nights together in the mansion. During these visits, some members of Elvis's old household staff would return to Graceland to care for their former charges. These visits continued even after Graceland was opened to the public. Mother and daughter would arrive at night, after the daily tours had ended, and then spend most of their time on the off-limits second floor. They talk about the good times, friends say, and remember Elvis.

Lisa Marie and Priscilla never visit Graceland during the month of August, however. On the anniversary of Elvis's death, when thousands of tourists are in Memphis, they make sure they are miles away.

★ ★ ★

The one disagreement between Lisa Marie and Priscilla that Scientology could not cure was the debate over Lisa Marie's career—or rather, her lack of one. Even though she was, by her teen years, the heir to what had become a $100 million fortune, Priscilla wanted her daughter to develop career goals and learn the value and satisfaction of earning her own money. She didn't want her to simply wait until she turned twenty-five and inherit her father's fortune. To try and instill in Lisa Marie a sense of the value of money, Priscilla once even restricted her to a ten-dollar-a-week allowance.

Despite Priscilla's efforts, Lisa Marie has only had one real job. For a short while, she worked in a travel agency owned by fellow Scientologists. With statements like "I had this normal nine-to-three, entry-level job," Lisa Marie made it quite clear that she knew very little about the real world of work. The truth was, she was just going through the motions for the sake of her mother.

★ ★ ★

In 1984, Lisa Marie met a young man at the Scientology Celebrity Center who would sweep her off her feet. Danny Keough was an aspiring musician with a group called D-BAT. His mother and stepfather were also active in the Scientology movement; they had cofounded a Scientology center in Los Angeles.

In Keough, Lisa Marie found everything she wanted in a man. According to close friends of the family, neither Lisa Marie nor her mother could find any reason to doubt Danny's motives. They say that Danny never showed any signs of interest in Lisa Marie's name or money. Here, at last, was someone who loved her for who she was, not because of what she had.

Danny and Lisa Marie soon began talking about marriage. Their marriage plans were hastened when Lisa Marie found out that she was pregnant. On October 3, 1988, Lisa Marie became Lisa Marie Presley-Keough.

Apparently Priscilla wasn't completely convinced of Danny's honorable intentions. At her urging, Lisa Marie and Danny signed a prenuptial agreement to protect her assets in case of a divorce.

When Lisa Marie married, she abandoned the use of body-guards and limousines. She also began to venture out into the real world more often. She was always in the audience when Danny's band was performing. She was even spotted doing her own grocery shopping. She seemed to be doing everything she could to live her life as Lisa Marie Keough.

Danny and Lisa Marie seemed to have the perfect marriage. They maintained their privacy by living in a series of high-security luxury apartments owned by the Church of Scientology. In 1989, Lisa Marie gave birth to Elvis's first grandchild, Danielle, who bears a strong resemblance to her mother. Not surprisingly, Lisa Marie was said to be the disciplinarian in the family; Danny was the play-ful, accommodating father.

In 1992, Lisa Marie gave birth to her second child, a boy she and Danny named Benjamin Storm. At the time of Benjamin's birth, the young Keough family was living in Tampa, Florida.

Shortly after Benjamin's birth *People* magazine asked Lisa Marie whether anything was missing from her life. She answered that her life was absolutely perfect.

★ ★ ★

On February 1, 1993, Lisa Marie celebrated her twenty-fifth birthday. According to the terms of Elvis's will, she was now free to take control of the Presley estate. Graceland, Elvis Presley Enterprises, the rights to Elvis's name and likeness—all were now hers to do with as she wished.

As Lisa Marie's birthday approached, rumors again circulated that, when she claimed her inheritance, she was either going to close Graceland or turn everything over to the Church of Scientology. The church would then turn Graceland into its headquarters. Lisa Marie quickly dispelled these rumors. Instead of giving her newly acquired empire away, Lisa Marie decided to leave things exactly as they were. In effect, she extended the trust for another five years. She also extended her mother's position as executor as a sign of her satisfaction with the job she had done. Priscilla and Jack Soden would continue to manage EPE.

"Everything remains the same," Lisa Marie said at the time, "except I am on the management team now." Lisa Marie had been attending EPE board meetings for several years, but she actually exercised no more authority after formally inheriting the estate than she had before. Though Priscilla has tried to prepare her daughter to assume a leadership role in EPE, to date, Lisa Marie has shown little real interest in the family business. She seems content to stay on the sidelines.

Leaving control of the family business to Priscilla was a wise move on Lisa Marie's part. It demonstrated the maturity others had observed in her in recent years. According to Jerry Schilling, a long-time associate of Elvis, the changes were a direct by-product of her marriage. "I think marriage and motherhood have made her a responsible person," Schilling says. "It prepared Lisa Marie for the day she would inherit Elvis's fortune. If the inheritance had happened five years ago, it potentially could have affected her."

Lisa Marie will have an opportunity to take control of the Presley estate and Elvis Presley Enterprises again in 1998. Most observers doubt she will make any changes then, either.

★ ★ ★

There was also another, less-publicized reason Lisa Marie decided to extend the estate trust. Her mother had lobbied her to do so because she felt it would provide Lisa Marie with an added measure of financial security. While the trust remained in effect, Lisa Marie's assets were protected in the event that she and Danny divorced. Priscilla wanted the trust extended so Danny would not be in a position to leave Lisa Marie and take half of the Presley fortune with him. He could have always contested the prenuptial agreement he signed earlier. By contrast, a trust is iron-clad.

Priscilla proved to be an uncanny judge of relationships when Lisa Marie's perfect marriage took a turn for the worse. In April 1994, Lisa Marie issued a statement saying that she and Danny Keough had separated and would be filing for a divorce. The separation was, by all accounts, amicable. "Danny and I will always love each other," Lisa Marie said at the time. "However, friendship was more suitable for us than marriage." They agreed, as her parents had, to share custody of their children.

Nothing could have prepared Danny or Priscilla for what Lisa Marie would do next. In fact, Lisa Marie was about to shock the world. A few months after her divorce, rumors started circulating that she had married, of all people, *Michael Jackson*—the same Michael Jackson who, only months earlier, had reached a multimillion-dollar settlement with the family of a teenage boy who had accused him of sexual abuse!

Lisa Marie and Michael met for the first time in Las Vegas in the mid-1970s. Lisa Marie was in town with Elvis, and Michael was in the middle of a concert engagement with the Jackson Five. Lisa Marie attended one of the Jacksons' performances, and then went backstage after the show. Despite their age difference—Michael was eighteen; Lisa Marie, eight—they reportedly hit it off right away. The two had only occasional contact over the ensuing years. While Lisa Marie was growing up, Michael Jackson was becoming one of the biggest pop stars in the world.

A decade after they first met, Michael saw a picture of Lisa Marie in a magazine. The little girl he had met so long ago had obviously grown up. Insiders say that the idea of seeing her again and possibly going out on a date with her intrigued Michael. However, he was too shy to call her himself. He would have to locate a matchmaker.

Michael and Priscilla both worked with an attorney, and Michael thought he would be the perfect person to arrange a date with Lisa Marie. But before he could approach him with the idea, Michael learned that she had married Danny Keough. Michael said Lisa Marie's marriage broke his heart.

Shortly after the rumors began circulating that Michael and Lisa Marie were married, a photograph of the two of them surfaced. The picture had been taken while the couple was visiting Disney World with Lisa Marie's children. Michael was wearing an almost comical disguise consisting of a cap, wig, and mustache.

The Disney World photograph intensified the marriage rumors, but even people close to Lisa Marie and Michael were unsure of their marital status. Some two months after the rumors first surfaced, Lisa Marie's publicist could neither confirm nor deny the stories. Even Priscilla seemed to be in the dark. When reporters questioned her, she seemed honestly unable to give them an answer.

On July 11, 1994, the Dominican Republic newspaper *Listin Diaro* printed a story claiming that Michael and Lisa Marie Presley were married. The judge quoted in the story, Judge Hugo Alvarez, said that he had performed the ceremony himself on May 26, in the small town of Lavega. It was believed that Lisa Marie and Michael chose the Dominican Republic because Lisa Marie wanted a quickie divorce from Danny Keough (they were separated, but their divorce was not yet final). However, Michael Jackson's publicist quickly denied the story.

Finally, on August 5, Lisa Marie issued a short press release confirming that she was, in fact, Mrs. Michael Jackson. "My marriage to Michael Jackson took place outside of the United States eleven weeks ago," she said in the release. "I am very much in love with Michael. I dedicate my life to being his wife." She also explained her reasons for denying the marriage for so long: "It was not formally announced until now for several reasons. Foremost being we were both very private people living in the glare of the public media. We both wanted a private marriage ceremony without the distractions of the media circus." She added that she looked forward to raising a family and living a healthy, happy life together with her new husband.

By all accounts, Priscilla had no idea that Lisa Marie was planning to marry Michael Jackson. She knew that the two were friends, but she was unaware of any romantic feelings between them. Friends say that Lisa Marie knew her mother would try and talk her out of the marriage, and so she kept her in the dark until after the ceremony. Priscilla learned of her daughter's marriage just before it was announced to the public. At the time, all Priscilla could say was that she was surprised. "When you are greeted with information that is shocking," she said, "you need to take some time to think about it and then you deal with it."

Some insiders speculate that part of what attracted Lisa Marie to marry Michael Jackson was the knowledge that Priscilla would not approve. While she had developed a good relationship with her mother since her troubled teen years, Lisa Marie had grown to resent the control that Priscilla continued to exert over her life. The marriage may have been a very public statement that Lisa Marie's mother could no longer tell her what to do.

When Priscilla Presley made an appearance on NBC's *Today* show in October 1994, the questioning quickly turned to Michael and Lisa Marie's marriage. When asked if she was surprised by the marriage, Priscilla said, "I think that is the way they wanted it." When asked how she felt about the marriage, Priscilla gave a very short and vague answer. "Lisa Marie is a very bright girl," she said. "I don't think she will do something detrimental to her."

Yet, recent events in Michael Jackson's life were enough to give any mother, or grandmother, cause for concern. Jackson had been accused of molesting a young boy, and he had reportedly paid the family millions in exchange for dropping the case. Similar accusations had surfaced involving other young boys. The thought that Danielle and Benjamin would be living with Jackson had to concern Priscilla.

While Priscilla made her opposition to the marriage quite clear, at least in private, we can only speculate what Elvis's opinion would have been. Most likely, Elvis would not have been happy about it, since Michael displays personal qualities that Elvis always disliked, such as phoniness and self-aggrandizement.

A case in point is the contrast in the way the two men have regarded their royal titles. Elvis was dubbed the "King of Rock 'n' Roll"; Michael Jackson is billed as the "King of Pop." Elvis, who was extremely religious, never embraced his title, saying that there was only one king, and he was in heaven. But Michael Jackson relishes his. In fact, Jackson insists on being billed as the "King of Pop" in all his public appearances.

Almost every Elvis fan I've talked to myself, or heard interviewed by others, was opposed to the marriage. Most fans seemed to disapprove of Michael's character. He had, after all, just made a financial settlement with the parents of a boy he was charged with abusing sexually. Many fans were outraged that Lisa Marie would allow her children to live with an accused child molester—let alone marry one. Many actually feared for the safety of Elvis's grandchildren.

After the news of Lisa Marie and Michael's marriage became public, rumors began to circulate that the couple would turn Graceland into a private home. Michael had constructed his home, Neverland Ranch, as a virtual amusement park. Perhaps Graceland would be a more suitable home for the family. So widespread was the rumor that Jack Soden felt compelled to issue a press release denying it. "I know very well that she is very content with the way things are," he said in the release. "Lisa Marie is very intent on leaving all of Elvis Presley's assets independent and intact."

★ ★ ★

At the time of their marriage, there was considerable speculation about their motivations (as well as over how long they would last). Was it for love, or was is it a public relations stunt? Did Michael want to convince the public that he was heterosexual? Was it a plot hatched by the Church of Scientology to recruit Jackson? Did Lisa Marie hope the marriage would springboard her own singing career? Mostly, people wondered, what could have brought these two people together?

Would marrying Michael Jackson have helped Elvis Presley's daughter become a singer? Does the sea need salt? According to Priscilla, one the first questions people ask Lisa Marie is, "Can you sing?" The answer is decidedly mixed, but it's no surprise that people ask: they're curious whether, through his daughter, Elvis might be resurrected. Ask Priscilla whether she thinks Lisa Marie will follow in her father's footsteps, and her answer will probably be no. She feels that Lisa Marie's musical talent lies in writing rather than singing or playing an instrument. Her friends say Lisa Marie has a good voice. A close friend describes her voice as sounding like Pat Benatar or Bonnie Raitt.

Does Lisa Marie even want to be a singer? She has stated publicly that, while she would be interested in making a record someday, her singing career is on hold until her children are older. Her decision may be motivated by the cool reactions of record companies to a home recording she made with her former husband's band, and which she decided to market as her demonstration tape.

Professionals who have heard Lisa Marie sing say that she does not have the talent to be recorded commercially. One record company exec is quite blunt in his opinion of Lisa Marie's singing: he says she has the talent of an anvil.

If a singing career doesn't seem likely, Lisa Marie may try her hand at acting. At one point she hired Jerry Schilling to be her manager. But before Lisa Marie could land any acting roles, she became pregnant with Benjamin, and they decided to wait to pursue her acting career. In any case, it is unlikely that Lisa Marie, by marrying Michael, would have gotten any more mileage out of the Jackson name than out of her own, no matter what aspect of show business she pursues.

Lisa Marie's only job in show business so far has been a small part in an Oldsmobile commercial, when she appeared with her mother. The slogan for the commercial was "It's Not Your Father's Oldsmobile." Clearly the viewer is supposed to think of Lisa Marie's very special father. The jingle might have been more effective had the advertisement been for Elvis's car of choice, the Cadillac. For appearing in the commercial, mother and daughter each received $250,000 and a car.

The Scientology recruitment plot is also an unlikely reason for Lisa Marie and Michael's marriage. Having Michael as a member would be of questionable public relations value to the church, given the controversy surrounding him, and there was little chance that Michael would become a Scientologist, even if invited. After many years as a Jehovah's Witness, Michael Jackson left the church altogether. He now looks upon his former church with cynicism. While Michael is extremely religious, he prefers to practice outside any organized religion. Michael did visit the Scientology Celebrity Center on a few occasions, at Lisa Marie's request. However, he reportedly showed little interest in becoming a member.

Is it possible that Michael and Lisa Marie were actually in love? A friend says that originally Lisa Marie dated Michael out of sympathy. She wanted to help him through the stress of the child molestation charges. As she spent more time with Michael, the friend says, her friendship turned into infatuation, and perhaps love.

Perhaps it's not so strange that the two high-profile celebrities would find they had a lot in common. They both have been in the public eye since they were children. Both are vegetarians. Both are very wealthy; their estimated combined net worth is in excess of $300 million. Michael Jackson is perhaps the only person in the world who can understand what it's like to be the daughter of Elvis Presley.

Michael and Lisa Marie showed little interest in the public's preoccupation with explaining their decision to marry. They concentrated on enjoying themselves. The newlyweds took up residence in New York's Trump Tower in a $110,000-a-month apartment. Michael wanted to spend some time away from California because it reminded him of the child molestation incident. After a few weeks, however, Lisa Marie insisted that they return to Los Angeles.

Lisa Marie quickly became involved in Michael's effort to rebuild his image. In August 1994, she went with Michael to Budapest to shoot a video. Lisa Marie's next project with Michael was a video for the song *You Are Not Alone.* In the video, Michael and Lisa Marie are nude from the waste up, though Lisa Marie keeps her back to the camera throughout. Nonetheless, Priscilla was reportedly quite shocked.

On September 8, 1994, Michael and Lisa Marie opened the *MTV Video Music Awards.* The couple walked to the microphone, and Michael said, "Just think, nobody thought it would last." Michael then kissed Lisa Marie on the lips and the couple walked off the stage.

Lisa Marie also appeared with Michael on a live, one-hour televised interview with Diane Sawyer. There was speculation that

Lisa Marie would announce on the interview that she was pregnant. This did not happen, but she did confirm that she and Michael were sleeping together. Diane Sawyer uncovered little of substance about her subjects. The only sign of tension was when Michael and Lisa Marie were asked where they would be living. Michael indicated that he would like to move to Europe to escape the American media. Lisa Marie made it clear that she was adamantly opposed to leaving the United States.

Michael and Lisa Marie visited Graceland for the first time on October 7, 1994, while in Memphis for an Elvis tribute concert. To the relief of many fans opposed to the marriage, they did not spend the night in the mansion. The majority of their visit was spent locked up in their hotel room, eating $300 worth of room-service exotic fruit trays.

Lisa Marie's relationship with Michael seemed to begin to deteriorate soon after their trip to Memphis. The couple began spending more and more time apart. Lisa Marie was soon living the majority of the time in a mansion some ninety miles from where Michael was living. She even went on vacation to Hawaii with her children and her ex-husband Danny Keough, while Michael remained at the Neverland Ranch. Though they had begun to live separate lives, Lisa Marie still publicly professed her love for Michael.

Perhaps inevitably, the union didn't last. The causes of the destruction of Lisa Marie and Michael's marriage were very similar to the reasons behind Priscilla and Elvis's divorce. The only difference was that Michael was not having affairs with other women. Lisa Marie disliked Michael's large entourage, just as Priscilla had resented the Memphis Mafia. She felt that Michael's people viewed her only as a tool to rebuild his sexual image. Lisa Marie also disapproved of the way Michael constantly showered expensive gifts on her children, just as Priscilla had fought Elvis's pampering of Lisa Marie. Finally, Lisa Marie grew tired of living in the bizarre world of the most popular and eccentric singer in the world.

In mid-August 1995, rumors began to surface that Lisa Marie was filing for divorce. The rumors suggested that Lisa Marie was distressed over a trip Michael had taken to Paris with two young boys. Michael was quick to deny the rumors, which he termed "garbage." He advised people not to read "that stuff."

Then, on December 10, 1995, Michael collapsed during a rehearsal for a televised concert. Jackson was hospitalized with symptoms of exhaustion and dehydration. Lisa Marie was spotted visiting him at the hospital, which, for the moment, quelled the rumors about their impending divorce.

One month later, however, Lisa Marie announced that the rumors were true. She and Michael had separated just four days after his collapse, and she was now filing for divorce, citing "irreconcilable differences" as the cause. She also gave the obligatory "but we are still friends" disclaimer. The marriage lasted a year and a half, and there were no children. People would be left to wonder just what musical talents such offspring would have inherited.

Most people predicted the marriage's failure. But Judge Hugo Alvarez, the Dominican judge who married Michael and Lisa Marie, also says he knew the marriage would never last. Alvarez has married hundreds of couples and as a result has become a fairly good judge of character. He says that Michael and Lisa Marie appeared less in love than anyone he ever has united. They seemed to treat the entire wedding ceremony as a joke.

Now that the royal marriage was over, public attention turned to the financial aspects of the dissolution. Fortunately, Michael and Lisa Marie had the good sense to arrange a prenuptial agreement. Under the agreement, there would be no divorce settlement. Both Michael and Lisa Marie would retain whatever they owned prior to the marriage. Lisa Marie asked only that her maiden name be restored and for Michael to pay her attorney's fees.

Lisa Marie has now been through two divorces and has surrendered none of the Presley fortune. With Priscilla around, it's doubtful she will ever pay a divorce settlement. Today, the only threat to Lisa Marie's continued, seemingly unstoppable accumulation of wealth is the public's fickle tastes. If they ever forget about Elvis, the money machine will grind to a halt.

As of this writing, no one seems to be losing any sleep over that prospect.

10

SELLVIS,
THE TRIBUTE CONCERT

On January 8, 1995, Elvis Presley would have been sixty years old. In honor of that occasion, and to commemorate the fortieth anniversary of the start of his career, Elvis Presley Enterprises organized a special concert performance, which it called *Elvis Aaron Presley, the Tribute Concert*. Nearly two years of planning went into the event. First-rank producers were hired. Top names in pop music were expected to perform. Thousands of advanced tickets were sold.

When the curtain went up, however, this much-ballyhooed "tribute" was, at best, disappointing, and, at worst, an out-and-out rip-off. What could have been a truly remarkable assembly of the greatest names in the music industry—a gathering of artists to honor the memory of the man who inspired their work and started it all—was, instead, just another opportunity to make a buck. In many ways, the story behind this concert seems to exemplify what Elvis Presley Enterprises has become.

The concert was the first Elvis tribute ever sanctioned by EPE. Until now, Priscilla had believed the time was not right for such an event. She gave this show her approval, she said at the time, because the production was to be of the highest quality and a portion of the profits were earmarked for charity.

Plans for the concert were hatched as early as 1993, when EPE and Avalon Tributes Inc. first formed a partnership to develop and produce the show. The multimedia, multiartist project would be built around a live concert of the today's top musicians performing songs Elvis had made famous. The event would be broadcast worldwide via a pay-per-view cable deal, and the performances would be collected on a video and a CD, both of which would be released commercially.

In February 1994, EPE and Avalon began looking for a record company to bring into their partnership. They needed a third party with production and marketing expertise, a roster of potential performers, and the resources to finance the entire project. They met with several major record companies, including Sony and MCA. (EPE's decision not to work with RCA provides some insight into the true nature of the Presley estate's shaky relationship with Elvis's record company.) Eventually, they settled on Polygram Holding Inc.

Polygram is a major international entertainment company that produces and distributes audio and video recordings and live concerts for television. Polygram was a good choice because it maintains a division devoted specifically to the type of multifaceted concert event EPE and Avalon had in mind. Also, Polygram had an impressive roster of recording artists—including Elton John, U2, and Sting—which it could influence to perform at the concert. Finally, Polygram agreed to release the album on its successful Island Records label.

In April 1994, the three organizations entered into an agreement to produce the tribute to Elvis. The agreement specified that the concert would be held in Memphis on October 8, 1994, exactly two months before Elvis's sixtieth birthday. EPE's role amounted to the granting of permissions for the use of Elvis's name and likeness. Avalon was charged with producing the actual concert, with assistance from Polygram. Polygram was responsible for producing the television broadcast, the video, the CD, and the merchandise. In addition, Polygram was to provide and collect funds for all activities associated with the concert. Polygram would then remit a share of the profits to EPE and Avalon.

Don Was, a well-known contemporary music producer, was hired as the musical director for the concert, the video, and the CD. He was to receive $75,000 plus a percentage of the revenue generated by sales of the recording.

The contract also specified that Priscilla Presley would be listed as the executive producer of the television broadcast and the video. This is a standard clause in every agreement for a video or television project with which EPE is closely involved. It's reminiscent of Colonel Tom Parker's insistence that he be listed as "technical advisor" in the credits of most of Elvis's movies. What Parker and Priscilla actually contributed to these projects to earn their titles remains unclear.

When news of the tribute concert first began to circulate, the rumored list of artists scheduled to perform included the biggest names in rock 'n' roll: Elton John, Bruce Springsteen, Paul McCartney, The Who—all were among the swarm of names buzzing around the project. Rumors even circulated that the remaining Beatles might reunite for the show. The fans believed such an all-star lineup was possible because the performers were, themselves, Elvis fans. The concert would be a once-in-a-lifetime chance to honor their hero.

EPE's vague statements to the press did nothing to discourage public speculation about who would perform at the concert. Jack Soden told the *Memphis Commercial Appeal,* "There are going to be some great names, but when people buy the tickets on September 10, there will still be some potentially big names in the show that they will not be aware of." The only performer Soden would explicitly rule out of the concert was Elvis himself.

There's little doubt that the rumors contributed to the tremendous demand for tickets, which all but exploded when they went on sale. Ticket prices ranged from $40 to $375—which were high even for the 1990s. But the high prices didn't deter buyers. The Pyramid Arena in Memphis quickly sold all seventeen thousand available seats. Ticket demand was so high, a lottery was held for their distribution. Requests for tickets came from all over the world. In fact, the requests received from Germany alone would have sold out the arena.

Total ticket sales for the event reached $1.2 million. Though the expense of producing the concert exceeded revenues collected from ticket sales, expected revenues from CD and video sales and the pay-per-view broadcast—as well as anticipated sponsorships from Sears and Harrah's Casinos—would provide EPE with a net profit of a million dollars.

In the weeks preceding the concert, Jack Soden continued to make vague public statements about the lineup of performers. Soden referred to what he called a great, broad-based desire on the part of the music industry to be involved in a tribute to Elvis. Exactly who would be appearing, however, remained a mystery. The closest Soden came to naming names was his statement that it was "highly likely" that people like Elton John would be performing at the concert.

On the day before the concert, Priscilla hosted a large party at Graceland for assorted VIPs. At the reception, she gave her guests a tour of Graceland. Priscilla made a point of telling them that Elvis, and not she, was responsible for the mansion's decor. (This can only confirm that she is embarrassed by the look, and she didn't want anyone to think she has bad taste herself.)

At the concert the following evening, the highlight of the show was the appearance of Priscilla, Lisa Marie, and Michael Jackson. After Priscilla opened the show, she went back to her private box, where Lisa Marie, Michael, and Michael's sister Janet Jackson were waiting. Michael hugged Priscilla and she gave him what was described as a mother-in-law kiss on the cheek.

Conspicuously absent from the festivities was Colonel Parker, but he was watching. The pay-per-view broadcast of the concert was beamed to millions of television sets in forty countries around the world—including the one in Parker's Palm Springs home. The concert was probably the first Elvis product the Colonel had ever actually paid for. It cost him $19.95.

Those who attended the concert and those who watched it live on television were amazed at the event's lack of organization. The performances on stage were often marred by noise from the next act setting up.

But by far the biggest disappointment was the lineup of performers. None of the previously rumored big-name stars were there. Not to disparage in any way the artists who did perform, but this was not the show the crowd expected. They thought they were going to see an all-star concert to rival Woodstock and Live Aid.

The list of artists who performed that night included Chet Atkins, Michael Bolton, Tony Bennett, Billy Ray Cyrus, Melissa Etheridge, Chris Isaak, Aaron Neville, Bryan Adams, Carl Perkins, Jerry Lee Lewis, and Dwight Yokum. Fans expecting to see a major-league lineup instead got the equivalent of the Grand Ole Opry.

The concert received mediocre reviews in the press. The September 15, 1994, issue of the *Memphis Commercial Appeal* featured a critical article titled, "Sizing Up the Downside of the Elvis Tribute." The choice of country singer Billy Ray Cyrus as the closing act was almost universally ridiculed. Apparently, as the concert date grew nearer, organizers became desperate for big names. According to an individual who worked on the show, Billy Ray agreed to appear only if he could close the show and sing "Amazing Grace"—hardly the closing act fans expected from this overly hyped tribute concert.

The performers who agreed to appear were also under the impression that many of the biggest stars in rock history would be there. Melissa Etheridge and others reportedly committed to the show with the understanding that it would be a once-in-a-lifetime gathering of rock music greats. Etheridge was said to be as disappointed as the audience when the big names failed to materialize.

★ ★ ★

So what happened? Where was Springsteen? Where were McCartney, Elton John, Prince, The Who? The answer was simple: the almost unanimous decision of the big-name stars to boycott the concert revolved around the issue of money. But they didn't boycott because they wanted money for themselves; they were volunteering to perform for free. They were upset because, despite original reports, only a small portion of the proceeds from *The Tribute Concert* were going to St. Jude's Children's Hospital and the T.J. Martell Foundation, the two designated charities. The concert was primarily a for-profit venture. Major stars like Springsteen only perform for free when all the proceeds from the concert are going to charity.

When I asked EPE how much of the concert's proceeds would be going to charity, they gave the following response: "The full proceeds from ticket sales and a percentage of sales on the sound track and home video sales (we have no idea when it will be released), etc., were for designated charities. Other than that, it was a for-profit venture. When video, CD, TV, and other profit components are part of any project, it complicates things as far as celebrity clearances and negotiations [are concerned]. Pure charity events with no TV, video, [or] sound track matters attached are much easier to get big celebrity involvement in."

Avalon said afterward that one of the reasons there were so few big-name stars was because of scheduling conflicts. Yet virtually none of the artists mentioned in the early rumors was on tour at the time of the concert. Many speculate that if the event had been a true charity tribute, the big names would have found the time to appear.

EPE's explanation was no more enlightening than that of its partners: "Many of the stars you heard about were never booked for the show. Many of the names that were publicized were names the press speculated about on their own when we weren't yet releasing official information. Many of the bigger names that had actually committed to the show, and were officially announced, backed out in the final weeks leading up to the show. This had to do with the varying complexities and negotiations between the stars and our coproducers who were handling star bookings. We really can't go into detail for legal reasons."

It's likely that some artists would still have performed if they could have restricted their involvement to the concert only, since all the concert proceeds were going to charity. But EPE and its partners refused to allow this. All the musicians had to agree to appear on both the CD and the video before they were allowed to perform. The appearance contract specifically stated, "No artist shall be permitted to perform at the concert unless that artist and their record labels have signed agreements authorizing all of the committed activities." The video and CD were where EPE planned to make its money.

★ ★ ★

In the end, *The Tribute Concert* did not prove to be as profitable for EPE as anticipated. Soon afterward, the partners had a falling out.

In June 1995, EPE filed suit against Polygram, charging breach of contract and demanding $4.36 million in damages. EPE claimed that Polygram had failed to pay an advance of $500,000, as well as $200,000 in concert expenses. EPE also charged that a million dollars in profits were lost because the concert soundtrack was not aggressively marketed and the promised home video was not produced. An additional $2.66 million dollars in compensatory and punitive damages was sought.

In its lawsuit, filed June 14, 1995, EPE claimed that, "In spite of the millions of dollars of revenue that Polygram received in connection with the Tribute project, it has willfully and inexcusably refused to pay Avalon and Graceland hundreds of thousands of dollars due under the contract since last October 1994."

Polygram justified withholding payment with a claim that the $2.87 million cost of the concert was much more than reasonably anticipated. Polygram sought to shift some of these costs to the other partners. EPE argued that Polygram could not use higher-than-anticipated production costs to excuse the payment of $500,000 due under the contract.

EPE also argued that Polygram was out of line in claiming it had not "reasonably anticipated" the increased production costs. Polygram had participated in changes made to the concert that resulted in an increase in expenses.

Part of the cost overrun, Polygram claimed, was the result of EPE's decision to use four stages instead of one, as originally planned. EPE countered that Polygram executives had agreed to that added expense in the interest of enhancing the program. In fact, it was Polygram's idea.

Originally, the concert was to have featured twenty-five performers on a single stage. Six television cameras would have been required for the broadcast. At a meeting on May 26, 1994, Polygram's television director and producer introduced the idea of using a rotating platform that would allow for the use of four separate stages, thus minimizing the delay between acts. While one act was performing, another one would be able to set up. Also, the stars would be able to perform with their own bands, instead of a single "house band." Polygram felt that more big-name stars would agree to appear if they could perform with their own people.

Polygram's program director later presented a scale model of the multistage setup for approval at a meeting of the three partners. (Priscilla was also present.) He demonstrated the staffing and equipment needs of the concert with the new setup. On July 20, Polygram's television producer submitted a new budget that reflected increased expenses of almost a million dollars. At no time did Polygram object to the format change or the resulting increase in expenses.

When Polygram later refused to pay the increased production expenses, Avalon's attorney contacted the record company. Polygram's refusal to meet its financial obligations was jeopardizing the concert, the attorneys said. Subsequently, Polygram provided additional funds to Avalon, but still maintained its objection to what it saw as budget overruns.

EPE's lawsuit against Polygram was not limited to the issue of improperly withholding advance and expense money. Polygram was also charged with breaching its fiduciary duty to EPE and Avalon. It seems that during preparations for the Elvis tribute concert, Polygram was working on a similar project commemorating the twenty-fifth anniversary of Woodstock. EPE charged that Polygram executives were unable to devote sufficient attention to the Elvis tribute because it was concentrating on the other show.

EPE also blamed Polygram for the lack of big-name performers appearing for the Elvis tribute. Their contract listed specific artists Polygram was to have recruited, including Elton John, Bruce Springsteen, Whitney Houston, Eric Clapton, Stevie Wonder, Willie Nelson, Cher, George Michael, Prince, The Eagles, Robert Plant, Jerry Garcia, The Who, R.E.M., Ray Charles, Billy Joel, Paul McCartney, and Rod Stewart. These were the artists the fans were expecting, and Polygram had failed to deliver them, EPE claimed.

Additionally, EPE charged that Polygram had not aggressively promoted the concert CD. It claimed that Polygram had promised to use every means possible to promote the album, including radio and television advertising. EPE called Polygram's actual marketing efforts "wholly deficient." In its suit, EPE stated, "The album which boasts a lineup of extremely popular artists has been relegated to the status of buried treasure." Also without consulting EPE or Avalon, Polygram released the CD on its Mercury Nashville country music label, instead of its Island Records label.

Polygram has also yet to produce a home video of the concert. The video was originally slated for a Christmas 1994 release. EPE and Avalon sought a total of a million dollars in damages for Polygram's failure to promote the album or release the video.

EPE may have been overstating its case when it described the CD of the tribute concert as featuring "a lineup of extremely popular artists." The roster of performers on the album was definitely more at home on a country label. It is true, however, that the album was not promoted very heavily. Polygram's decision not to invest more in marketing the CD was reportedly based on its assessment of the limited potential of the album. In the end, it just wasn't a very marketable product.

Polygram also failed to list Harrah's Casinos as a concert sponsor on some items of tribute merchandise. Polygram was notified of the omission prior to the concert, but planned on selling the merchandise anyway. Only after Avalon insisted was the merchandise pulled off the market. When Polygram failed to provide promotional time for another concert sponsor, Northwest Airlines, during the broadcast of the concert, Northwest reduced its sponsorship payment.

Damages in the amount of $2,662,500 were sought to compensate EPE and Avalon for injuries suffered due to Polygram's breach of its fiduciary duty. Avalon sought payment of the $125,000 in unreimbursed expenses for the concert, as well as $37,500 it had spent providing audience lighting for the television broadcast. According to the agreement, Polygram should have paid this expense directly to the lighting supplier. Avalon paid for the lighting in the interest of keeping the project going.

Polygram never filed an answer to EPE's lawsuit. About two months after filing its complaint, EPE dropped the suit. Apparently, EPE, Avalon, and Polygram reached a mutually satisfactory agreement out of court. As of this writing, no video of the tribute concert has been released, and none appears to be forthcoming.

So far, the fans aren't complaining.

11

IT CAN'T GO ON FOREVER, CAN IT?

THE ELVIS BUSINESS TODAY is a $100-million-a-year industry. The story of the twenty-year evolution of that industry is truly a fascinating one. But how long can such an industry continue to flourish, dependent as it is on the past works of a single individual? How long before the public's interest in Elvis fades? The fans from the fifties won't live forever. Will those who were raised on Madonna and Michael Jackson, on Pearl Jam and Nirvana, continue to fill the Graceland tour buses? Will they have a reason to make the pilgrimage to Memphis?

For the present, interest in Graceland shows no signs of abating—or even slowing. The crowds continue to grow every year. "There is no reason to think people won't be coming here in 2050, 2060, or 2089," says Jack Soden. "Look at Stephen Foster [composer of 'Oh! Suzannah,' 'Camptown Races,' and 'My Old Kentucky Home']; his home is one of the top two to three biggest attractions in Kentucky, and Stephen Foster hasn't had a hit song in a long, long time."

In a 1995 survey, *USA Today* asked its readers, "Who is the greatest performer in rock music history?" Respondents chose Elvis Presley by a seven-to-one margin. Number two in the poll was Elvis's former son-in-law, Michael Jackson.

Elvis's records continue to sell at a phenomenal pace. In 1987, ten years after his death, seven of his recordings went gold. In 1992, a five-disc set of Elvis's 1950 recordings appeared in record stores with a seventy-five-dollar price tag. The set quickly achieved platinum status and produced over $15 million dollars in revenue for RCA. *Music* magazine reported that, for the first six months of 1993, Elvis was the best-selling deceased singer, with 750,000 units sold.

There are more than four hundred active Elvis Presley fan clubs worldwide. This is true of no other artist, living or dead. And these aren't tiny, backyard, *Little Rascals,* no-girls-allowed clubs, either. One Elvis fan club in Great Britain claims over twenty thousand members.

From the beginning of his career, Elvis's appeal has known no national boundary. Russian president Boris Yeltsin is a fan; his favorite song is "Are You Lonesome Tonight?" In the Marshall Islands, there is a coin bearing Elvis's image that serves as legal tender. A hostage released from captivity in Lebanon reported that the furnishings in the room in which he was held consisted of a bed, a toilet, and an Elvis poster on the wall.

The financial success of Elvis Presley Enterprises has been recognized in a variety of publications, including *Forbes* magazine. In 1988, *Forbes* ran a story listing the ten top-earning deceased entertainers. Elvis was number one. In 1995, *Life* magazine devoted an entire issue to Elvis on the occasion of his sixtieth birthday.

EPE has also been recognized as the leading expert in its unique field. The heirs of other famous Americans have looked to the Presley estate's managers for guidance in commercializing their famous ancestors. Dexter King, the son of Dr. Martin Luther King, has met with Jack Soden several times for his advice on how best to capitalize on his late father's fame. A gift shop has subsequently been opened at the King Center in Atlanta, Georgia, which sells books, T-shirts, posters, and even a water bottle on which portions of Dr. King's speeches have been printed. The King estate has also contracted with an intellectual properties management firm to control the licensing of Dr. King's name and likeness. An entertainment complex along the lines of Graceland could be a future venture for the King estate.

It is almost impossible to go through an entire day in this country without hearing or reading the name Elvis Presley. Anyone or anything associated with Elvis continues to draw the attention of the press. In April 1995, newspapers across the country carried the story that Elvis's barber had died. And, of course, the life of Lisa Marie continues to be standard tabloid fare.

New books about Elvis are released by major publishers on a regular basis. There is even a movement by a group of college astronomy students to name a constellation after Elvis. (Of course, Elvis Presley Enterprises would probably demand a licensing fee. Perhaps there is a line of "Belt of Elvis" constellation T-shirts and mugs in our future.)

Demand for Elvis Presley merchandise continues to be strong. On the eighteenth anniversary of Elvis's death, the cable shopping channel QVC ran a three-hour segment devoted entirely to Elvis-related products. The products sold during that segment included 24-carat gold Elvis baseball cards and four drinking glasses, each devoted to one of Elvis's hit records. The price of the glasses: fifty-five dollars each. Almost every item on the show was billed as a "limited edition," despite the fact that tens of thousands of dollars of Elvis merchandise were sold during these three hours.

A recent auction of Elvis memorabilia netted several million dollars. Among the items at that auction was a television set Elvis had shot when Robert Goulet appeared on the screen. The winning bid was several thousand dollars.

It seems likely that Elvis Presley Enterprises is nowhere near the end of its amazing climb to prosperity. EPE has its representatives searching the world for new business opportunities. After the success of Graceland, it plans to open several other Elvis theme attractions. Elvis amusement parks are currently under construction in Nashville and England, while the one in Japan waits only for proper financing—the interest is already there. Elvis is closely associated with Las Vegas, so an Elvis casino would be a natural collateral enterprise. Even closer than Vegas is Tunica, Mississippi, just a twenty-minute drive from Graceland, where ten other casinos are already in operation. EPE is also discussing a plan to build a chain of Elvis museums across the country.

And new foreign markets are opening up every day, including countries that had previously been closed to the West. Jack Soden anticipates an influx of new consumers and the release of a "pent-up demand for western products" that should last for years. "Elvis Presley Enterprises believes that Elvis products will be one of the things these people are interested in buying," he says. That's millions of people who don't yet own an Elvis mug or an Elvis clock, millions who will at last be able to leave their countries and vacation in America. Surely many of them will want to include Graceland on their itineraries. If any one individual symbolizes America to the rest of the world, it's Elvis Presley. "It's almost like starting over," Soden says.

EPE plans to continuously expand and enhance the Graceland facilities to keep visitors coming, much as Disney does at its facilities. Long-range plans include tearing down the Graceland Plaza across the street and replacing it with a hotel and convention center, a museum, and a concert hall. The cost of the hotel and convention center alone would be $40 million—a far cry from the $500,000 the estate had available when it opened Graceland in 1982. There are even suggestions that Graceland's sacred second floor will be open someday.

The estate's managers are also exploring the possibility of creating a chain of Elvis retail outlets. The Disney and Warner Brothers stores have been tremendous successes, and they would follow in their footsteps. EPE is currently working with Host Marriott, the Memphis airport concessionaire, to establish an experimental Elvis store at the airport.

EPE has also discussed the possibility of developing a Saturday morning cartoon show with Hanna-Barbera. The Elvis cartoon series would begin with a sixty-minute, prime-time feature that would be expanded into a regular series. Presumably, the cartoon would be a vehicle for licensing a line of Elvis dolls and toys. If the show were a success, it could create another generation of Elvis fans.

No doubt the city of Memphis hopes the Elvis phenomenon continues for at least few more years. The opening of Graceland had an impact on the city much like the impact Disney World had on Orlando. Graceland is the number-one tourist destination in Memphis, but it prompted the development of several other attractions, and today tourism pumps over a billion dollars annually into the Memphis economy. Because of Graceland, the city has become an international tourist destination.

EPE is even expanding into non-Elvis tourist attractions. The Hunt-Phelan mansion in Memphis is EPE's first try at breaking out of the strictly-Elvis business. After pumping $1 million into refurbishing the 166-year-old mansion, they are hyping it as an important Civil War relic. Among other things, their promotional literature claims that the home—originally built by William Richardson Hunt, a Confederate colonel who helped supply the South with armaments—was the site from which Ulysses S. Grant planned the Battle of Vicksburg. They also claim that the mansion was a stop on the underground railroad.

A Memphis Civil War historian, Charles Crawford, disputes these claims. He accuses EPE of inventing the stories to sell tickets. Only time will tell whether EPE can work the same magic with the Hunt-Phelan mansion as it has with Graceland.

★ ★ ★

In the years since his death, Elvis has evolved into something more than just a marketing dream—though he is that. He has been transformed by time from a symbol of juvenile delinquency and moral decline into an example of the American dream. Elvis's transformation has been so profound that in the 1992 presidential campaign, both candidates mentioned him. At the Republican National Convention, George Bush mentioned Elvis *twice* in his speech accepting his party's nomination.

Not to be outdone, Bill Clinton quickly professed his love for Elvis Presley, and he continued to make Elvis references throughout the campaign. He sang a verse of "Don't Be Cruel" in a television interview, and he played "Heartbreak Hotel" on his saxophone during his appearance on the *Arsenio Hall Show*. In fact, he mentioned Elvis so often that Bush began to refer to Elvis in his attacks on Clinton. "Clinton compares himself to Elvis," Bush said, "because the minute he tries to take a stand on something he starts wiggling." If Clinton were elected, Bush said on another occasion, "America would be checking in to Heartbreak Hotel."

At the Democratic National Convention, even Al Gore mentioned Elvis. In his speech, he confessed that his dream had always been to come to Madison Square Garden and be the opening act for Elvis.

In the opinion of the Secret Service, Clinton has clearly won the Elvis candidate competition. Their code name for him is Elvis. The agents reportedly get a kick out of saying, "Elvis has left the building."

In recent years, Elvis seems to have graduated from mere pop icon to true cultural phenomenon. A sure sign of this change is the number of academic institutions studying "the Elvis phenomenon." Emory, Alcorn State, Mercer, and several other universities offer classes devoted to Elvis.

In August 1995, Elvis took his place alongside da Vinci, Shakespeare, and Mozart as the subject of a serious academic symposium. A week-long conference was held at the University of Mississippi devoted to the analysis of the Elvis Presley phenomenon. The 1995 International Conference on Elvis Presley, "In Search of Elvis: Music, Race, Religion, Art, and Performance," brought together Elvis experts from around the world. The conference also featured lectures from scholars of music, history, literature, sociology, and anthropology, who covered every conceivable facet of the Elvis Presley phenomenon. Some 150 participants paid $350 each to attend the conference. The attendees were a mixture of academics, journalists, and Elvis fans.

The conference drew considerable criticism from the academic community. Professors across the country voiced their objections, feeling such a serious look at Elvis Presley trivialized academia. Supporters insisted that a study of the most popular entertainer in the history of the world was a perfectly reasonable academic pursuit. His impact on American culture is unparalleled, they argued. Elvis changed our attitudes on subjects as disparate as sex and race relations. Elvis's influence on this country is much more profound than that of Shakespeare, Mozart, or da Vinci. Average Americans are much more likely to know the words to "Hound Dog" than to a soliloquy from *Macbeth*.

Since his death, Elvis has become almost a religious figure to some fans. Jeffrey Sigglezzorri, for instance, has been listening to messages from the King for fifteen years and spreads the word through rendering Elvis's songs as sermons. Certifying himself as an "Elvis Worker," he imbues the holy message of "less lips, more hips" into his Yoga classes in Sebastopol, California. He says there are currently ten to fifteen certified Elvis Workers, with many more people interested in becoming one in the future. Jack Soden is a little uncomfortable with the extreme devotion of some of Elvis's followers, such as one physically handicapped admirer who claimed that Elvis inspired her to walk again. "Let's not take it all too seriously," he says. "The fans are so intense, we make a joke about jelly donuts and they are pained by it." Priscilla, however, seems to reinforce the reverence with which many fans regard her former husband. At times, she seems to be in awe of him herself. When a fan reveals that he or she met Elvis, Priscilla has been heard to say, "Oh, he touched you."

Not all fans are so seriously devoted, of course. Stephanie Pierce runs the 24 Hour Church of Elvis and Coin Operated Art Gallery in Portland, Oregon, where she "worships" the things you can't get rid of. As she puts it, "The church's holy trinity is plastic, Styrofoam, and Elvis."

Reports of Elvis sightings are giving UFOs a run for their money, both in terms of frequency and credibility. When Elvis was alive he was almost never seen in public, outside of a concert hall. After his death, Elvis became a social butterfly, if we are to believe the tabloids. However, it seems doubtful that he would have gone to all the trouble of faking his death and then risked exposure by making frequent appearances at fast-food restaurants.

It's not easy to explain the multifaceted cult that has developed around Elvis. Its causes are diverse, but clearly the myth of Elvis has taken root in our national psyche. Bill Morris Jr., former mayor of Memphis and a friend of Elvis, says, "The Elvis Presley syndrome after death continues to startle and amaze even the people close to Elvis." The man who discovered Elvis, Sun Records founder Sam Phillips, says that Elvis's continuing appeal is due to the fact that the public sees him as a common man who made it big. Phillips likens him to Abraham Lincoln in that respect.

Elvis was devoted to his family, generous to a fault, a strange combination of icon and everyday guy. In many ways, he personifies the American dream. He was a poor boy who started out with nothing and caught a brass ring bigger than he could hold.

A recent newspaper editorial ranked Elvis's death along with the bombing of Pearl Harbor, the assassination of JFK, and the first moon walk as a "generation marker." And yet, fan mail arrives daily at Graceland from thirteen- and fourteen-year-olds, fans who hadn't even been born when Elvis died. Is it the media circus that draws these young fans? Does Elvis's music matter anymore, or has it become superfluous, nearly irrelevant? Children who have never seen a Mickey Mouse cartoon happily wear T-shirts adorned with his face. Why should Elvis be any different?

In truth, Elvis Presley the man has ceased to exist, literally and figuratively. He's now a mythical being, a caricature, a cartoon with a twitchy lip and a shaky leg. Elvis Presley Enterprises will continue to prosper because Elvis the icon can never die.

★ ★ ★

Ultimately, it's somewhat beside the point asking whether the Elvis commercial juggernaut *can* roll on forever or even if it *should*. In 1980, Elvis Presley Enterprises was begun with a noble purpose: to save Graceland and preserve an inheritance for Lisa Marie Presley. EPE has been so successful that Lisa Marie now has more money than she could ever spend—which means she no longer needs EPE, which has been the central force behind the marketing and exploiting of Elvis. But even if she wanted to stop it, could she? Elvis became an icon before EPE ever existed, and since his death, he has become a cultural phenomenon beyond the power of any one person or organization to control.

Lisa Marie has made it clear, however, that she has no intention of changing anything having to do with Elvis Presley Enterprises in the foreseeable future. So we can rest assured that the Elvis circus will continue, aided, abetted, and organized by EPE. His face will continue to be plastered on belt buckles, shot glasses, and women's underwear. Today, the tackiness and crass commercialism is almost expected, as if it's supposed to be that way. If some people find it offensive, the majority do not. Lisa Marie doesn't seem to mind that millions of people will continue to parade through the house in which her father died, and to which she could legally retire if she chose to.

The corporate line has always been that EPE continues to serve faithfully as the chief guardian of Elvis's memory. But if there's any charge against EPE that seems entirely justified, it's that they have perpetuated the tasteless and tacky exploitation of Elvis just as vigorously as they have tried to honor his memory in more dignified ways. They have zealously guarded their exclusive rights to Elvis's name and likeness—not to fend off heartless attempts to profit at Elvis's expense, but to make sure they always get a piece of the action. If Elvis was generous to a fault, Elvis Presley Enterprises never gives anything away for free. EPE's primary concern has been, and will continue to be, the making of money; rather than preserving Elvis's memory, it has manipulated and shaped our image of him to the one that was most profitable.

When all is said and done, things haven't really changed that much for Elvis Presley. From the moment he hit it big in 1956 until the day he died, he was surrounded by people who used him. The gifted boy from Tupelo who simply wanted a nice home for his mother, the loyalty of friends and family, and the chance to do what he did best, died lonely in a crowd.

The story of Elvis Presley is, ultimately, a tragedy. It's a tragedy that one so talented, who rose so fast and inspired so many, died so young; and that, to a great extent, he brought his death and so much of his estate's mismanagement on himself. It's also a tragedy that those closest to him—those who helped him achieve such incredible stardom and who shared his life—betrayed his trust, generosity, and, finally, his memory for as much cash as they could get.

APPENDIX

COMPLAINT FILED BY THE PRESLEY ESTATE AGAINST COLONEL PARKER

IN 1979, SHORTLY AFTER the death of Vernon Presley, Probate Judge Joseph Evans ordered an investigation into the relationship between the Presley estate and Elvis's longtime manager, Colonel Parker. On August 14, 1981, following the completion of that investigation by Memphis attorney Blanchard Tual, Lisa Marie Presley's court-appointed guardian *ad litem,* the Probate Court of Shelby County, Tennessee, issued an order demanding the cessation of all payments to Colonel Parker. The judge further directed the Presley estate to bring suit against Colonel Parker for improper activities related to his managerial service for both Elvis and his estate. RCA Records was to be named in the suit as Colonel Parker's accomplice. The following is excerpted from the complaint filed by the Presley estate against Colonel Parker:

> In February, 1955, Elvis met Parker for the first time when Parker assisted Elvis's then manager, Bob Neal, in arranging a concert for

Elvis in Carlsbad, New Mexico. At all times referred to herein, Elvis was without knowledge or understanding of the business and financial aspects, customs, and usages of the music and entertainment industries, whereas Parker held himself to possess, and upon information and belief, in fact, possessed, expertise in such matters.

On August 15, 1955, Elvis and Parker signed their first agreement, pursuant to which Parker agreed to act as "special advisor" to Elvis and Neal in consideration of an annual salary of $2,500.

On November 21, 1955, Parker in Shelby County, Tennessee, caused Elvis, who was still a minor, to enter into a management agreement, pursuant to which Parker agreed to act as Elvis's "sole and exclusive advisor and personal representative" and to use his "best efforts" to advance and benefit Presley's career in the entertainment industry, in consideration of which Parker was entitled to receive 25 percent of Elvis's gross income. At that time, because Elvis was also signed to a management agreement with Neal, pursuant to which Neal was entitled to receive 15 percent of Elvis's gross income, Parker and Neal on November 21, 1955, entered into a co-management agreement, pursuant to which they agreed to both serve as Elvis's personal representative and mutually share in the collective 40 percent management commission.

On March 26, 1956, two months after Elvis had reached his majority, Parker caused Elvis to enter into an agreement with Parker, pursuant to which Elvis and Parker ratified their prior management agreement of November 21, 1955, and Elvis appointed Parker his sole and exclusive "advisor, personal representative and manager."

On January 2, 1967, Parker caused Elvis to enter into an amendment to their existing management agreement, which Elvis executed in Memphis, Tennessee, pursuant to which Parker's management commission, for no apparent consideration, was increased from 25 percent to 50 percent with respect to a substantial portion of Elvis's future gross income.

Parker served as Elvis's sole and exclusive personal manager and fiduciary for a twenty-one-year period commencing in 1956 and terminating upon Elvis's death on August 16, 1977. As a result of this continuing contractual relationship, Parker, at all times relevant, occupied a position of trust and confidence as his sole advisor and manager, and was under a strict fiduciary duty to act solely in Elvis's best personal and professional interests.

As Elvis's fiduciary, Parker was at all times under the mandate of law required to avoid circumstances in which his personal interests came into contact with the best personal and professional interests of Elvis, and to scrupulously avoid acting in a manner calculated to promote his personal interest to the detriment of Elvis's personal, financial, and professional interests.

On or about March 1, 1973, Parker, as Elvis's fiduciary, caused Elvis to execute six interrelated agreements between RCA on the one hand, and Elvis and/or Parker on the other hand.

The buyout agreements called for a total purchase price of $5,400,000 payable [at] $2,800,000 to Elvis and $2,600,000 to Parker. As a result of the buyout agreement, Elvis relinquished all of his rights to further royalties from the continued marketing and sales of records embodying his pre–March 1, 1973, recorded performances.

As a result of the six agreements, which agreements were negotiated by Parker on his own behalf and purportedly on behalf of Elvis as Elvis's personal manager and fiduciary, RCA agreed to pay the following amounts to Elvis and Parker. To Elvis: $4,650,000; to Parker: $6,200,000, plus 10 percent of the net profits of RCA tours.

As a result of the six agreements, Parker arranged for himself to receive $1,550,000 more than Elvis plus 10 percent of RCA's net profits from tours.

With respect to the six agreements Parker breached his fiduciary duty to Elvis and/or his duty of loyalty and reasonable care by, among other things: a) Causing Elvis to acknowledge or execute agreements which were not in his best interest, including but not limited to agreements with RCA, which collectively provided for Parker to receive 57 percent of all of the capital money due and payable to RCA plus 10 percent of RCA's net profits from tours, and by structuring the aforesaid agreements in such a manner that the total collective effect of said agreements would be and was to provide Parker substantially more monies than they would provide Elvis. b) Causing Elvis to acknowledge agreements which collectively permitted Parker to self-deal in his role as Elvis's personal manager in violation of all fundamental precepts and duties owed by a fiduciary to his charge to Elvis's severe detriment and damage. c) Causing Elvis to execute the agreements without the benefit of individual counsel or business advice. d) Failing to raise any objection to royalty statements, failing to conduct audits of financial books and records for the purpose of verifying the accuracy of royalty statements, and waiving certain claims with respect thereto to Elvis's damage and detriment.

Accordingly, the six agreements are either saturated with or constitute an embodiment of Parker's mismanagement, self-dealing, overreaching, and breach of trust.

Throughout the course of Elvis's career and subsequent to Elvis's death, Parker, by means of self-dealing in breach of the absolute trust which Elvis and later his estate placed in him, and in further breach of his fiduciary obligations and his duty of loyalty and reasonable care as imposed by law, engaged in the exploitation of Elvis in a manner designed to maximize his own private financial gains and profits to the detriment of Elvis's financial interest and career and to the detriment of his estate. This conduct, in addition to the conduct previously described herein, included among other things: a) Creating corporate vehicles which enabled Parker to acquire and profit from properties to which Parker was not entitled and capture income in excess of Parker's purported contractual entitlement in the area of music publishing and the merchandising of Elvis's name and likeness, to the severe financial detriment of Elvis and the estate. b) Causing Presley to enter into disadvantageous contracts with Parker and with a company substantially owned or controlled by Parker. c) Causing Presley, without the benefit of independent counsel or business advise, to enter into the contracts referenced above, which contracts upon information obtained were drafted and prepared by Parker, rendering Parker's interest in such contracts presumptively invalid under Tennessee law. d) Causing Presley to enter into disadvantageous contracts with third parties in order to accommodate Parker's personal financial requirements. e) Misusing his position as Elvis's, and later the estate's, personal manager and fiduciary by requiring third parties interested in commercially exploiting Presley to compensate Parker personally, which compensation was accepted and utilized by Parker for his own personal financial gain and profit. f) Limiting Elvis's concert appearances to the territory of the continental United States notwithstanding the enormous demand for and financial gain to be had from such appearances worldwide, which limitation was the result of Parker's not having secured a passport when he entered the United States and his fear that, once abroad, he would not be permitted reentry into this country. g) Failing to incorporate into recording contracts negotiated on Elvis's behalf any legal protection which would enable Elvis's accounting representatives to audit financial books and records for the purposes of verifying the accuracy of royalty statements and payments rendered to him to Elvis's damage and detriment. h) Failing to provide Elvis with any tax planning to Elvis's damage and detriment.

The attorneys for the Presley estate went to great lengths to demonstrate that Shelby County, Tennessee, was the appropriate jurisdiction for the case. They wanted to keep the case in their home court in Memphis because they felt they would have the advantage of public sentiment there.

Parker, throughout the years, regularly and systematically had dealings with Elvis at Elvis's business office in Shelby County, Tennessee, conducted discussions of business affairs with Elvis, either in person or by telephone, made payments to Elvis of sums of monies earned pursuant to contracts, rendered accounting statements to Elvis pursuant to contracts, attended public performances by Elvis, and provided, in conjunction therewith, promotional services pursuant to his obligations as personal manager, and made contracts in connection with personal performances by Elvis. b) Following Elvis's death, Parker made payments and arrangements in Shelby County, Tennessee, for the purpose of continuing his managerial and fiduciary relationship with Elvis.

As a result of the foregoing, Parker breached his fiduciary duty to Presley and to the estate thereafter, and accordingly, all of Parker's interests, rights, powers, and contracts, oral or written, with Presley and/or the estate, and with Presley and/or the estate and others should be forfeited in favor of the estate.

By reason of the foregoing, Parker breached his fiduciary duty to Presley and the estate thereafter causing Presley and the estate to suffer monetary damage in an amount to be determined by this honorable court and requiring the defendant to provide plaintiffs with a full and complete accounting of all monies received by Parker as a result of the professional activities of Presley.

Parker alleges that in 1967 his relationship with Elvis changed from one of Artist/Manager to that of a joint venture, and as a result, 50 percent of the assets of which the estate is presently comprised, and 50 percent of all income payable to the estate in the future belongs to Parker.

The estate says that no joint venture relationship ever existed between Elvis and Parker. Parker violated his fiduciary duty to Elvis by diverting to himself, for his own private gain and profit and to Elvis's financial detriment, money substantially in excess of 50 percent of all income generated by Elvis's personal concert appearances.

The Presley estate concluded their complaint, in part, by summarizing their claims against RCA.

RCA, pursuant to its payment obligations under the terms of the recording agreement, acknowledges that it owes royalties to either the estate or Parker in the amount of $152,354.14.

The estate says that, as a result of Parker's repeated and systematic breaches of fiduciary duty to Elvis, Parker's interest in all contracts with Presley and/or the estate and with Presley and/or the estate of others is forfeited in favor of the estate and all monies presently or herein after payable by RCA under the terms of the recording agreement, including the $152,000 presently in the possession, custody or control of RCA is payable to the estate.

Parker contends that the $152,000 is payable to him under the expressed terms of the recording agreement.

As a result of the foregoing, a substantial controversy concerning the proper distribution of the $152,000 royalty payment and all future royalty payments payable under the recording agreement presently exists between the estate and Parker, requiring judicial resolution by this court.

The Presley estate also concluded their complaint by summarizing their claims against Colonel Parker/Boxcar Enterprises.

On May 25, 1963, Parker caused Elvis to enter into a merchandising agreement with Parker in connection with special souvenir folios and pictures. The 1963 merchandising agreement provided that, in recognition of Parker's creation of special projects in the field of merchandising in furtherance of the "artistry and exposure of Elvis Presley," such "special projects" would be commercially exploited by Parker with all net profits derived therefrom to be divided 50 percent to Elvis and 50 percent to Colonel Parker.

At some point in time, Parker purports to have signed to Boxcar, a company substantially owned and controlled by Parker, all rights which Parker acquired from Presley relating to the merchandising of Presley's name and likeness.

Plaintiffs contend that Boxcar's merchandising rights, which were acquired from Parker, were limited to special merchandising projects in connection with Elvis Presley's personal appearance tours. Accordingly, upon Presley's death, Boxcar's right terminated.

Boxcar contends that it continued to possess the exclusive rights to commercially exploit Presley-related merchandise pursuant to the rights originally acquired by Parker from Presley, whereas the estate claims that such rights are property assets of his estate.

In 1974, Parker formed Boxcar and purported to convey to Boxcar the rights which Parker had acquired from Presley in connection with the marketing and promotion of Presley's name, image, and likeness.

At the time Boxcar was incorporated, Parker caused the shares of Boxcar to be distributed as follows: Parker 40 percent—worth $8,000, Elvis 15 percent—worth $3,000, George Parkhill 15 percent—worth $3,000, Fred Bienstock 15 percent—worth $3,000, Tom Diskin 15 percent—worth $3,000.

Parkhill and Bienstock thereafter sold their shares of stock to the corporation and said shares were redistributed by Parker as to alter the ownership of Boxcar as follows: Parker 56 percent, Elvis 22 percent, Tom Diskin 22 percent.

Parker caused salaries to be paid to Boxcar officers from 1974 through 1976 in the following amounts: 1974—Parker $27,560, Diskin $4,750, Presley $2,750, Parkhill $4,750, Bienstock $2,750, Patty Diskin $1,375, Mary Diskin $1,375. 1975—Parker $24,000, Diskin $6,000, Presley $6,000, Parkhill $6,000, Bienstock $6,000, Patty Diskin $3,000, Mary Diskin $3,000. 1976—Parker $36,000, Diskin $46,448, Presley $10,500, Parkhill $2,500, Bienstock $2,500, Patty Diskin $2,500, Mary Diskin $2,500.

Not only did Elvis possess a small percent of the ownership interest in Boxcar—between 15 and 22 percent—but, in 1974, 1975, and 1976, Elvis received only 6 percent, 11 percent, and 10 percent, respectively, of the distributable salaries.

Boxcar became the vehicle by which Parker diverted [to] himself approximately 61 percent of all income generated by the distribution and sale of Presley-related merchandise, an amount substantially in excess of Parker's entitlement under the terms of his merchandising agreement with Elvis Presley, and in violation of Parker's contractual and fiduciary duties to Presley.

At all times relevant, Boxcar had knowledge that the fiduciary relationship existed between Parker and Elvis and that Parker's conduct in the creation and operation of Boxcar constituted a breach of Parker's fiduciary duty to Elvis. As a result thereof, Boxcar conspired with Parker and aided and abetted Parker to breach his fiduciary duty to Presley.

Wherefore plaintiffs pray: On the first claim a declaration that all of Parker's interests, rights, and/or powers in contracts oral or written with Presley and/or the estate, including but not limited to record royalties, song writer royalties, and motion picture and television participation, should be forfeited in favor of the estate. An order requiring Parker to provide plaintiffs with a full and complete accounting of all monies received by Parker as a result of the professional activities of Presley, including but not limited to disclosure of Parker's income tax returns for the years 1973 to the present. Enjoining Parker from disposing of his assets or property pending final determination of this action and awarding the plaintiffs compensatory damages together with punitive damages all to be determined at the trial of this action. A declaration that no joint venture existed in fact between Parker and Presley or any company substantially owned by Parker or Presley for any purpose so as to entitle Parker to 50 percent of the assets which comprise the estate or 50 percent of future income of the estate. A declaration that all monies presently and hereafter payable by RCA are to be paid to the estate to the exclusion of Parker and that the royalties which are presently due and owing and are within the custody and control of RCA in the amount of $152,000 and all additional royalties herein after to become due be placed to the clerk of this court pending the final determination of this action. A declaration that Boxcar's rights to commercially exploit the name, image, and/or likeness of Elvis Presley for any purpose are terminated and that the exclusive right to commercially exploit the name, image, and/or likeness of Presley resides in the estate. An order enjoining Boxcar from disposing of its assets pending final determination of this action and an award of compensatory damages together with punitive damages all to be determined following an accounting at the trial of this action. On all claims interest provided by law, costs, reasonable attorney and accounting fees, and such other and further relief as this court deems just and proper.

BIBLIOGRAPHY

———. "Sellvis." *Economist* (April 10, 1993): 66.

Adler, David. *Elvis, My Dad.* New York: St. Martin's Press, 1990.

Bronikowski, Lynn. "The Elvis Business." *Rocky Mountain News,* August 11, 1992, 57.

Brown, Tony. "Elvis Tries to De-Elvis Play Miracle at (wherever)." *Charlotte Observer,* January 14, 1994, 1C.

Clayton, Rose. *Elvis Up Close.* Atlanta: Turner Publishing, 1994.

Collins, Elise. "Certifiably Elvis." *Psychic Reader,* July 1996, 15.

Cotton, Lee. *All Shook Up.* Ann Arbor, MI: Popular Culture, Ink., 1993.

Dundy, Elaine. *Elvis and Gladys.* New York: St. Martin's Press, 1988.

Dunning, Al. "Memphis States Its Case." *The Baltimore Sun,* October 20, 1993, 1D.

Frank, Robert. "Suspicious Minds: Some Doubt Tales of Memphis Mansion." *Wall Street Journal,* June 24, 1996, A1.

Guralnick, Peter. *Last Train to Memphis.* Boston: Little, Brown and Company, 1994.

Haight, Kathy. "Empire Keeps King's Memory Alive and Well." *Charlotte Observer,* August 16, 1986, 1D.

Hopkins, Jerry. *Elvis, the Final Years.* New York: St. Martin's Press, 1981.

Mitchell, Justin. "If Elvis Economics Is Everywhere, Chances Are Brain Power Is in Hiding." *Rocky Mountain Press,* August 28, 1992, 105.

Neill, Michael. "All Shook Up." *People* (February 27, 1995): 50.

Parker, John. *Elvis, the Secret Files.* London: Anaya Publishers Limited, 1993.

Richardson, John. "Scientology." *Premiere* (September 1993): 88–92

Schroer, Andreas. *Private Presley.* New York: William Morrow and Company, 1993.

Shelby County, Tennessee, Probate Court. *Report of the Guardian Ad Litem in re the Estate of Elvis A. Presley, deceased.* Memphis, 1981.

Shepard, Scott. "Elvis' Empire Worth a King Sized Ransom." *The Daily News of Los Angeles,* August 16, 1993, L2.

Thompson, Charles. *The Death of Elvis.* New York: Delacorte Press, 1991.

Tunzi, Joseph. *Elvis Sessions.* Chicago: JAT Publishing, 1993.

Vellenga, Dirk. *Elvis and the Colonel.* New York: Delacorte Press, 1988.

Worth, Fred. *His Life from A to Z.* New York: Contemporary Books, 1988.

INDEX